CITIZENS WITHOUT SHELTER

CITIZENS WITHOUT SHELTER

HOMELESSNESS, DEMOCRACY, AND POLITICAL EXCLUSION

LEONARD C. FELDMAN

CORNELL UNIVERSITY PRESS
Ithaca and London

First published 2004 by Cornell University Press

Design by Scott Levine

Printed in the United States of America

Library of Congress Cataloging-in-Publication Data

Feldman, Leonard C., 1971–
   Citizens without shelter : homelessness, democracy, and political exclusion / Leonard C. Feldman.
     p. cm.
Includes index.
  ISBN 0-8014-4124-2 (cloth : alk. paper)
  1. Homelessness—United States. I. Title.
  HV4505.F45   2004
  362.5'0973—dc22

                             2003024990

Cornell University Press strives to use environmentally responsible suppliers and materials to the fullest extent possible in the publishing of its books. Such materials include vegetable-based, low-VOC inks and acid-free papers that are recycled, totally chlorine-free, or partly composed of nonwood fibers. For further information, visit our website at www.cornellpress.cornell.edu.

Cloth printing   10 9 8 7 6 5 4 3 2 1

TO MY PARENTS,
GORDON AND JANET FELDMAN

CONTENTS

ACKNOWLEDGMENTS

This book could not have been completed without the intellectual guidance and kind support of a great many people. At the University of Washington, Christine Di Stefano, Stuart Scheingold, Jamie Mayerfeld, Michael McCann, and Nancy Hartsock gave me the freedom and gentle guidance I needed to pursue my interests in political theory and public law. I have been lucky enough to continue to benefit from their wisdom, good humor, and encouragement in the years since graduate school. In Seattle, I had the chance to volunteer with a street newspaper, and my thanks go to the office of *Real Change* and its director, Tim Harris, for letting me see homeless activism from the inside while I helped around the office.

A belated thank you goes to my professors when I was an undergraduate at Yale. Victoria Hattam first got me excited about political science, and Ian Shapiro, David Plotke, Shelley Burtt, and Cathy Cohen introduced me to various ways of doing political theory with a practical orientation.

The Andrew W. Mellon Foundation provided support for this project by way of a postdoctoral fellowship at Grinnell College, where I had the good fortune to be mentored by Ira Strauber, who gave generously of his time and provided close readings of several chapters of the manuscript. Biljana Bijelic offered loving support, a patient ear, and excellent advice as I revised the manuscript. At the University of Oregon, I have benefited from political theory conversations with many colleagues and friends, including Irene Diamond, Dan Gil, Lars Skålnes, Gerry Berk, Joseph Lowndes, and André Lambelet. In addition to kind encouragement, Deborah Baumgold

and Julie Novkov provided extensive comments on portions of the manuscript, greatly helping me to clarify my arguments.

Many other people have given generously of their time to read and comment on earlier versions. My thanks go to Samira Kawash, Susan Bickford, Patchen Markell, Austin Sarat, Morris Kaplan, Russell Muirhead, and the two anonymous reviewers for Cornell University Press. I also want to thank Courtney Smith and Robin Jacobson, who did a magnificent job as my research assistants in the final stages of manuscript preparation. Finally, I am most grateful to Catherine Rice of Cornell University Press for her support and guidance throughout the publication process.

Chapter 3 contains material from "Redistribution, Recognition, and the State: The Irreducibly Political Dimension of Injustice," *Political Theory* 30 (June 2002): 410–440, © 2002 by Sage Publications, Inc., and reprinted by their permission.

LEONARD FELDMAN

Eugene, Oregon

CITIZENS WITHOUT SHELTER

State Power and the Polarities
of Homeless Politics

The Atlanta Union Mission, on its website, advertises "700,000 nourishing meals," "300,000 nights of safe shelter," and "Spiritual, Physical and Emotional Healing." Its home page presents a collage of images: a man sitting on the street in a dejected and submissive posture, his head slumped toward his chest; a closely cropped photo of a young boy's face, his eyes large and gazing upward; an elderly man with gray scraggly hair and a cap, eating soup with a spoon; and a younger man lying asleep on the street covered by what appear to be newspapers. Click to the page devoted to shelter programs, and you find advertised the Atlanta mission's capacity—"Emergency shelter for over 400 men, women and children every day"—alongside the following text:

Today's untouchables are homeless men, women and increasingly children.

Men—Frightening—Avoided on the street

Women—invisible or blamed.

But more than ever—Children—Innocent Victims.

The average age of a homeless person in the U.S.

9 years old!

Warm Food and Shelter

TOUCH

These "untouchables"[1]

In addition to presenting its goals, and images of the suffering people it helps, the mission website urges people to volunteer and contribute money. It presents a compelling and not uncommon example of the politics of compassion for homeless persons—inflected by the particular orientation of Christian charity. But do the images and words of the rescue mission's website *resist* the construction of homeless persons as "untouchables," or do they *reinforce* such a representation?

According to many observers, the "politics of compassion" as advocated by the Atlanta mission was increasingly overtaken in the 1990s by a "politics of compassion fatigue," manifest in a new war against the homeless.[2] Indeed, in the early 1990s, municipal governments shifted the focus of their policies: rather than seeking primarily to ameliorate the conditions of homelessness, cities across the United States turned to a more punitive approach, targeting the homeless themselves through a new field of illegalities. As Samira Kawash writes, "Since the magnitude of the problem of homelessness came into widespread public consciousness in the early 1980s, the discourse surrounding the homeless has slowly shifted from a guilty compassion to an exhausted and often vengeful disavowal. Communal responses to homelessness in the 1990s aim not to eliminate the causes of homelessness, but to eliminate the homeless themselves by denying them any place."[3] Marking the transition from compassion to compassion fatigue in the early 1990s was the emergence of new "public-space" ordinances, including bans on public sleeping and restrictions on panhandling.

Accompanying these ordinances were new forms of policing that targeted "disorder," such as the confiscation of street persons' property and police sweeps of homeless encampments.[4] For instance, in Santa Ana, California, police on August 15, 1990, engaged in the mass arrest of homeless persons at the city's civic center, citing sixty-four for various minor offenses such as jaywalking, littering, and public urination. Through a coordinated effort involving officers atop buildings with binoculars and officers on the ground with handcuffs, those arrested were taken to a local stadium, which served as the command post for the operation. There, they were chained to benches for up to six hours and had numbers marked on their arms. Afterward, they were driven to the edge of the police district and released.[5]

In New York, police officers in the mid-1990s enforced an obscure Sanitation Department ordinance, prohibiting people from abandoning boxes and erecting obstructions on city streets, against homeless persons sleeping in such boxes in public spaces. This police practice, part of Mayor Rudolph Giuliani's approach to public disorder, was defended by city officials as "necessary after homeless people who left debris in [a] park, across from the Manhattan Criminal Court building . . . refused offers of shelter."[6]

The city of Philadelphia passed a "Sidewalk Behavior Ordinance" in 1998. The law prohibits panhandling on highways and "aggressive solicitation," which includes panhandling within eight feet of a building or vendor and seeking funds within twenty feet of a bank or automatic teller machine (ATM).[7]

The city of Dallas passed an ordinance in 1994 prohibiting, among other things, sleeping in public: "A person commits an offense if he (1) sleeps or dozes in a street, alley, park, or other public place; or (2) sleeps or dozes in a vacant lot adjoining a public street or highway."[8]

These four cases are examples of the four main strategies cities have employed in what critics call the new "war against the homeless." These strategies can be identified, according to the National Law Center on Homelessness and Poverty (NLCHP) as (1) police actions, including mass arrests and confiscation of homeless persons' property; (2) selective enforcement of older statutes not originally targeting the homeless; (3) the passage of new laws restricting certain forms of panhandling; and (4) the passage of new laws restricting sleeping and sitting in public spaces.[9]

Scholars of homelessness investigating this turn to punitive policies have dug beneath the concepts of compassion and compassion fatigue that circulate in media discourses in order to understand the broader ideological and cultural significance of the new punitive approach. Commentators have noted the ways in which a proprietary and exclusionary conception of public space is reflected in and constituted by anti-homeless ordinances and the more general war against the homeless of which they are a part.[10] An ideology of public space as "owned" by a normatively enshrined "we" of home-dwelling citizens is both cause and effect of the punitive homeless policies, which, these scholars note, beyond simply targeting the problem of homelessness or street disorder, become part of a broader pattern of hegemonic identity constitution.

This scholarship is valuable in rejecting the instrumentalist view of homelessness as a discrete social problem to be solved by a public that happens upon it. Studies in geography,[11] sociology,[12] culture,[13] political communication,[14] and architecture,[15] have developed a *dialectical* and *constitutive* approach to the phenomenon of "homelessness." Rather than seeing it as an isolated problem to be solved by the public and a positive fact to be explained by the researcher, they investigate the complex, co-constitutive relationship between culturally contingent categories of "homeless," and "housed," between "street person" and "public citizen." For instance, April

Veness argues that homelessness cannot be seen only as an economic or psychological problem to be solved "by corrections in the distribution of resources or moral fortitude." Rather, confronting homelessness requires "a detailed analysis of the cultural context of home as promulgated by middle-of-the-road policy makers and middle-class reformers."[16] Some of this work develops poststructuralist insights concerning the role of a constitutive antagonism in structuring social relations.[17] As Samira Kawash puts it, "The aim of the vengeful homeless policies of the last decade is not limited to the immediate goal of solving the problem of homelessness by eliminating the homeless. This 'war on the homeless' must also be seen as a mechanism for constituting and securing a public, establishing the boundaries of inclusion, and producing an abject body against which the proper, public body of the citizen can stand."[18] The picture of homeless politics that emerges reveals a complex and dialectical process involving culturally contingent understandings of home and homelessness, postindustrial redevelopment of urban spaces, and processes of abjection in constituting a public identity against a "dirty" and "improper" homeless other.

CONNECTING THE POLITICS OF COMPASSION WITH THE POLITICS OF COMPASSION FATIGUE

These various studies have been extremely productive in presenting an ideological critique of the 1990s war against the homeless, but less successful in articulating the linkages between the "politics of compassion fatigue" under critique and the "politics of compassion" that it is said to partly displace. (I say "partly" because of course compassion fatigue does not entirely displace compassion. A burgeoning social service system for the homeless—emergency and specialized shelters that include Christian rescue missions, substance abuse programs, job training programs—represents the continuation of a politics of compassion.) As Kim Hopper asserts, a duality in policy responses to homelessness can be seen in "the tension between providing sanctuary for the helpless and disciplining the unruly."[19] That tension reflects the distinction frequently made between the "deserving" and the "undeserving" poor.[20]

Figuring out the connections between the politics of compassion and the politics of compassion fatigue is made all the more necessary in light of recent efforts by neoconservatives to defend punitive public-space ordinances as a form of compassion. Defenders of public-sleeping and panhandling bans sometimes justify them as elements of a broader "holistic" social service policy of outreach, treatment, and rehabilitation—the "tough love" needed to end homelessness.[21]

While neoconservatives fold punitive politics into a compassionate conservatism of tough love, critics on the left make the reverse move, arguing that compassionate forms of welfare and shelter themselves work to
stigmatize and discipline the homeless. A long tradition of left-Marxist criticism has shown the alliance between criminal law and liberal welfare-
state programs for the poor along the lines of social control.[22] In the specific context of homelessness policy, Ingrid Sahlin examines the
complementarities between punitive and helping policies in terms of their
shared goal of *enclosure;* she argues that in Sweden, policies and programs
that aim to help the homeless by ameliorating the conditions of homelessness frequently end, instead, by complementing the exclusionary practices of homeless criminalization.[23]

If ameliorative and punitive approaches both reinforce the separation of
the homeless population from a normative public of home-dwelling citizens,
and if punitive policies are justified by neoconservatives as an element of
compassionate aid, then one must pause before simply reasserting the desir-
ablity of compassionate policies over and against a punitive approach. As the
left critique of welfare makes clear, one should not assume that whatever is
not explicitly punitive (emergency shelters, drug treatment programs, etc.)
is an ideologically distinct alternative to be bolstered and shielded from critical examination.[24] Yet it is also a mistake simply to dismiss compassionate
and welfare efforts as nothing more than punitive, disciplinary social control measures in disguise. Although sympathetic to this critique, I believe
it moves too quickly toward finding a hidden unity of the two approaches.
Explaining such unity in terms of an economic functionality (the requirements of urban reinvestment, the needs of capitalism), or a cultural logic
(the ever present dynamic of identity/difference) leaves unanswered the
question of why the homeless *need* to be contained, enclosed, disciplined,
or excluded. Furthermore, it fails to appreciate that whatever similar goals
may orient welfare and punishment, and however much neoconservatives
may try to justify punishment as a form of welfare, there are real ideological differences. In other words, both the differences between sanctuary and
discipline *and* the underlying logics that connect them need to be examined.

Thus, the important question to ask is not how "we" came to exhaust
our compassion for "them." Rather, the important question is how the
politics of compassion and the politics of compassion fatigue might be
so related that it is easy to move from one to the other. Is there some hidden link between charitable appeals for food and shelter, such as the one
made by the Atlanta Union Mission, and the punitive policies of displacement, harassment, and exclusion? Is there an underlying structure or process

that links compassion with compassion fatigue, and permits the relatively easy slide from calls to *eliminate homelessness* to calls to *eliminate the homeless?* Lest we keep endlessly circling from shelter to punishment, from compassion to compassion fatigue, from containment to prohibition, we must examine critically both what unites these two poles on the policy spectrum and what divides them. Doing so requires an investigation of culture and politics.

Given that oscillations between sanctuary and discipline, shelter and punishment may reflect evaluative judgments concerning "deserving" and "undeserving," "worthy" and "unworthy," it is necessary to consider in depth the patterns of cultural representation and, in particular, the way that homeless persons are represented in popular media and texts ranging from newspaper articles to films to sociological studies.[25] In this regard, I see cultural constructions of the homeless as both more complex and more visceral than a simple distinction between the deserving and the undeserving poor.[26] These cultural representations are more deeply connected to contemporary norms of agency and freedom and contemporary dynamics of romanticized investment and disgusted disavowal than a cognitive vocabulary of desert might indicate.

Sometimes the homeless are represented as truth-seekers and saintly heroes; at other times the homeless are imagined as a threatening, criminal other—"matter out of place."[27] Furthermore, sometimes the homeless are imagined as completely free, choosing agents; at other times the homeless are viewed as totally constrained, helpless victims of misfortune. The first dimension of representational variation I call the sacred/profane axis. Along this axis representations range from an identification of homelessness with the spiritually superior to an identification of homelessness with dirt, the abject, and criminality.[28] The second dimension of representational variation I call the free/unfree axis. Along this axis, representations range from the notion of homelessness as a lifestyle choice and a situation marked by a kind of natural liberty to the idea that homelessness is involuntarily acquired and a condition defined by social constraint and the compulsions of bodily need. Thus, as sacred or profane, free or unfree—a *set* of polarities marks the representation of homelessness as much as it marks policy responses.

These two axes of representational variation intersect, creating cross-cutting possibilities. For instance, the homeless as radically free (as homeless by choice, their condition defined by resistance and a lack of subordination to social control) can either be invested with romantic longing or condemned as a dangerous class. Similarly, the homeless as unfree (as involuntarily homeless, their condition defined by necessity, constraint, and deprivation) can either be invested with sympathy, pathos and fantasies of saving missions or excluded as "matter out of place." The most typical opposition is between a vision of the homeless as dangerously and profanely free (justifying criminalization) and a vision of the homeless as sacralized, helpless sufferers (justifying shelter). It is this opposition that, for instance, structures the legal debates concerning the rights of the homeless (discussed in chapter 2) and that underlies the policy polarity between punishment and sanctuary.

In examining various positions on the free/unfree, sacred/profane grid, I argue that in political discourse, sociology, and film the homeless are marked by a certain undecidability along one or both of these two axes. This undecidability manifests itself as a kind of doubleness in which polar opposite images overlay each other. First, in two contemporary academic commentaries, mirror images of the homeless as free-sacred and free-profane emerge in the debate between leftist critics and conservative defenders of punitive policies. Second, in the sociological literature on "disaffiliation," homelessness is alternately imagined as profane-freedom and profane-unfreedom. And finally, in the 1991 movie *The Fisher King,* images of the homeless oscillate between the sacred freedom of the spiritually superior to the sacred unfreedom of the helpless victim.

As Kathleen Arnold argues, leftist scholars who celebrate resistant subcultures (in my terminology, the homeless as free and spiritual heroes of the open road) echo their conservative opponents who see in the homeless a dangerous form of rebellion (the homeless as profane and unconstrained outlaws of contemporary public space).[29] Homelessness as a form of freedom may thus be invested with a romanticized longing for the open road, or it may be a receptacle for the resentments of a domesticated citizen.

Homelessness as freedom is given a positive valuation by political theorist Thomas Dumm who seeks to embrace a form of "spiritual homelessness." Identifying the homeless with the spirit of the nomad, Dumm argues that a just society would be one in which homelessness is enabled. Thus, Dumm argues that we should move toward a society in which "homelessness is supported and made possible." He suggests that the homeless are resisting the "containment fields" of modern life and identifies contemporary homeless persons with traditional hoboes. Thus, homelessness is a form of oppositional freedom and resistance to the disciplinary institutions of contemporary U.S. society: "This old-time hobo . . . and anyone who has sought to take to the open road, . . . anyone who has imagined the possibility of getting lost, disappearing from the constraints of containment

. . . could *almost be said to be homeless by choice*. The circumstances that govern organized, normalized life are oppressive to such people, they seek out alternatives, they seek to live outside the containment fields that govern modern experience."[30]

A great deal is elided in that "almost." It indicates a certain hesitation about identifying homelessness as a form of spiritual freedom and rebellion. To be fair, Dumm wants to encourage a spiritual homelessness while "ameliorat[ing] the material condition of homelessness." But because his focus is almost exclusively on the psychological and spiritual dimensions of homelessness, he provides little in terms of what such an amelioration of the material conditions would look like except to offer support for lives "outside the containment fields that govern modern experience." The main thrust of his argument is the identification of homelessness with a form of (sacred) freedom: "If the material conditions that enable . . . any one of us . . . to be homeless disappear, the spiritual possibility of homelessness as the open road, as a possible path of freedom, disappears as well."[31]

Homelessness as freedom is given a negative valuation by legal scholar Robert Tier. Sacred, positive freedom ("resistance to the containment fields of modernity") becomes profane license ("rebellious threat to the social order"). Tier is one of the leading legal defenders of public-space restrictions and "broken windows" policing (see chapter 1). Tier dislikes the term "homeless," preferring the older categories of vagrant and vagrancy. Furthermore, he argues that cities make a mistake when they view vagrants as helpless victims "of economic dislocation or . . . an inevitable feature of market capitalism." Rather, the visible homeless in urban public spaces are a "troubled population" that, due to substance abuse problems and mental illness "engag[e] in . . . anti-social and disorderly conduct."[32] Tier's language works relentlessly to stereotype and demean homeless persons, yet he manages to claim that it is the legal defenders of the rights of the homeless who "promote the most pernicious stereotypes about poverty in America." They do this, he claims, by identifying street homelessness with poverty instead of with antisocial disorder. Tier quotes expert court testimony to make the distinction between the deserving and undeserving poor: "Poor people in America do not live on the streets, under bridges, or in parks, do not carry all of their belongings in shopping carts or plastic bags, wear layers of tattered clothing, pass out or sleep in doorways, urinate or defecate in public places, sleep in their cars or in encampments, do not harass or intimidate others, ask for money on the streets, physically attack city workers and residents, and do not wander the streets shouting at visions and voices."[33]

Although he acknowledges mental illness and addiction, Tier's purpose is not to accept a vision of the homeless as helpless and unfree (by virtue of a condition or illness) but rather to deepen the pathologization of homelessness and to posit them as individuals who can be held accountable for their (freely chosen and disorderly) behaviors. The abject images (tattered clothing, urine) that appear in his argument promote not sympathy but disgust, maintained by emphasizing the agentic dimension of the "disorderly" behavior that arouses the disgust. For instance, public urination is not an indication that cities have made their public spaces incredibly inhospitable to persons without a private space of their own; rather, it is a freely chosen disorderly behavior. Public-space restrictions do not criminalize homelessness; they are simply evidence that "communities have decided to cease tolerating everything that any deviant wants to do." Bad choices have made homeless street dwellers a dangerous threat to the vitality of urban public spaces, but laws prohibiting urban camping, aggressive panhandling, and the like will help turn homeless people from disorderly and rebellious outlaws to upstanding citizens who "are capable of being good citizens and are capable of obeying these new laws."[34]

Tier's political position is the mirror opposite of Dumm's. Tier worries about a liberalism that has made urban public spaces a zone of license where disorderly and rebellious vagrants drive out upstanding citizens, especially the "deserving" (that is to say, housed) poor and the middle class. Dumm worries that precisely those public-space restrictions Tier supports will make homelessness (and, by extension, other forms of resistance and oppositional freedom) impossible. Tier is wholeheartedly on the side of the "containment fields of modernity" that Dumm is interested in escaping. Tier identifies street homelessness with abject and dangerous disorder—tattered clothes, urine, feces, and aggression. Dumm identifies street homelessness with the open road and a spiritual freedom to which housed citizens might aspire, should they seek to break out of their containment fields. Dumm and Tier romanticize and demonize, respectively, the agency of homeless persons. But what they agree upon is that homelessness is to some extent a choice, and a rebellious choice at that. What neither really problematizes is the idea that homeless persons are rebellious outsiders of the social order.

The doubleness of representations of the homeless can be seen in the pioneering work of sociologist Howard Bahr. In his 1973 work *Skid Row* (and, together with Theodor Caplow, in *Old Men Drunk and Sober*), Bahr recasts homelessness as a wider social process of "disaffiliation" from social structures, reward systems, and kinship relations.[35] The depiction of disaffiliation oscillates between an image of natural liberty and an image of social constraint. As someone who is outside the social order, "disaffiliated man" presents an alternating image—he is either completely free, or he is completely constrained. It all depends how you look at him, and this depends, in turn, on how you regard the social processes of "affiliation," responsibility, sanction, and reward.

Bahr's account of disaffiliation as both freedom and constraint occurs in a discussion of the reasons why the housed public fears the homeless: "There are some functional bases for the generalized distrust of the disaffiliate. It is not so much that he is a deviant as that *he is outside the usual system of sanctions,* and hence his behavior cannot be predicted with any certainty." And furthermore, the homeless person "poses a threat because he has moved beyond the reward system. . . . Being functionally, if not actually devoid of significant others, property, and substantial responsibility, he is not subject to the usual social restraints. It is no threat to the fully disaffiliated to threaten the forfeiture of his property, the imprisonment of his family or the loss of his job. He has none of these."[36]

Despite (or perhaps because of) the neutral-sounding functionalist language, there is a certain undecidability in Bahr's account. Is disaffiliation a form of freedom or a form of constraint? Although on one level it is no doubt correct to say that it is both, homelessness is not, in these passages, recognized as containing a mixture of freedom and constraint but rather as oscillating between complete freedom from constraint and absolute deprivation—a double image. On the one hand, disaffiliation is portrayed as a condition of natural liberty, a lack of social constraints. Thus, Bahr describes the disaffiliate as someone who is "outside the usual system of sanctions"—a person within the boundaries of the political community but outside the social contract. In so doing Bahr echoes Rousseau's observation that (in the late stage of the state of nature) the rich see themselves as having everything to lose, whereas the poor have nothing to lose but their natural liberty. Of course, the functionalist spin on having "nothing to lose but one's natural liberty" is to be "outside the usual system of sanctions" and "not subject to the usual social restraints." But the passages cited above alternate between this image of disaffiliated man as having transcended all social discipline in moving beyond the reward system and another image of disaffiliated man as having lost all social goods and attachments. It is almost as if the natural liberty must be disavowed because "affiliated man" might otherwise long for an escape from those containment fields. Thus, the text shifts registers, describing the state of being above or beyond social sanction in the language of constriction and dispossession: the homeless are untouched by conventional forms of discipline because they have none of the investments, attachments, or possessions that make the domestic(ated) citizen so receptive to a system of reward and sanction. No property, no family, no job—the freedom from social constraints and sanctions is a consequence of the absolute deprivation of social goods.

As Charles Hoch and Robert Slayton, the authors of *New Homeless and Old*, point out, this theoretical framework contradicts the rich ethnographic evidence presented by scholars of "disaffiliation," which offers a glimpse of a complex culture of skid row, a social world that despite its marginalization has its own structures of affiliation, social networks, and sanctions.[37] Although this ethnographic detail points to more productive ways of understanding homelessness, the theoretical framework is itself instructive, as it unwittingly displays the structure of representation in which the homeless are always double. Bahr and Caplow's social-functional explanation of the "generalized distrust" of the disaffiliated glosses the resentment of the socially constrained and affiliated toward the bearers of natural liberty. We distrust them because they are not subjected as we are—they are unpredictable—and so homelessness is invested with the ambivalent attitudes we have to our own subjection and civil freedom.

Where the sociology of disaffiliation presents a double image of the homeless as either dangerously outside the bounds of the social (profane liberty) or pathetically deprived of the affiliations of the social (profane constraint), a popular motion picture, *The Fisher King*, consistently positions the homeless as bearers of a spiritual consciousness. Like the sociology of disaffiliation, however, the film retains an undecidability about agency along the free/unfree axis: are the homeless free spirits, or does the pathos of their suffering and constraint bring them closer to the sacred? Directed by Terry Gilliam, the 1991 film centers on the relationship between Jack (Jeff Bridges), a Howard Stern–like disc jockey, and Parry (Robin Williams), a homeless squatter with mad, enthralling visions of quests and demons. Jack's life falls apart after his callous comments to a radio caller spark the caller's shooting rampage at a "Yuppie watering hole." Jack and Parry are brought together by chance, but it turns out that Jack has been indirectly responsible for the death of Parry's wife, a victim of the enraged radio caller. Jack, having lost his career, flirts with homelessness himself, is mistaken for homeless, and is saved from marauding anti-homeless youths by Parry and his gang.

Though haunted by visions, Parry is marked by his actions and wisdom as a sacred outsider, unconstrained by social discipline. As one commentator puts it, "Parry dances and, in general, is able to behave with greater freedom than the socialized and more normal people in the city."[38] Parry is not just wacky and wise; he is also a free spirit, closer to the divine and the "spiritually superior."[39] In one scene, this disaffiliated free spirit is naked in Central Park while Jack voices the disapproval of the (literally) surrounding society:

> **PARRY:** Have you ever done any cloudbusting? You lie on your back and you concentrate on the clouds . . . and you try to break them apart with your mind. It's wild.

> **JACK:** You can't do this! This is New York! Nobody lies naked in a field in New York. It's . . . it's too Midwestern.

> **PARRY:** Come on, try it. Ya feel the air on your body—ya little fella's flappin' in the breeze. . . . [E]verybody in the city is busy with their business and no one knows we're bare assed in the middle of it.[40]

But Parry is not the only image of homelessness in the film. A particularly moving scene presents an eloquent soliloquy by Sid, a disabled, homeless panhandler toward whom a passerby has just tossed a coin:

> He's paying so he don't have to look. What he don't know is, he's paying for a service. Guy goes to work every day and for eight hours, seven days a week, he bends over a[nd] gets it right up the ass till he can't stand. . . . But one day, right before quitting time on Friday, his boss is going to say something like "Say Bob—come into my office and kiss my ass" . . . and Bob is going to think—"The hell with it! I don't care what happens. All I want right now is to see the expression on his face when I stab him with this pair of scissors." . . . But then he thinks of me—"Wait a minute!" he says, "It's not so bad. At least I got two arms and two legs and I ain't beggin' for money." He puts down the scissors and puckers up. . . . I'm what you call a moral traffic light. It's like I'm saying "Red—go no further."[41]

Sid's speech (and his demeanor as the passive, hunched-over supplicant) presents homelessness as sacralized suffering and unfreedom, but it is not unfreedom in relation to the freedom of housed persons. Rather, homeless deprivation is the limit point that helps to maintain the disciplinary forms of subjection and petty humiliations in the everyday life of "Bob," the imagined commuter. This scene is a striking illustration, then, of Piven and Cloward's point that "some of the aged, the disabled, the insane, and others who are of no use as workers are left on the relief rolls, and their treatment is so degrading and punitive as to instill in the laboring masses a fear of the fate that awaits them should they relax into beggary and pauperism."[42] The encounter with homeless deprivation keeps the resentful

worker in control of himself and subordinated to his boss, for from the perspective of the disciplined worker, homelessness as unfreedom becomes not
a call to compassion but rather an implied threat, a looming and terrify-
ing possibility. Sid's serene awareness of his role in propping up a system
of social discipline marks him, like Parry, as a sacred outsider.

Jack adopts Parry and makes his amends by bringing Parry together with
his new love interest. Jack appears to have redeemed himself for his sins
as a career-obsessed and amoral disc jockey. But Parry is then beaten by the
homeless-hating thugs, and Jack blithely restarts his career, having had only
the appearance of a cathartic transformation. The turning point in the film
comes soon thereafter when a television executive pitches Jack a sitcom idea
that would cap off his reborn career: "It's a weekly comedy about the homeless. . . . But it's not depressing in any way. We want to find a funny upbeat
way of bringing up the issue of homeless to television. There are three wacky
homeless characters but they're wise, . . . they're wacky and they're wise.
. . . And, the hook is, they love being homeless. They love the freedom, . . .
they love the adventure. . . . It's all about the joy of living, . . . not all the
bullshit we have to deal with, . . . the money, the politics, . . . the pressures.
. . . And we're gonna call it 'Home Free.'"[43] Jack bursts out of the room—
the insulting and callous studio executive has sparked in him an epiphany
concerning his duty to Parry.

When read in relation to Sid's speech, however, the "Home Free" sitcom pitch becomes more complex. Not only does the entertainment industry's callous disregard of suffering reawaken Jack's compassion; it simultaneously undoes the moral traffic light of homelessness as looming threat.
"Home Free" becomes attractive because it presents an alternative to the
hierarchy and to the humiliation-maintaining traffic light of homelessness
as destitution: an imaginary space of freedom to which the humiliated and
disciplined worker might become attached.

The complexity of the superficially offensive sitcom idea lies, furthermore, in its complex relationship to the film as a whole. The pitch, played
as a decisive catalyst in pushing Jack to save Parry and seek his own true
redemption, works only to the extent that the viewer bracket his or her
own enjoyment of Robin Williams's wackiness as a free-spirited and mad
bum.[44] Whether it is running around Manhattan seeking his love interest Lydia, lying naked in Central Park, or plotting the theft of what he
believes to be the Holy Grail from an Upper East Side mansion, Parry
represents more than just a figure of trauma; he is also the embodiment
of a romanticized freedom. Thus, the film as a whole undermines the deci-
siveness or univocality of the home-free scene by embracing the equation

of homelessness with freedom. The viewer is thus required both to identify with Parry's free-spirited nature and to disavow the studio executive's callous and self-serving embrace of it. The viewer must identify with both the spiritually wise (and free-spirited) Parry and the spiritually wise (and helpless) Sid.

What is noteworthy about these variations in policy responses and representations is not so much the variety as the consistency of the polar oppositions. On three registers—agency (free or unfree), valuation (sacred or profane), and policy response (sanctuary or criminalization)—homelessness is marked by a doubleness, a recurring set of oppositions. The most common one is between a view that sacralizes the helplessness of the homeless, to be given sanctuary, and a view that demonizes the agency of the homeless, to be disciplined by the laws (see chapter 2). The variable oppositions along one or more axes, however, sometimes occuring within a single text, dramatize the cultural underpinnings of ambivalence that enable the movement from compassion to compassion fatigue.

THE ROLE OF SOVEREIGN POWER

In order to explain the representational doubleness and cultural ambivalence, one could well discern here traces of the abject—that complex mixture of attraction and repulsion in the unsettling zone of the liminal—in the homeless other who literally unsettles (home-less) and attracts (home-free). Abjection, Christine Di Stefano writes, "is implicated . . . in the creation of boundaries and in archaic memories of the nonexistence, fragility, and violation of those boundaries. . . . Abjection attracts and repels simultaneously."[45] Much good recent work in political theory has observed that relations of identity/difference (hierarchical orderings of social groups whose identities are mutually constitutive) are structured by abjection and ambivalence, through psychodynamic processes that assign the marginalized group to the realm of the dirty and impure. Policy responses to the homeless, for instance, are understood in the context of the liminal position of the homeless in society, a position that stirs feelings of the uncanny, of that which disturbs identity.[46]

But the doubleness of the homeless other and our response, the ambivalence encoded in the movement from compassion to compassion fatigue, disclose a set of relations more fundamental than either enclosure in the interests of urban redevelopment or abjection as a psychocultural dynamic of collective life. I do not mean to suggest that the concepts of enclosure and abjection are not helpful as ways of understanding the anxiety experienced by a home-dwelling citizen in his or her encounter with a homeless person or of explaining the emergence of new forms of social control in urban public spaces. Rather, I am arguing that these ways of framing homelessness, by emphasizing the social, serve to deflect attention from the political dimensions of homelessness and cannot make full sense of the dualities and oscillations outlined above. To take seriously the idea of homelessness as a problem of politics, and to think seriously about what it means to say that homeless persons are (and ought to be) citizens, requires a thorough analysis of the mechanisms and dynamics of political exclusion. This is where recent trends within the field of political theory can be of help. As scholars in political theory display a renewed interest in the role of the state and the political sphere in constituting relations of hierarchy, exclusion and identity/difference that were hitherto traced to culture or society, it is time to pry homelessness loose from its usual frame as a social problem and to see the state and sovereign power as deeper causes, not as superstructural with respect to society.[47] The recurring polarities of homeless policies and cultural representatives disclose a fundamental relationship between political power and "bare life."

The idea of bare life has been explicated by Giorgio Agamben, who sees the most basic opposition in the Western political tradition as the one between bare life and political existence. Bare life is a concept that can be thought of in contrast to "the good life." Bare life is necessity, mere physical existence, and, for ancients such as Aristotle, what humans have in the household, as opposed to their lives as speaking citizens in the polis. The ancients excluded bare life from the polis, the political sphere, which concerned questions of the good life, whereas bare, natural, reproductive, biological life was confined to the realm of the household. This is where Agamben complicates the story: the bare life confined to the household is not "natural," because it is its exclusion that constitutes bare life as such. Furthermore, according to Agamben, the confinement of bare life to the household is "at the same time an implication of . . . bare life in politically qualified life," since the exclusion of bare life from politics constitutes the sphere of the political in the first place. The sphere of the political and the sphere of bare life retain traces of each other in this double separation. Their opposition, which at first glance seems natural or necessary to politics, forms a puzzle for Agamben: "We must . . . ask why Western politics first constitutes itself through an exclusion (which is simultaneously an inclusion) of bare life."[48]

It was with the Romans that this (paradoxical) distinction, fundamental to the Western political tradition, was first mapped onto a particular figure as the bearer of the bare life that is both included and excluded by politics. This bearer of bare life was *homo sacer*, an obscure figure from ancient Roman law, a peculiar, and seemingly contradictory figure. According to Agamben, it was not permitted to sacrifice the sacred man, yet he could be killed by anyone, and this killing did not constitute a crime, a homicide. *Homo sacer*, who may not be sacrificed but who may be killed with impunity, is "beyond both penal law and sacrifice," isolated and exposed by sovereign power. Indeed, *homo sacer* "preserves the memory of the originary exclusion through which the political dimension was first constituted." This is so because it is precisely in the zone of sovereignty that it is permissible to kill (the sovereign decision over life and death) without committing a homicide or a sacrifice. *Homo sacer* represents the paradigmatic inscription/constitution of bare life by political power. Again, bare life is not a natural life in any sense of being prepolitical—that is, simple life in the state of nature or the common animality of humans—because it is constituted by political power, in the form of the "ban." The ban linking sovereign power and bare life marks the fundamental political relationship: "In Western politics, bare life has the peculiar privilege of being that whose exclusion founds the city of men."[49]

This ban is double: it signifies both expulsion from the political community and the mark of the sovereign; it is both an exclusion and an inclusion. The person who has been banned from the city—the outlaw—is reduced to bare life. *Homo sacer* and other outlaws are "not . . . simply set outside the law . . . but rather *abandoned* by it, . . . exposed and threatened on the threshold in which life and law . . . become indistinguishable." *Homo sacer*, in being banned, is abandoned by law, since the law withdraws from him and permits anyone to kill him. Agamben also describes the ban as "the force of simultaneous attraction and repulsion that ties together the two poles . . . bare life and power."[50] The ban includes bare life by inscribing it with the mark of sovereign power; the ban excludes bare life by abandoning and exposing it.

The doubleness of the ban as inclusion and exclusion, attraction and repulsion, is reflected in a certain doubleness of the banned figure, which Peter Fitzpatrick describes:

> *Homo sacer* is still of the profane. He fugitively occupies an all-too solid world in which he can be killed without sacrifice. Yet *homo sacer* is also of the transcendent beyond. He has already been sacrificed. These two dimensions can only be combined in *homo sacer* because of the confident reference beyond, because of a sacrifice which has brought the beyond into the measure and contingency of a profane world. The life of this sacred man is "bare," then, only because it has been consigned to an empyrean, leaving nothing for it in the profane world but to be killed.[51]

As Fitzpatrick argues, the doubleness of the ban and the sacred/profane duality are related.[52] The ban isolates a bare, naked life that appears as both sacred (excluded by the political community and thus transcending the political community) and profane (isolated by the political community and thus captured by the ban).

Agamben writes in an earlier work: "That which is excluded from the community is, in reality, that on which the entire life of the community is founded. . . . Thus the sacred is necessarily an ambiguous and circular concept. (In Latin sacer means vile, ignominious, and also august, reserved for the gods; both the law and he who violates it are sacred.)"[53] In other words, that which is held in an inclusive exclusion, held in a ban which is in some sense foundational for the community, is marked by an ambiguity, a doubleness, as both spiritual and base. Thus, when the politics of compassion seizes upon a sacred form of life, it is saving a bare life that has been prepared for rescue by the sovereign ban. Humanitarian discourses that proclaim the "sacredness of life" do not oppose punitive and violent forms of political power; they are embracing a bare life that has been constituted by sovereign power: "The sacredness of life, which is invoked today as an absolutely fundamental right in opposition to sovereign power, in fact originally expresses precisely both life's subjection to a power over death and life's irreparable exposure in the relation of abandonment."[54]

The inclusive exclusion of the ban also marks the figure of bare life as simultaneously free and unfree. In romanticized depictions, the outlaw, pursued by the police, is captured by power; his status as outlaw bears the inscription of a sovereign that has, in a sense, always already captured him. On the run from the law, however, the outlaw is also a figure of natural liberty, a romanticized daredevil who resists not only capture but also the everyday forms of disciplinary subjection that constrain the lives of law-abiding subjects. The doubleness and ambiguity of the ban, as both an inclusion and an exclusion, both attraction and repulsion, marks banned bare life with ambiguity: vile and august, constrained and free. Agamben points to exile as a form of the ban that manifests this doubleness and ambiguity: the exile is simultaneously "removed" and "captured," "excluded" and "included."[55] This is why, Agamben says, there is an undecidability surrounding exile: Is it a refuge or a form of punishment? The difficulty in answering this question reflects the doubleness and ambiguity of the sovereign ban on bare life.

Agamben's account of sovereign power and bare life has the advantage of bringing back into view the specifically political dimension of otherness. Rather than approaching the doubleness of the other from a purely psychosocial perspective (abjection as attraction and repulsion) or from a cultural/anthropological approach (identity/difference and the ambivalent reaction to liminality), Agamben helps us to bring back a traditional category of political theory—sovereign power—into the field of exclusion, difference, and biopower.[56]

The disruptive yet foundational status of bare life in the modern political order is visible, according to Agamben, in the way the very concept of "the people," essential to modern notions of democratic legitimacy, carries a double meaning: both as sovereign citizens and as the wretched, the common, the poor, the masses. This fracture within the very concept of the people, Agamben writes, haunts the modern nation-state, since it is based on a concept of "popular sovereignty" requiring that "the people" be understood as an undivided whole. The fracture between people-as-citizens and people-as-excluded-poor is a modern manifestation of the very old split between the naked life of the private sphere and the political life of the public sphere.

But because naked life is represented by whole groups of people, such as the poor (and refugees, and the homeless), modern states seek political solutions to recover the fiction of "the people" as a unity, of bare life as fully morphed into the citizen. Policies of exclusion and containment in relation to the homeless are one example of this process. Not only does the state (through laws and institutions of governance) carve out a second-class political status for homeless persons, but citizenship as full membership is constituted as the exclusion of bare life, and homeless persons figure in legal and political discourse as the embodiments of that bare life. In other words, the political exclusion of homeless persons is a constitutive exclusion. As a result, one must be wary of thinking of homelessness as a problem that states and citizens stumble upon. One must be wary of viewing the state, law, and the sphere of citizenship as somehow superstructural with respect to the problem of homelessness.

Abjection, ambivalence, social anxiety—none of these can fully explain the dualities of homeless representations and policy responses. All of them treat homelessness as a problem of society rather than a problem of sovereign state power. Agamben's account of the sovereign ban on bare life helps make sense of the peculiar polarities of the homeless and homelessness in media representations and public policy. It is as they are held in the sovereign ban that homeless persons appear as free and unfree, as sacred and profane. And it is as subjects of the ban on bare life that homeless persons are subject to the various inclusive exclusions (public-sleeping bans, stigmatizing shelters) that constitute the typical range of policy responses to homelessness in contemporary urban America. The dualities of homelessness—sacred or profane, unconstrained or helpless—and the attendant policy responses are the dualities of an inclusive exclusion and the fundamental ambivalence surrounding it.

For instance, held in the inclusive exclusion of the sovereign ban, the figure of bare life appears both entirely constrained (the homeless person who is captured by the ban on the public performance of life-sustaining activities) and entirely unconstrained (the "disaffiliated" outlaw who transcends all sanctions). Held in the inclusive exclusion of the sovereign ban, the figure of bare life appears both profane (the "dirty beggar") and sacred (the outsider whose exclusion signifies contact with a spiritual beyond or, in the left's secularized version, a romanticized refusal of the "containment fields" of modernity). Compassionate shelter programs and punitive public-space bans each reflect and constitute the homeless-as-bare-life, a hidden affinity the likes of which Agamben uncovers in the context of refugee policy: "Humanitarian organizations . . . can only grasp human life in the figure of bare or sacred life, and therefore, despite themselves, maintain a secret solidarity with the very powers they ought to fight. . . . The 'imploring eyes' of the Rwandan child, whose photograph is shown to obtain money but who 'is now becoming more and more difficult to find alive,' may well be the most telling contemporary cipher of the bare life that humanitarian organizations, in perfect symmetry with state power, need."[57] From the Atlanta Union Mission depicting homeless "untouchables" to the Santa Ana police chaining homeless persons to benches; from the identification of spiritual homelessness to the construction of vagrancy as dangerous rebellion; from disaffiliation as the transcendence of all social sanctions to disaffiliation as the deprivation of all social goods; from the home-free sitcom to the panhandler as moral traffic light—all these polarities have been structured by political power's isolation of bare life.

But Agamben does not simply view bare life and the political as mutually constitutive; he also argues that in modernity "the realm of bare life" has gone from being a constitutive exclusion to the rule. No longer only the constitutive outside, bare life "gradually begins to coincide with the political realm," and bare life and political existence "enter into a zone of irreducible indistinction." This statement leads to one of his more sweeping claims: "Contrary to our modern habit of representing the political realm in terms of citizens' rights, free will, and social contracts, from the point of view of sovereignty, *only bare life is authentically political.*"[58] I am not persuaded by Agamben's contention that *only* bare life is authentically political, nor by his contention that discourses of citizenship, rights, and publicity are essentially a masking of our collective status of bare life, caught within the sovereign ban.[59] Such an apocalyptic vision leads to the suggestion that "every attempt to found political liberties in the rights of the citizen is, therefore, in vain."[60] This strong version of the argument seems to me to empty the category of bare life of its critical content. It is helpful to return to Agamben's earlier insights into the Roman *homo sacer*, a figure whose complete identification with bare life becomes foundational for the political community. Agamben moves too quickly from an analysis of how specific figures (*homo sacer*, the outlaw, refugees) embody bare life, to the apocalyptic and totalizing claim that in modernity we are all virtually bare life. In so doing, he misses an opportunity to examine how the politics of bare life is implicated in the production of political injustices and subordinate political statuses. Outlaws of various forms are not the victims of particular injustices but rather signifiers of a new universal condition. Instead of viewing "citizens' rights, free will, and social contracts" as fictions in relation to the "authentically political" relation of sovereign power over bare life, I examine how the bare life predicament intersects with modern political discourses of citizenship, agency, and the public sphere, producing differential and hierarchically arranged political statuses.

Home-dwelling citizen and homeless bare life are political statuses, not social statuses or elements of personal identity. Although the liberal state's self-image is one of being founded on contract, not status, I argue that the liberal state is actively involved in producing differential political statuses, including the mutually constitutive categories of home-dwelling citizen and homeless bare life.[61] Law (legal statutes, judicial opinions) effectively produces status while at the same time "eliminating the evidence" of its own involvement—pretending to re-cognize a preexisting sociocultural or personhood status "out there" and effacing the traces of its own constituting power to produce hierarchically ordered categories of persons (see chapter 3). In other words—and here I am selectively appropriating—Agamben's account of the fundamental role of bare life in constituting political power, and the fundamental role of political power in constituting bare life, does help make sense of the forms of political inequality in contemporary society through which *some* people are reduced to the status of bare life, the status of an outlaw, the constitutive outside of an exclusionary model of citizenship.[62]

If the recurring traps, blind alley, and polarities of homelessness policy and representation reflect a political dynamic, is there also a political response—a recovery and reimagination of practices of citizenship and democracy—that can respond to the unproductive polarities of the bare life predicament? Am I thereby simply restating the fundamental problem— political life as covering over bare life—as if it were the solution?[63] Well, yes and no.

Agamben dismisses rhetorics of citizenship as being simply nostalgic when confronted by the modern saturation of bare life, but his dismissal is too hasty. As saints and outlaws, as the emblems of the freedom of the open road and as the signifiers of total helplessness and compulsion, the one thing that the homeless are not (recognized as) is citizens. It is citizenship as a protective artifice (as Hannah Arendt puts it) that helps to overcome the bare-life reduction, and it is an ethic of robust pluralism that can promote the extension of this protective artifice to those most in need of it.

I take my cue from Arendt, whose *Origins of Totalitarianism* Agamben cites approvingly. In this text, Arendt displays a keen concern for the predicament of people who were reduced to bare life—refugees whose predicament lay in their status as abstract humanity, as being "nothing more than human," and subject to "humanitarian" concern that looked suspiciously like the response of organizations dedicated to fighting cruelty to animals. Arendt's response involves the articulation of "a right to have rights," and this right is not grounded in the bare life rescued by humanitarianism but is emergent in political action.[64] That the "right to have rights" might be emergent in political action and not grounded in the image of a bare, sacred life indicates a way out of the bare-life predicament: nurturing forms of political action that trouble and contest the citizenship/bare-life opposition. In the context of homeless politics I propose as a response to the bare-life predicament a defense of a *pluralized* citizenship that (a) recognizes the dangers of a strict separation between bare life and the political (a distinction that must be endlessly maintained with violence), (b) does not as a result give up on traditional categories but instead (c) nurtures political practices that run across the distinction between bare life and the political, refusing the isolation of bare life and reinvigorating democratic politics.

As William Connolly puts it, "A pluralizing political society would foster cultural diversity. . . . [E]ach pluralizing movement, if and as it succeeds, migrates from an abject, abnormal, subordinate or obscure Other *subsisting* in a nether world *under* the register of justice to a positive identity now *existing* on the register of justice/injustice."[65] An ethos of "critical responsiveness" helps to nurture such pluralizing movements through their migration, according to Connolly, and my project develops such an ethos in relation to the movements that resist the bare-life predicament. Pluralizing movements are the forms of political action through which the right to have rights emerges on the register of justice. The sites I examine—homeless shelters, homeless encampments, the modern home ideal, the public sphere—may be thought of as the frontiers of democratic pluralism, as the sites where pluralizing movements seek to change registers—from the register of abject bare life that is the seemingly logical and natural outcome of economic forces or personal inadequacies (though in fact a product of political power) to the register of justice/injustice and political resistance to contestable practices and institutions.

At this point, however, a critic might argue that "pluralism" is the *last* thing we need in responding to (domestic) homelessness; what we need are homes, and any attempt to pluralize, relativize, and decenter the home works only to legitimate the deprivations of the homeless. We know what is required, and that is to put everyone into homes; the only difficulties are the *instrumental* ones concerning how to achieve the desired end-state of universal home-dwelling. Indeed, it is tempting to imagine, alongside this critic, that our categories and concepts do not need reworking, that all we have is a failure of will, not a failure of thought. But I believe that the dream of putting everyone into homes is not only unrealistic in the current political climate but also insufficient. The dream of "everyone in a proper home" is like the dream of "everyone a member of a nation with its own state."[66] This dream *produces* the bare life of refugees. Refugees are reduced to bare life not because of a scarcity of material resources but, as Arendt notes, as a consequence of a decidedly nonpluralistic political organization of space: the nation-state system in which birth-nation-territory are presumed to constitute a seamless whole and where there exists, says Nicholas Xenos, "no uncontrolled space."[67] The dream of proper homes—even in its redistributive progressive form—is implicated in the production of bare life when grand schemes for ending homelessness are based on the destruction or conversion of nonnormative dwellings such as residential hotels and collectively organized homeless encampments deemed "substandard housing." The dream to put everyone in homes is a manifestation of the dream for a completely unified "people" purified of bare life, a dream that perversely and paradoxically creates the bare life it seeks to eradicate; it is the dream that orients the violence of a war on poverty toward the destruction of working-class neighborhoods in the name of slum clearance. This is not to reject calls for affordable housing; it is rather to insist that such policies be developed in a pluralistic spirit that avoids the production of an excluded bare life as the "other" against which singular norms of home and home-dwelling citizen stand.

As calls either to eliminate homelessness or to eliminate the homeless from valued public spaces are made with increased urgency, norms about proper homes and home-dwelling citizens and images of the bare life of the homeless insinuate themselves ever more deeply into the programs and policies designed to eliminate homeless(ness). The bare life of the homeless appears to confirm the inevitability and desirability of the modern ideal of home (after all, isn't "home" the solution to this nightmare?) and all it connotes about success and normalcy. As William Connolly puts it, normalizing societies "apply intense institutional pressures to secure [a restrictive set of] identities as norms against which a variety of modes of otherness are defined and excluded." In normalizing societies, where a "cramped" pluralism is treated as something to be defended, not extended, norms of home and the public sphere are fortified, and the bare life of the homeless is produced as their other.[68] It is here that the limits of our "cramped" and domesticated version of democratic pluralism appear to have been found.

These limits, though, are more like frontiers. Frontiers are not simply boundaries; they are openings into unknown territories and may be pushed—pluralized, renewed, reworked. Although Agamben says that from the perspective of sovereign power only bare life is political, from the perspective of democratic action the political emerges as (in Connolly's words) "the multifaceted medium through which the multiple dissonances within it are exposed and negotiated."[69] In this spirit of robust democratic pluralism, the polarization of society into home-dwelling citizens and homeless bare life (whether punished or sheltered) is to be resisted; democratic pluralism manifests an aversion to normalization and the otherness produced as a result of the logic of the norm. This resistance occurs primarily not through the drive for the universalization of the home ideal, which will relentlessly produce the bare life of the homeless as its other, but through a pluralizing movement.

In other words, Arendt's argument about the need for the artifices of political community to protect us from the reduction to the "merely human" is supplemented by the recognition that those artifices are best extended not through nostalgic invocations of past practices of citizenship but through the pluralizing movement of nurturing alternative spaces of dwelling (residential hotels, democratically organized encampments) and alternative spaces of political activity (the street newspaper movement, homeless encampments protesting distributive injustices and shelter policies, alliances between homeless and non-homeless activists, litigation challenging the constitutionality of public-space restrictions). Such pluralization of the categories of home and public sphere can enable multiple forms of dwelling "through which new possibilities of being might be enacted."[70] Pluralization of the category of justice can respond to the multiple forms of injustice that afflict the homeless and resist the legal logics that use punishment and confinement to inscribe the homeless as bare life in the legal order.

I seek to pry loose the problem of homelessness from the dominant discursive frameworks of charity, need, punishment, and pathology. Viewed in connection, not as discrete perspectives along an ideological spectrum, these frameworks conceal as well as reveal. They exhibit some of the doubleness of the ban on bare life while they simultaneously seek to depoliticize the phenomenon of homelessness by bringing it within the orbit of personal failures or social failures. My study brings to light the hidden (but fundamental) political nature of homelessness as caught within the sovereign ban on bare life, and I propose a reimagination of our categories of public, citizenship, home, and justice in responding to the contemporary traps and blind alleys of homeless politics. I argue that legislative and judicial responses to homelessness ought to incorporate an alternative understanding of the agency of homeless persons, one that does not convert that agency into an accusation against outlawed bare life; a trivalent approach to the injustices of homelessness—economic, cultural, and political; a pluralization of our normative conceptions of home; and a pluralization of our normative conceptions of public space. These are required to resist the sovereign ban, the political processes that polarize society into home-dwelling citizens, on the one hand, and the bare life of the homeless, on the other.

OUTLINE OF CHAPTERS

Chapter 1 begins the project of critically examining the contestable discursive and material production of "the public sphere" and its nonpluralistic characteristics that are elaborated through anti-homeless legislation. I argue that anti-homeless legislation marks the boundaries of the contemporary consumptive public sphere and entails a significant shift away from older vagrancy law and its preoccupation with productivity and idleness. The consumptive public sphere entails at best the "cramped" pluralism that Connolly criticizes; it ascribes to public space as a natural, self-evident function the free movement of goods and consumers. The consumptive public sphere stands in contrast to an aspirational, pluralizing conception of public space that fosters encounters with difference and what Richard Sennett calls "the visceral experience of freedom."[71]

Chapter 2 proceeds from the analysis of anti-homeless legislation to its review by federal courts. I examine the discursive construction of homeless persons within legal discourse, and I argue that key judicial opinions *upholding* anti-homeless legislation and key judicial opinions *overturning* anti-homeless legislation are in agreement, in troubling ways, in their representations of homeless persons. These opinions dramatize the polar oppositions discussed earlier, ranging from a vision of homelessness as sacred unfree-dom (the homeless as entirely helpless and deserving of rescue) to a vision of homelessness as profane freedom (the homeless as criminally respon-sible lifestyle choosers). These polar opposite representations are united, though, in their underlying reduction of the homeless to the status of bare life. Though they disagree as to whether or not homelessness is a voluntary "lifestyle choice" or an involuntary status, they imagine the homeless not as citizens but as persons who, in their naked humanity, are at best to be kept alive with a blanket or the floor of a shelter. In other words, these judi-cial opinions reflect and reinforce political power's isolation of bare life.

From the legal misrecognition of the homeless as bare life, chapter 3 moves to consider whether or not the concern for "recognition" is essen-tially misplaced, getting in the way of redistributive programs designed to end homelessness. My central claims in this chapter are that recognition *is* important for homeless persons and that the injustices of homelessness are trivalent: in addition to maldistribution, the homeless face misrecognition and political exclusion. Anti-homeless legislation should be viewed as enforc-ing a specifically political form of exclusion: the ban on bare life that turns the homeless into outlaws. I suggest that legal recognition of the rights of homeless persons (including the right to sleep in public space) and political activism (such as that of tent camps) aimed at realizing those rights can develop into a broader politics concerning housing distribution and shelter policies. Politicized homeless encampments should be understood not as a counterproductive "identity politics" but rather as a pluralizing movement contesting the multiple injustices of homelessness.

Since the public shelter emerged as the central institution for dealing with street persons, appeals to "do more" for the homeless have often essen-tially come down to the call to build more shelters. Implicit in that demand is the assumption of what it is that is being sheltered: in Agamben's words, bare, biological life. Having explored some of the unjust "misrecognition" effects of homeless shelters, I go on to examine the process, in the 1980s and 1990s, whereby homeless shelters essentially replaced residential hotels at the bottom rung of the housing ladder. The result, I argue in chapter 4, is of serious consequence to the theory and practice of democratic plural-ism: the polarization of society into home-dwelling citizens, on the one hand, and dependent clients of a shelter system, on the other. State hous-ing policies such as legal codes concerning proper and substandard dwellings (not simply "market forces" or "social forces") are implicated in this process. And state housing policies are shaped in part by prevailing models of the rela-tionship between household and public sphere. So I argue that Hannah

Arendt's own commitment to political plurality, and her diagnosis of modern displacement and the vulnerabilities of being "merely" human, point *beyond* the model of household and polis presented in *The Human Condition* to a more robust form of pluralism (in Connolly's language, "pluralization"), extending to household forms themselves.[72] The availability of housing options, particularly of options between the degrading conditions of warehouse-like shelters and the normatively enshrined private houses and apartments of mainstream middle-class life, is crucial for the development of a democratic and pluralist response to the bare-life predicament.

In the conclusion I return to the theme of the law's treatment of the bare-life predicament. The exclusion of the homeless from the category of citizenship is made strikingly manifest through a reading of two federal cases concerning organized "public sleeping" protests, one by housed demonstrators and the other by homeless demonstrators. In going to great lengths to distinguish the civic dimensions of a public-sleeping protest from the supposedly nonpolitical actions of homeless persons, the courts constitute the opposition between citizenship and bare life. In response, I turn to a California appeals court opinion and recent ethnographic work that breaks down the opposition between citizenship and bare life by gesturing towards an ethic of dwelling. Such an ethic of dwelling nourishes the practices of democratic pluralism and weakens the isolating power of the sovereign ban on bare life.

The sovereign ban on bare life constitutes the status of homelessness and marks it with a recurring ambivalence. The sovereign ban as manifest in prohibitions against public sleeping and homeless encampments is a specifically political form of injustice. Legal discourses reproduce this political injustice by reducing the homeless to the status of bare life, to be punished as profane outlaws or sheltered as helpless sufferers. And yet the state's fundamental role in all this seems continually to vanish from view: the language of "social problems," of economic redistribution versus cultural recognition, rests on the premise shared by liberals and Marxists alike that the liberal state is not in the business of producing status. Homelessness serves, ultimately, as an example of (a) the political production of status through the sovereign ban on bare life, (b) the successful effacement of that production, and (c) the need for discourses and practices of democratic pluralization to resist both (a) and (b).

CHAPTER 1

From Vagrancy Law to Contemporary Anti-homeless Policy

We must learn to recognize this structure of the ban in the political
relations and public spaces in which we still live.
—Giorgio Agamben, *Homo Sacer*

Defenders of punitive policies such as panhandling restrictions, public-sleeping and sidewalk-sitting bans, and police sweeps of homeless encampments tend to justify these policies with reference to a vision of the homeless as "profane outlaws," disorderly and unconstrained subjects who require the discipline of the laws. Critics of these punitive policies tend to present a vision of the homeless as sacralized sufferers, helpless victims of misfortune who require shelter, not punishment. Even though critics and defenders have polar opposite visions of the homeless, however, they do tend to agree that contemporary punitive policies continue a tradition of vagrancy legislation stretching back to fourteenth-century England. I complicate this shared narrative, developing a genealogy of punitive anti-homeless policies that explores both continuities *and* discontinuities.

Both critics and defenders of the new public-space ordinances targeting the homeless tend to find a great deal of continuity between these policies and common-law prohibitions against vagrancy that stretch back to fourteenth-century England. Critics of current anti-homeless laws frequently trace their origin to centuries-old vagrancy laws in order to denounce these policies as "old wine in new bottles." As Harry Simon argues, "Official efforts to punish homeless indigents are not new. For more than six centuries, vagrancy and loitering statutes made it a crime to wander without visible means of support." When the Supreme Court in 1972 struck down vagrancy statutes as unconstitutionally vague, cities turned to more targeted ordinances that "changed the form, but not the substance, of official efforts to control the homeless."[1] Since critics contend that the essential goal of these ordinances and policies remains the same—the criminalization of homelessness and poverty in order to control the displaced poor—Robert Humphreys asserts that "in many ways, the plight of the modern-day street homeless is strikingly similar to that of roving vagrants and vagabonds of former times."[2] And Don Mitchell argues that anti-homeless laws have "roots in long-standing ideological or cultural concerns about the relationship between the deviant poor and the upstanding bourgeoisie."[3]

Defenders of the current policies make much the same argument—describing a historical continuity in social policies to control the poor and displaced. Like the critics, one prominent advocate of current anti-homeless ordinances, Robert Tier, sees a common underlying goal to these various efforts. But this goal is not to wage war against the homeless so much as it is to satisfy the perennial need of social orders to defend a culture of work and responsibility from the disorders of idleness and begging. What has improved is the method: we now have more focused laws (bolstered by social scientific knowledge about the causes and consequences of disorder) that apply directly to the conduct that societies have long recognized as subversive. So, Tier says, although "westerners have historically and consistently sought to prevent, or at least control, begging" the new statutes "do not criminalize the status of being a beggar (or being poor)" but reach "only conduct which is egregious, dangerous or intrusive." The new public-space ordinances gain *constitutional* legitimacy in their discontinuity from past efforts but they gain a broader *moral* legitimacy from their connection to that tradition. Tier says he wants "to distinguish the current efforts from the more sweeping measures of the past, but also to demonstrate that the current efforts are part of a long tradition of community efforts to maintain safety and civility in public spaces."[4]

Thus, although legal defenders and critics disagree fundamentally about the legitimacy of these punitive policies, they tend to agree on the existence of historical continuities between newer and older policies toward the poor and displaced. Whether the new policies are one more chapter in a sorry history of social intolerance and antagonism or a new and improved effort (more targeted, less constitutionally problematic) by society to cope with the perennial problem of disorder, their historical basis is reiterated in almost every law journal article on the topic, and in many judicial opinions as well.

There is a good deal to recommend these narratives of historical continuity, both the legitimating defense and the delegitimating critique, for the affinities between vagrancy law and newer public-space ordinances are hard to miss. The displaced poor have indeed been viewed as a threat in many times and places, and this fact can be given a plausible critical interpretation (the continuing war against the poor) or a plausible status quo–legitimating interpretation (the perennial need of social orders to protect themselves from disorder). Moreover, both sides of these legal debates have good rhetorical reasons for emphasizing historical continuities: critics may succeed in undermining the policies by connecting them to vagrancy statutes that have been declared unconstitutional; defenders may succeed in gaining a broader moral legitimacy for these policies by uncovering the wisdom of tradition.

These rhetorical strategies, however, produce a history of very broad strokes that hinders efforts to understand the contemporary political and cultural processes at work. The result is that the critiques and justifications tend to have a certain timeless, ahistorical character.[5] Is it really the *same* threat across societies and historical periods? Is it really the *same* animus or anxiety motivating efforts at social control? What is obscured from view when new punitive policies toward the homeless are imagined as either a further installment of the battle between rich and poor or a new and improved effort of society to cope with the debilitating effects of begging, disaffiliation, and idleness?

First, I would argue that these views may prevent an appreciation of the particular contradictions, anxieties, and normative idealizations of self, citizenship, and public sphere that lie behind particular punitive policies; thus, both the legitimating and the delegitimating narratives of continuity shield the political order from examination. Another way to put this is that although the bare-life predicament may recur across historical periods—from *homo sacer* to the refugee—the specific contours of the opposition between bare life and the political sphere change quite dramatically. Therefore, I seek to trace a genealogy of the punitive policies surrounding beggars, homelessness, and vagrancy. The movement from vagrancy law to anti-homeless legislation, I argue, involves a significant transformation in the identification of the very problem or threat to which the laws address themselves. This transformation reveals, in turn, a larger shift in the very constitution of the public sphere: from the productive public sphere and its preoccupation with idleness to the consumptive public sphere and its preoccupation with aesthetic appearance.

Thus, I connect vagrancy law and contemporary anti-homeless legislation to historically contingent constructions of the public sphere and forms of governance through work and consumption. These constructions are not completely discontinuous. Concerns about "idleness" link older vagrancy prohibitions with contemporary discourses of welfare reform, and arguments about the "future criminality" of the displaced poor constitute a thread that links vagrancy law to anti-homeless legislation. But there has also been a significant shift: Rather than incorporate (through coercion) the idle into a world of work and discipline, contemporary anti-homeless laws protect (through exclusion) a consumptive public from threats to its security.

VAGRANCY LAW

My goal is not to present an exhaustive history of vagrancy law but to paint a brief picture of it in seventeenth- and eighteenth-century Europe in order to raise some critical questions about the continuity thesis. William Blackstone's *Commentaries on the Laws of England,* first published in 1765–1769, forms the basis of my account of how vagrancy was identified as a problem, and what sorts of concerns, anxieties, and categories became linked to that problem. But I begin with the comments of Michel Foucault, whose interest in vagrancy in the seventeenth and eighteenth centuries stems from his interest in the history of madness.

In *Madness and Civilization,* Foucault asserts that the institutions of confinement that sprang up in seventeenth-century Europe first targeted idleness. By the nineteenth-century, madness had taken the place of idleness as the central target of confinement, but the roots of the confining impulse, and the institutions and discourses surrounding confinement, were located within the problematic of labor and idleness. The seventeenth-century institutions originated, Foucault contends, in an "imperative of labor," not philanthropic benevolence: "Our philanthropy prefers to recognize the signs of a benevolence toward sickness where there is only a condemnation of idleness." In that "classical" age, the age of reason as an age of confinement, "idleness is rebellion—the worst form of all, in a sense: it waits for nature to be generous. . . . [T]he sin of idleness is the supreme pride of man once he has fallen, the absurd pride of poverty." Foucault suggests that the rituals of confinement, excommunication, and reintegration of the vagrant and vagabond reproduced in the sphere of production the earlier social boundaries around leprosy: "Between labor and idleness in the classical world ran a line of demarcation that replaced the exclusion of leprosy."[6]

One should not draw too strict a line between a classical age and what came before it, however. Even preceding the seventeenth-century, the efforts of ruling elites to control vagrancy centered on the question of idleness. The historian A. L. Beier describes the way in which the idleness of vagrants was construed as a threat to the economic productivity of English society in the sixteenth century: "It was not just vagrants' numbers, though, that worried officials. Rather, it was their disruption of the labour system and political order. . . . Above all, they were dependent workers, that is, servants and apprentices, who formed the bulk of the labour-force in early modern England. If they were idle, production in all sectors would grind to a halt, and unimaginable disorders might ensue." Beier traces the condemnation of the idleness of vagrancy neither to a functionalist economic logic nor to a specifically Protestant conception of worldly productivity as a sign of salvation. Rather, like Foucault, he sees a particular version of humanism as a source of the condemnation of idleness and of the confinement of vagrants in institutions dedicated to self-improvement through labor: "Humanists generally viewed worldly activity as a good thing and saw no value in idleness. . . . Thus, contrary to the Franciscan ideal of poverty, so powerful in the High Middle Ages, . . . the humanists saw dangers in material deprivation."[7]

In both the sixteenth and seventeenth centuries, vagrants were subject to corporal punishments such as flogging and to new institutions of confinement—houses of correction—in order to eliminate "that loathsome monster idleness (the mother and breeder of vagabonds)," wrote Robert Hitchcock.[8] Vagrants were confined and taught the virtues of labor, in contrast to the medieval charity provided in monasteries and almshouses.[9]

Alongside the prevention of idleness, preventing "future criminality" was a prominent justification for vagrancy statutes and prosecutions. Some scholars point to a gradual shift in the focus of the application of vagrancy laws, from the concern with labor mobility and idleness to the prevention of such criminal activities as theft. William J. Chambliss locates this shift as early as the sixteenth century with the revision of English vagrancy laws to include restrictions on games and pastimes and to increase penalties.[10] Other scholars place the shift in emphasis later. Tier, for instance, says that "in England, the focus of vagrancy law changed from motivating unproductive members of society to preventing crime" in the nineteenth century.[11]

Nevertheless, concerns about idleness persisted as well. Kenneth Kusmer, in his historical study of homelessness in the United States, points to productivity and idleness as key to society's response to vagrancy in the late nineteenth century. Discussing the subcultures of tramps and hoboes in that period, he argues that "although they operated within industrial society, their pattern of intermittent work and leisure, as well as the social organization of the hobo jungles, reflected a commitment to preindustrial values." With work and productivity emerging as central values, "the vagrancy problem" became "a recognized national issue." As Kusmer writes, "In a nation comprised, ideally, of sturdy yeomen, small capitalists, and upwardly mobile working men, [the vagrant] seemed a footloose, goalless wanderer, living not by his hands but by his wits and—worst of all—in the dissipation of idleness."[12]

The rationale of preventing crime also continued. Caleb Foote, in his study of vagrancy law application in post–World War II Philadelphia, documents how prominent a justification it was for arrests, frequently offered by early twentieth-century courts to defend vagrancy statutes. Arresting vagrants was a form of crime prevention, explained by metaphors of disease and reproduction: vagrancy statutes "check the spread of 'a parasitic disease'"; "the vagrant mode of life denounced by the statutes is of itself a crime breeder"; and the vagrant is "the chrysalis of every species of criminal."[13]

Although there is, then, disagreement as to the relative significance of these two concerns at different points in time in the history of vagrancy law, it is safe to say that idleness and future criminality have constituted twin rationales for vagrancy law for a considerable time.

William Blackstone deals with vagrancy in chapter 13 of the fourth book (1769) of his *Commentaries on the Laws of England,* titled "Offences against the Public Health, and the Public Police or Economy," where he delineates a sphere of governmental concern that, following Foucault and Agamben, can be called "biopolitical": the investment of power in "the population," its health, habits, and reproduction. From laws concerning "public health," he moves on to the "public police and economy," by which he says he means "the due regulation and domestic order of the kingdom: whereby the individuals of the state, like members of a well-governed family, are bound to conform their general behavior to the rules of propriety, good neighbourhood, and good manners; and to be decent, industrious, and inoffensive in their respective stations."[14] Included here are felonies such as clandestine marriages and bigamy, but several sections of this chapter discuss laws that are preoccupied with idleness.

Vagrancy, in the English common law, is defined by idleness and the absence of productive labor. As Caleb Foote says, "At common law a vagrant is an idle person who is without visible means of support and who, although able to work, refuses to do so."[15] Blackstone introduces his discussion of vagrancy law by calling idleness a "high offence against the public economy." Prohibitions against the idleness of vagrants meets with his approval. "Idle persons or vagabonds," those people who sleep in the daytime and frequent alehouses at night, are divided into three classes: "Idle and disorderly persons, rogues and vagabonds, and incorrigible rogues." Blackstone says that all three groups "are offenders against the good order, and blemishes in the government, of any kingdom," and "they are therefore all punished, . . . idle and disorderly persons with one month's imprisonment in the house of correction; rogues and vagabonds with whipping and imprisonment not exceeding six months; and incorrigible rogues with the like discipline and confinement, not exceeding two years." Proceeding from vagrancy and vagabondage to a discussion of the sumptuary laws governing conspicuous consumption, Blackstone is more circumspect: "It may still be a dubious question, how far private luxury is a public evil; and, as such, cognizable by public laws." Although many laws governing extravagance in dress had been repealed, he notes one remaining statute that prohibits a man from being served more than two courses for dinner, except on specific holidays, when he may have three.[16]

The close textual relation between vagrancy and sumptuary law is curious. Certainly, not too much should be read into the conjunction of idleness and luxury as objects of sanction under the heading of public economy. Blackstone logically connects the prohibitions against gaming (which follow) with sumptuary law ("Next to that of luxury, naturally follows the offence of *gaming,* which is generally introduced to supply or retrieve the expenses occasioned by the former"), but makes no such transitional statement connecting vagrancy law and idleness with sumptuary law and luxury. Furthermore, he explains at the beginning of this "public economy" chapter that the accumulated offenses are something of a grab bag of crimes and nuisances: "This head of offences must therefore be very miscellaneous, as it comprises all such crimes as especially affect public society, and are not comprehended under any of the four preceding species." Nevertheless, a certain logic can be traced out that links vagrancy, luxury, and gaming, and this is the issue of idleness, which figures so prominently in the "public economy" chapter. Indeed, after discussing sumptuary law, Blackstone returns to the issue of idleness when he explains that gambling is "an offence of the most alarming nature" in part because, among the lower classes, it encourages "public idleness."[17]

He returns to the theme again in discussing a last category of public crimes, poaching. Blackstone disapproves of the game laws, which are "so numerous and so confused, and the crime itself so questionable in nature," yet he says that if there is a rational basis for the hunting restrictions and the extra penalties placed on landless poachers, it is idleness: "I have ranked [hunting] under the present head, because the only rational footing, upon which we can consider it as a crime, is that in low and indigent persons it promotes idleness, and takes them away from their proper employments and callings, which is an offence against the public police and economy of the commonwealth."[18]

Idleness, then, linked prohibitions against vagrancy, against excessive consumption and gambling, and, to a certain extent, against poaching. Alan Hunt argues that "the moralization of idleness was a central component in the regulatory discourses of the late Middle Ages," connecting vagrancy law to sumptuary regulation of consumption and appearance: "The persistent moralization of customary recreation and idleness, while not being sumptuary in the narrow sense, nevertheless was directed against the cultural consumption and practices of the masses in a moralization that was given coercive inflexion through the linkage to the regulation of labour which was the root of the criminal laws against vagrancy." Sumptuary law, particularly regulations in the Middle Ages concerning apparel, were often explicitly linked to vagrancy law: "On the borders of modernity there were two connected but never fused discursive targets, luxury and idleness. . . . Idleness as a second focus of preoccupation was particularly significant in that while it resonates with the critique of luxury, it has its own distinctive thrust again directed against the labouring classes." Idleness became a central focus of regulation when "the regulation of labour became an increasingly significant object of governance as labour shortage and the displacement of feudalism proceeded with increasing rapidity."[19] Idleness and luxury, then, resonate insofar as both signify an absence of productive activity. The idleness of the vagrant, like excessive consumption, violated norms of worldly activity and productive labor.

THE UNCONSTITUTIONALITY OF VAGRANCY LAW

Vagrancy laws, imported directly and almost word for word from the English common law, existed on the books in American cities and states up through the first half of the twentieth century. Not until 1972 did the Supreme Court invalidate such legislation, striking down a Jacksonville, Florida, vagrancy ordinance on due process grounds for being unconstitutionally vague.[20] The Jacksonville ordinance under consideration in *Papachristou v. City of Jacksonville* explicitly targets disorderly persons and provides an extensive classificatory scheme of vagrancy—a catalogue of colorful characters:

> Rogues and vagabonds, or dissolute persons who go about begging, common gamblers, persons who use juggling or unlawful games or plays, common drunkards, common night walkers, thieves, pilferers or pickpockets, traders in stolen property, lewd, wanton and lascivious persons, keepers of gambling places, common railers and brawlers, persons wandering or strolling

around from place to place without any lawful purpose or object, habitual
loafers, disorderly persons, persons neglecting all lawful business and habitually spending their time by frequenting houses of ill fame, gaming houses,
or places where alcoholic beverages are sold or served, persons able to work
but habitually living upon the earnings of their wives or minor children shall
be deemed vagrants and, upon conviction in the Municipal Court shall be
punished as provided for Class D offenses.[21]

Although the Supreme Court rejected this ordinance on the grounds of
vagueness, what is as remarkable is its extensive specification of individuals
and character types.

Justice William Douglas discusses the roots of Florida's vagrancy statute
in English law, noting the central place of labor control: "The breakup of
feudal estates in England led to labor shortages which in turn resulted in
the Statutes of Laborers, designed to stabilize the labor force by prohibiting increases in wages and prohibiting the movement of workers from their
home areas in search of improved conditions. Later vagrancy laws became
criminal aspects of the poor laws. The series of laws passed in England on
the subject became increasingly severe."[22] Tracing vagrancy laws to the
decay of the feudal system paves the way for their rejection as archaic, ill-
suited to contemporary social conditions. Douglas cites the case of *Ledwith
v. Roberts* in a footnote to this effect: "The early Vagrancy Acts came into
being under peculiar conditions utterly different to those of the present
time."[23] He situates vagrancy law within the problematic of labor and idleness in an emerging industrial order and the breakup of feudalism, thus
establishing the law as an anachronistic throwback.

After suggesting that the ordinance is a historical anachronism, Douglas
rejects it as unconstitutionally vague, a violation of due process in that it
does not allow someone to know in advance whether his or her conduct
is covered. Furthermore, it "encourages arbitrary and erratic arrests and
convictions" and criminalizes conduct considered innocent by modern
norms and outside the scope of governmental police powers. Douglas points
to various forms of conduct that are either considered neutral or positively
endorsed by our culture but that could possibly fall within the vague parameters of the Jacksonville ordinance: the portion of the ordinance directed
at drinkers and barflies, for example, "would literally embrace many members of golf clubs and city clubs." Evincing a romantic attachment to the
vagabond as a kind of saintly and free hero of the open road, he cites
Walt Whitman as lauding a poetic form of vagabondage. Douglas identifies with the romantic, vagrant soul, discussing the freedom to wander as
one of the "amenities" that nourish freedom, dissent, and individuality in

American political culture.[24] (Indeed, the specification of identities in the Jacksonville ordinance, with its elaboration of disorderly character types, rogues, and wanderers, seems to invite that very identification.)

Douglas also notes that "future criminality . . . is the common justification for the presence of vagrancy statutes," but he rejects that defense of vagrancy laws: "A presumption that people who might walk or loaf or loiter or stroll or frequent houses where liquor is sold, or who are supported by their wives or who look suspicious to the police are to become future criminals is too precarious for a rule of law. The implicit presumption in these generalized vagrancy standards—that crime is being nipped in the bud—is too extravagant to deserve extended treatment."[25]

Justice Douglas's argument that vagrancy law is a relic of a previous order is substantively correct, but not, I contend, on the basis of his optimism about the progress of individual rights or on the basis of his romantic embrace of the wanderer as central to American identity. Rather, vagrancy law becomes archaic, I argue, when its central preoccupation with idleness and production comes into dissonant contact with an emerging postindustrial order. What the postindustrial spaces of American consumer society require is not the elimination of idleness but rather the disappearance of abject poverty.

POST-PAPACHRISTOU: CONSUMPTIVE SPACES AND DISORDERLY ACTS

Idleness has remained a prominent rationale for policy toward the poor. Welfare reform in the 1990s—seeking to reintegrate welfare recipients into the sphere of productive labor and to link shelter benefits to labor—provides evidence of the degree to which idleness, conceived of as nonparticipation in the world of wage labor, animates welfare policies. Future criminality too, in a modified form, remains a justification for anti-homeless policies (discussed below). But a specifically postindustrial logic has emerged in post-*Papachristou* anti-homeless ordinances: the exclusion of the displaced poor from consumptive public spaces means that the relationship between begging and sumptuary practices articulated in Blackstone's commentaries has not disappeared but rather has been reversed. Whereas the older vagrancy prohibitions were discursively linked to restrictions on "conspicuous" consumption, it is precisely conspicuous consumption that is *protected* by the new laws against aggressive begging, sidewalk-sitting, and urban camping.

We often hear that we live in a consumer society, and this comment is usually meant as a criticism. The criticism comes from a variety of directions, however. Most famously, the critique has been articulated by Daniel

Bell as a conservative defense of the values of thrift, hard work, and self-denial in the face of an emerging ethos of hedonism, immediate gratification, and credit.[26] Theorists of American culture such as Warren Susman imagine a conflict between a "Puritan-republican, producer-capitalist culture and a newly emerging culture of abundance."[27] But the criticism has also been presented from a left-Marxist perspective in which the emergence of "consumer values" is imagined not as a dangerous and anarchic hedonism erupting from below but as a new regime of normalization that ultimately serves the goal of capital accumulation. As Jean Baudrillard argues, consumption is a disciplinary practice, not a sphere of individual freedom: "The consumer, the modern citizen, cannot evade the constraint of happiness and pleasure, which in the new ethics is equivalent to the traditional constraint of labor and production." In this account, producer and consumer values are not considered to be in direct contradiction; rather, consumptive pleasure over productive thrift is viewed as "an internal substitution in a system essentially unchanged."[28]

From a Foucauldian perspective, Nikolas Rose's picture of "advanced liberal" societies in his *Powers of Freedom* places consumption at the heart of the project of governance. Whereas the governance of conduct once occurred primarily through bureaucracies and expert interventions into the field of the social, neoliberal reforms, the rollback of the welfare state and the extension of market logics have led to new forms of advanced liberal governance: "Individuals are now to be linked into a society through acts of socially sanctioned consumption and responsible choice, through the shaping of a lifestyle according to grammars of living that are widely disseminated yet do not depend upon political calculations and strategies for their rationales or their techniques."[29]

In Baudrillard's view, aids to consumption, such as credit and the ideology of consumptive pleasure, are the most recent disciplinary mechanisms of capitalism, "the equivalent and the extension, in the twentieth century, of the great indoctrination of rural populations into industrial labor which occurred throughout the nineteenth century."[30] In Rose's view, consumptive technologies have more recently come to fill a regulatory void created by the rollback of the social state. As individuals center their identities on an ideology of choice, the need for governmental projects of normalization is less acute, at least for the mainstream public of consuming and desiring selves: "As these mechanisms of regulation through desire, consumption and the market . . . come to extend their sway over larger and larger sectors of the population, earlier bureaucratic and governmental mechanisms of self-formation and self-regulation begin to be dismantled and refocused upon marginalized individuals who through ill will, incompetence, or misfortune are outside these webs for 'consuming civility.'" Rose points, then, to a bifurcation in governance strategies and projects: regulation through consumption and desire "in the name of identity and lifestyle" for most of us, and a focusing of explicitly political, state-sponsored regulatory regimes on the marginal, dispossessed, otherized populations.[31]

These strategies are realized in particular kinds of spaces, spaces that perfectly dramatize the bifurcation in social control strategies that Rose discusses. Postindustrial redevelopment of urban public spaces is centered on consumptive and leisure activities, and many critics note that the result is "pseudo-public space" or "privatized public space." Shopping malls that seek to evoke the ambiance of the agora while maintaining sharp restrictions on expression and assembly, privately owned plazas and parks constructed adjacent to office towers in exchange for "increased density allowances" from city zoners, the transformation of airports and train stations into spaces of shopping and entertainment, business improvement districts that create forms of private governance and fund private security guards to keep tourists and shoppers secure and homeless street dwellers in perpetual movement[32]—all of these developments, alongside the public-space ordinances discussed below, help constitute what Alexander Kluge and Oskar Negt call the "privately owned public sphere, in which 'the public' is defined as a mass of consumers and spectators."[33] This consumptive public sphere is the space in which consumer identities are formed and at the same time the space where intensified police powers are deployed against excluded others, such as the homeless. These developments, writes Susan Bickford, "work not simply to privatize formerly public spaces, but to purify both public and private space—especially to purify them of fear, discomfort, or uncertainty."[34]

In describing this vision of consumptive space under the term "consumptive public sphere," I differ slightly from some analysts who denote the consumptive spaces of redeveloped urban centers, shopping malls, and business improvement districts as "pseudo-public spaces" and "nonpublic urban" or "postpublic" space.[35] Although these terms helpfully point toward the purifying, heavily policed, exclusionary, and depoliticized nature of such spaces,[36] the terms fail to incorporate a recognition of the fact that these consumer spaces are defended *as public spaces,* designed to re-create an idealized vision of a "lost" public space, and constitute a particular (consuming) subject as a member of "the public." Thus, when left critics attack the privatization of public space, or the loss of public space, they echo the very discourses of urban nostalgia they are attempting to confront. As Rosalyn Deutsche argues, "Within this idealizing perspective, departures from established arrangements inevitably signal the 'end of public space.' Edge cities, shopping malls, mass media, electronic space . . . become tantamount to democracy's demise." In describing the *loss* of public space, the critic, Deutsche argues, becomes an unwitting bedfellow of designers of nostalgic re-creations of public space in urban redevelopment projects.[37]

A second critical strategy, rather than presenting a narrative of the end of public space, points to the exclusions and ideological visions that establish a particular vision of the public sphere. This approach describes the shifting constructions of publicness and the exclusions through which they are generated. Such a genealogy of the public sphere, as Deutsche argues, rejects the notion of an essential nature of publicness such as full inclusivity or the exposure to difference: "Precisely because the 'essence' of publicness is a historically constituted figure that grows and changes, the public is a rhetorical instrument open to diverse, even antagonistic uses." Rather than positing an ideal of "real" public space which we have lost with the creation of "false" or "inauthentic" public spaces (nonpublic, postpublic), a genealogical investigation exposes the exclusions, displacements, acts of violence and interpretations that produce contingent versions of public space.[38]

I employ such a genealogical approach, describing the shifting nature of publicness from the productive public sphere to the consumptive public sphere. It is important, however, not to abandon the critical purchase one gains with critiques of "nonpublic" or "postpublic" spaces. What these critiques have going for them is an aspirational ideal (sometimes explicit, sometimes implicit) of public space. Clarissa Hayward articulates this ideal of democratic publicness in terms of a space that "cultivates, not citizen virtue, understood to require freedom from need and to imply shared ends, . . . so much as a citizen identity founded in moments of exposure to the diverse perspectives, needs, and claims of the strangers with whom one cohabits public urban space."[39] Bickford describes such an aspirational ideal of public space as a space of multiplicity and exposure, seeking to separate this ideal from nostalgic invocations of a lost public space: "My argument is not that through building modern urban and suburban life we have 'lost' the public realm, but rather that the possibility of achieving a genuinely public realm inhabited by multiple 'we's' is blocked through these practices."[40]

The difficult but necessary task is to hold on to an ideal of public space as nurturing a robust pluralism, on the one hand, while acknowledging, on the other, that the public sphere, in Deutshe's words, "is not only a site of discourse; it is also a discursively constructed site" and that as such it can never be "a fully inclusive, fully constituted realm." The genealogical investigation of exclusions that enable particular discursive constructions of the public sphere is not incompatible with an ideal of democratic public space as a space of plurality, exposure, and the multiplicity of perspectives; indeed, such an ideal is what motivates such genealogies in the first place. The genealogical spirit, however, does caution against treating the ideal of democratic public space as a fully realizable space of multiple identities, "a fully inclusive, fully constituted realm."[41] The goal is a public space that nurtures and is nurtured by the spirit of democratic pluralization, but one must recognize that (as Connolly argues) pluralization is always an emergent process to be encouraged, not an end state (pluralism) to be defended or mourned.[42]

The consumptive public sphere is nonpluralistic insofar as it ascribes to public space a single, natural, pregiven purpose: the circulation and movement of goods and persons. Following the analysis of Bell, Baudrillard, and Rose, it signals a shift in normalizing strategy, ideology, and spatial organization from production to consumption. As Bickford argues, "The space in malls and renovated downtown shopping complexes is policed in part by asserting an unambiguous and singular function: consumption. The policing of function is a way of determining what kind of public is present."[43] A vision of public space as not itself marked by contestation or dispute is the vision expressed by defenders of public-space restrictions on the homeless, whom they view as intruders from the outside, interfering with and disrupting the fulfillment of public space's proper purpose. As Deutsche puts it, "When public space is represented as an organic unity that the homeless person is seen to disrupt from the outside, the homeless person becomes a positive embodiment of the element that prevents society from achieving closure."[44]

Extending this line of analysis, Andrew Mair argues that the displacement of the poor is not incidental but necessary to postindustrial redevelopment: "The very nature of the post-industrial city *demands* the removal of the homeless." Postindustrial space is marked by the absence of production and poverty, a space where office workers live, work, consume, and are entertained, and "the very presence of the homeless provokes a significant crisis in the ideological security of the post-industrial space." Reclaiming public spaces as middle-class consumptive spaces, postindustrial redevelopment seeks to create "a space which is internally homogeneous, . . . separated from the sites of industry and poverty which continue to exist." The homeless become a threat to this meaningful space, Mair argues, because of what the homeless signify to the status-seeking, middle-class gentrifiers. The homeless appear to "deviate from virtually all of the social norms associated with status-seeking society," such as norms about work, family, and public behavior.[45] Attempts to remove the homeless from the postindustrial city include the eviction of shelters from the gentrifying neighborhoods that Mair discusses; the criminalization of panhandling near key sites of consumptive activity (ATM machines, outdoor eating establishments, queues of "five or more persons waiting to gain admission to a place or vehicle");[46] urban-camping ordinances criminalizing public sleeping; the redesignation of public trash receptacles as government property, off limits to the homeless; and street sweeps that confiscate the property of homeless persons, redesignating it as trash. Ordinances against aggressive panhandling in places such as Los Angeles, Santa Monica, and Baltimore map the postindustrial city; in constructing new fields of illegalities these ordinances seek to construct a danger- and anxiety-free zone around the pleasures and pathways of consumptive space and its legitimate middle-class users.[47] Postindustrial redevelopment surrounds urban space by new walls that divide consumptive pleasure and choice from poverty and homelessness.[48]

Not all spaces in contemporary postindustrial cities are consumptive spaces, of course. Geographers have explored the division of public spaces into the "prime" or "pleasure" spaces of middle-class consumption and the "refuse" or "marginal" spaces that remain untouched by gentrification (such as those under bridges and highway overpasses) and are sometimes used by homeless persons as makeshift encampments. David Snow and Leon Anderson note that there is a continuum between prime and marginal spaces, and that these spatial definitions and investments of value are continually shifting and subject to contestation. Processes of gentrification reduce the extent of marginal space and render homeless persons' daily survival strategies more precarious. Indio, a homeless man in Austin, Texas, reported to Snow and Anderson, "There used to be lots of places down here where no one would bother you. But it ain't that way no more. Too many fancy buildings going up." As marginal spaces become redeveloped, homeless persons find themselves forced to occupy prime space more and more, coming into greater contact with domiciled citizens and producing the political conflicts exemplified by the panhandling and urban-camping ordinances. For homeless persons navigating postindustrial urban space, strategic engagements with prime consumptive spaces (those invested by domiciled citizens with value and subject to extensive policing) and strategic retreats to marginal spaces (where one can be left alone, to sleep, eat, drink, and congregate) become key to survival.[49]

The punitive response of cities seeking to protect the aesthetic appearance and economic vitality of prime spaces is to create a "secure" border
around the spaces and activities of normative consumptive activity. But
everyone must consume: consumption is essential to the life process.
Homeless people must eat and drink, and if they live their lives on the
street, they must accumulate and maintain some amount of personal property without the security of a place governed by a private-property right
of exclusion. Yet not only do panhandling and anti-sleeping laws seek
to exclude the homeless from consumptive spaces, but programs aimed
at helping the homeless also seek to delegitimate their claims to be consumers. And this exclusion of the homeless from consumer identity is not
incidental; it is a constitutive exclusion, marking out the boundaries of
consumptive space and consumer identity. Programs have been instituted
in various cities to encourage the non-homeless to give homeless panhandlers not money but tokens redeemable for shelter or food, to prevent
convenience stores in skid row neighborhoods from selling fortified alcohol, and to confiscate and redefine street-dwellers' property, as trash that
produces a public health hazard (see the discussion of *Love v. Chicago* in
chapter 2).

What Kawash calls "processes of containment, constriction, and compression" include the attempt to restrict the consumption of the homeless.
She argues that anxiety over consumption by the homeless is part of a larger
anxiety.[50] It emerges when the fantasized wholeness of a disembodied,
abstract public subject confronts the abjected homeless body that is its product, its constitutive outside, and its threatening other:

> The public view of the homeless as "filth" marks the danger of this body *as
> body* to the homogeneity and wholeness of the public. The desire or ambi-
> tion for such wholeness thus faces an obstacle that may be ideologically dis-
> avowed but that always returns as an irreducibly materialist challenge. The
> solution to this impasse appears as the ultimate aim of the "homeless wars":
> to exert such pressures against this body that will reduce it to nothing, to
> squeeze it until it is so small that it disappears, such that the circle of the social
> will again appear closed.[51]

The fantasy at work behind anti-homeless policies is the fantasy of so
constricting and displacing this homeless body that it will "go away." In
other words, it is the fantasy of eliminating bare life, of recovering an "uncon-
taminated" public citizen. But it is a fantasy that is doomed to repetition
and failure and more repetition, since the very identity of the public consumer citizen is formed through the constitutive exclusion of bare life.

The new public-space ordinances regulating panhandling and prohibiting sidewalk-sitting and sleeping or camping in public parks are thus the punitive underside of the consumptive public sphere. Whereas vagrancy statutes stressed the need to incorporate the idle into the civilization of productivity, panhandling and sidewalk-sitting laws seek to exclude abject poverty from "prime" consumptive spaces. Rather than incorporate (through coercion) the idle into a world of work and discipline, contemporary anti-homeless laws protect a consumptive public (which they constitute) from threats to its security and enjoyment.

The city of Seattle's sidewalk ordinance and its legal defenses manifest the ideology of public space as an "organic unity" with a pregiven purpose: the unobstructed movement of goods and persons in commercial activity. In the fall of 1993 the Seattle City Council passed an ordinance that, among other things, banned sitting on sidewalks in downtown Seattle and in neighborhood commercial areas between 7:00 A.M. and 9:00 P.M.[52] Designed by City Attorney Mark Sidran in response to concerns over the loss of viable urban commercial space in the wake of "urban blight," the ordinance was a tool to control the homeless population of Seattle in order to make downtown and other retail zones more friendly to consumers. As cited by Judge Barbara Rothstein, who upheld the ordinance as constitutional, its purpose was "to facilitate the safe and efficient movement of pedestrians and goods on the public sidewalks of commercial areas."[53] Mark Sidran, architect of the bill and its chief defender, argued that the legal question involved "the balancing of the rights and interests of people who have the right to use the sidewalks, especially senior citizens, against having to navigate around people who are sitting or lying down."[54]

The city of Seattle, defending the ordinance, presented in its memorandum to the court the testimony of a business leader who stressed this problem of obstruction: "Walking down the Ave can feel like running a gauntlet. Pedestrians have to dodge aggressive panhandling, lewd and derogatory comments, and the residue of urine, alcohol and worse. They also *have to step over people* individually or in groups on our sidewalks."[55] In all these comments, what Richard Sennett terms the "mechanics of movement" triumphs over "the visceral experience of freedom." Public space is not to be constructed so as to "arouse the body . . . by accepting impurity, difficulty, and obstruction as part of the very experience of liberty."[56] Public space is not to be constructed so as to facilitate encounters with difference, exposures to otherness. Rather, public spaces become instrumental to the free circulation of goods, consumers, and workers.[57] The homeless, described by Sidran as "lounging on busy sidewalks," are obstacles the

upstanding citizen/worker/consumer must "step over."[58] A vision of the
"upstanding" citizen is established in opposition to the bare life of the
homeless street-dweller and panhandler, who are viewed as physical block-
ages preventing the achievement of a unified public space in which consumer goods and consumers move unobstructed. To sit in public space is
to resist the social discipline of the body that demands efficient and pur-
poseful movement. The (homeless) body, at rest, not only obstructs
other citizens on the go but also threatens the ideology of the disciplined, upright, body-in-motion.

The majority opinion of the Ninth Circuit Court of Appeals, also upholding the ordinance, articulates a similar view of the purpose of public space.
With an almost Hobbesian zeal for definitional precision, Judge Alex Kozinski's opinion constructs mobility as the raison d'être of sidewalks. "The first
step to wisdom is calling a thing by its right name," he asserts. "Whoever
named 'parkways' and 'driveways' never got to step two; whoever named
sidewalks did." By properly defining the sidewalk as "an area for walking
along the side of the road," and proceeding from the "wisdom" of this correct definition, Kozinski is able to conclude that the sidewalk ordinance is
a legitimate legislative regulation of behavior.[59]

In this discourse of mobility and obstruction, public space serves only an
instrumental function—facilitating the movement of goods and people from
one space (of consumption, residence, labor, or leisure) to another. To sit
in public space is to bring behavior proper to another sphere (the home, office,
or recreational park) into public, commercial space. As Don Mitchell argues,
"By being out of place, by doing private things in public space, homeless people threaten not just the space itself, but also the very ideals upon which we
have constructed our rather fragile notions of legitimate citizenship. . . . [T]hey
threaten the ideological construction which declares that publicity . . . must
be voluntary."[60] The discourse of unimpeded motion, then, is one way in
which public space has become, in Michael Shapiro's term, "sanctified."[61]
Public space assumes a "natural" function, so self-evident as to be manifest
in the very term "side*walk*." But of course, this "natural" and "obvious"
meaning of public space is politically produced by a judicial decision that is
thoroughly enmeshed in a conflict over space. In this discourse of motion,
commerce, and consumption the homeless street-dweller becomes the constitutive outside of the consumptive public sphere, a blockage—both physical and ideological—to the free movement of goods and consumers but a
blockage that simultaneously constitutes the boundaries of public space. As
Kawash argues, "The increasingly violent forms of exclusion of the homeless
from public spaces correspond to a rigorously normative definition of the

public." As a constitutive exclusion, the "'war on the homeless' must also be seen as a mechanism for constituting and securing a public, establishing the boundaries of inclusion, and producing an abject body against which the proper, public body of the citizen can stand."[62]

The contours of the public sphere of consumption and circulation are also made clear in the exceptions established by the sidewalk ordinance, the occasions when normative members of the public may have reason to sit down. People may sit on the sidewalk if they are suffering from a medical emergency, using a wheelchair, waiting for a bus, "operating or patronizing a commercial establishment conducted on the public sidewalk pursuant to a street use permit, or . . . participating in or attending a parade, festival, performance, rally, demonstration, meeting, or similar event . . . pursuant to a street use . . . permit."[63] As customers at espresso carts and as spectators at parades, those included within the boundaries of the normative vision of the public are entitled to sit, and their activities must be distinguished, as exceptions, from the excluded behavior of homeless street-dwellers and panhandlers. Even though not all these exceptions mark consumptive activities, in establishing normative uses of public space the ordinance identifies the legitimate user—shopper, spectator, office worker.

Panhandling ordinances display a similar logic. Whereas the begging prohibitions contained within vagrancy statutes historically centered on the problematic of idleness and the need to constitute a disciplined workforce (and were thus part of an ensemble of disciplinary practices including the poorhouse and other forced labor institutions), the contemporary regulation of begging is oriented toward a different problem: the need to maintain a purified space of consumption. Just as Seattle's sidewalk-sitting ordinance constitutes a normative model of public space as a space of mobility and consumption against the "blockage" of the street-dweller "lounging" on the sidewalk, aggressive-solicitation laws seek to construct a legal barrier around citizen-shoppers and the spaces they frequent.

Baltimore, Los Angeles, and Santa Monica have all passed laws against "aggressive solicitation" or "aggressive panhandling," ordinances that map the pleasure spaces of the postindustrial city.[64] Baltimore's ordinance was upheld by the federal district court on all grounds except its impermissible distinction between aggressive panhandling and aggressive solicitation by charities and organizations (a constitutional deficiency that was easily remedied by broadening the statute to prohibit *all* forms of aggressive solicitation). The ordinance, like the laws passed in Santa Monica and Los Angeles, prohibits both solicitation in an aggressive manner and solicitation in certain places.

Prohibited forms of begging (the "manner" restrictions) include panhandling "in a manner that would cause a reasonable person to fear bodily harm," touching the person being solicited without the person's consent, continuing to solicit or following the person after a refusal, blocking passage while soliciting, using obscene or abusive language while soliciting, and "acting with the intent to intimidate another person into giving money."[65] These restrictions function to create a legal barrier around the normative public navigating public spaces. The "place" restrictions on panhandling create an absolute ban on all panhandling in certain public spaces, where it is adjudged to be "inherently intimidating," such as within ten feet of any ATM, in a bus or at a bus stop, and next to a car stopped at a traffic light. The Santa Monica ordinance includes these restrictions and adds others: solicitation is prohibited in "outdoor dining areas of restaurants or other dining establishments serving food for immediate consumption" and "a queue of five or more persons waiting to gain admission to a place or vehicle, or waiting to purchase an item or admission ticket."[66]

These punitive policies aimed at criminalization and exclusion are complemented by "compassionate" alternatives that work through the logic of assimilation, not criminalization.[67] Yet strategies of assimilation, seeking to reintegrate homeless persons (considered as damaged or incomplete subjects) into full citizenship as economic actors, actually produce a similar division between the upstanding citizen and the homeless. For instance, charitable groups, business improvement districts, and neighborhood associations have established voucher and referral programs whereby citizen-consumers can give nonmonetary aid to panhandlers in shopping districts, thus ensuring that they will not be funding drug or alcohol use. Although the voucher programs do not display the same logic of literal exclusion (excluding the homeless from valued consumer spaces through the force of legislation on panhandling, sidewalk-sitting, and public sleeping), their ultimate goal may be to drive panhandlers away by closing the spigots of liberal guilt. Furthermore, these programs symbolically mark off the homeless from the status of consumer (and legitimate occupant of the consumptive public sphere), reinforcing the link between homeless people and nonmarket providers of social services. For instance, the "Helping Hands Panhandling Cards" program sponsored by a business association in Durham, North Carolina, provides citizen-consumers with cards listing social service referral information. The campaign, as Kawash points out, addresses citizen-consumers as the "we," instructed in how to avoid giving "them" cash.[68]

A more elaborate program has been developed in the North Beach neighborhood of San Francisco, where "Community Coupons" give more than just referrals; vouchers distributed by neighborhood residents to panhandlers are redeemable for services and cash at a homeless resource center. To redeem the coupons, however, a person must enroll in the resource center's "Step Program" of rehabilitation: "If the citizen declines enrollment within the North Beach Citizens Step Program, they will be unable to use the coupon. On the positive side, that means our resource center retains *full* face value of the coupon, plus, the homeless person has been informed of our outreach efforts and existence." The Community Coupons program makes distinctions, first, between home-dwelling citizens and homeless clients who need help and, second, between (deserving) homeless clients who belong to the neighborhood and (undeserving) "transients" who do not: "As awareness grows within the community, declining a coupon will also be a quick way to determine if this is a *'local' citizen that needs help,* or *a transient person* that is not aware of our community's proactive campaign for change."

In other words, the North Beach Citizens association conflates the distinction between "local citizen" and "transient person" with the distinction between *submissive* and *resistant*. The program turns the local homeless citizen who resists the disciplinary strings of the Community Coupons into an outsider who is just passing through. An assimilative project turns out to have its own exclusionary force in converting the resistant subject into the outsider. Accepting a coupon and enrolling in the Step Program leads to "database enrollment as a Citizen of North Beach" and a photo identification. For a home-dweller, of course, "citizenship" in North Beach proceeds from physical residence. For a street dweller, on the other hand, neighborhood membership is contingent upon his or her agreement to enter into a social worker–client relationship as a damaged subject in need of rehabilitation.[69]

The Step Program in which a Community Coupons client must enroll entails a heavy dose of normalizing assimilation supplemented by meager supplies: a blanket, clothing, and meals in step one; counseling, meetings, bus tokens, and laundry in step two. In what can only be described as a jarring combination of therapeutic normalizing discourse and pseudorespect for the homeless as "citizens," the North Beach Citizens website describes the transition from step one to step two as follows: "As pride, trust, and receptiveness to change develop, citizens are inspired to make the progression to the next level of services."[70] But the language of citizenship here is disingenuous: as the program makes clear, *homeless* citizenship is not an entitlement of birth or residence but rather a contingent and subordinate status premised upon one's willing subjection to a hierarchically structured program of normalization. Thus, the separation of the homeless panhandler from the consumptive public sphere is effected not only through the force of legal exclusion and police but also through the compassionate efforts of "civil society" to assimilate homeless persons into the status of normal subject. Home-dwelling citizens, the legitimate occupants of the consumptive public sphere, are thereby enlisted in the project. The homeless are excluded from the market and the money economy, becoming clients with needs, subjects of a bureaucratic social service apparatus.

The transition from vagrancy law to anti-homeless legislation is part of a wider shift from, as I have argued, a producer-oriented industrial order to a postindustrial consumer-oriented society. In an explicitly political context, anti-homeless measures can also be understood as part of the punitive underside of the neoliberal and neoconservative rollback of the liberal welfare and regulatory state (as the refocusing of punitive mechanisms on demonized others while a majority of the population is absorbed into consumer society).[71]

Placing the transition from a producer public to a consumer public in the context of neoliberal reform of the welfare state makes it clear that concerns about idleness and productivity do not disappear. Indeed, concern about idleness remains prominent in welfare-to-work programs and the various forms of disciplinary and normalizing incorporation (job training, transitional housing, "life skills" classes, and addiction treatment) aimed at making homeless persons "productive members of society." But as Robert Desjarlais argues, these concerns may best be seen as traces of an older order. Desjarlais, describing social control in and around a Boston homeless shelter, theorizes a transition from a productive/disciplinary society to contemporary society, which contains only vestiges of that tradition: "The age of discipline, taking 'humanity as its measure,' celebrated the positive benefits of human activity and encouraged the detailed organization of human thought and agency. The present age, taking government budgets as its measure, upholds vestiges of this tradition. . . . [N]ow, not all people are needed as productive forces. It is no longer necessary or important to work the entire population of society into a positive economy of bodily discipline."[72] Still, those "vestiges" of an older tradition of discipline do remain. Sanford Schram, for instance, views the welfare-to-work reforms of the 1990s as an attempt to prop up a vision of a fading industrial order in the face of postindustrial realities.[73] It would thus be fair to say that the homeless are targeted both through exclusionary, punitive policies aimed at securing a postindustrial consumptive public space and through disciplinary incorporation into the world of work.

Judges, legal activists, and those who emphasize the maintenance of "order" all contend that the new public-space ordinances target "conduct" and not "status." They see the new laws, therefore, as constitutional; they are not unconstitutionally vague like the Jacksonville vagrancy ordinance struck down by the Supreme Court, and they do not unconstitutionally target a status like "the vagrant."[74] George Kelling and Catherine Coles stress that an "order maintenance" approach to policing public space differs from older vagrancy law administration in that the maintenance of order, done correctly, targets conduct, not the status of vagrancy or homelessness or poverty: "The *act* of panhandling, the *act* of public drinking, are disorderly behaviors of concern here—not being poor, or even being recognized widely as a prostitute or public inebriate. The issue is behavior." Punishing behavior, they claim, is in sharp contrast to vagrancy laws, which "punished status—the poor and idle, able-bodied individuals who could work, but did not. No illegal act was required: vagrancy alone was sufficient cause for arrest." Cities concerned to maintain civility and reduce fear in public spaces turn to narrowly targeted ordinances proscribing specific forms of conduct: "The permissible constitutional alternative to vague and overbroad status-based legislation was greater specificity and behavior-directed statutes and ordinances."[75]

The move from status to conduct is a reflection of the due-process and equal-protection revolutions in American constitutional law in the 1960s and 1970s. The transition constituted a move toward a more complete liberalism in which individuals were held responsible for their specific, voluntary actions and not subjected to criminal penalties on the basis of a status over which they had no control or of a vague catchall category applied through unfettered police discretion. This move from status regulation to conduct regulation would also *seem* to overcome the bare-life predicament. As Arendt argues, a key feature of the rightless condition of being "merely human" is the absence of all responsibility—bare life is not "guilty," just superfluous, and it is more dangerous to be part of a wretched excess of humanity than it is to be an accused criminal held to standards of responsibility. According to Arendt, the position of the refugee, who suffers from the absence of the protective artifices of citizenship, actually *improves* when he or she commits a crime, thus gaining the status of responsible subject accused by the law.[76]

But despite both Arendt's argument and the standard liberal narrative that views the movement from "vague" status laws to "specific" conduct laws as progressive, this making-responsible of the homeless through a regulatory discourse of prohibited acts works less to accord respect to homeless persons as responsible agents than simply to widen and thicken the legal net of harassment and persecution—which it does by (a) creating the ideological figure of the homeless person who willfully and irresponsibly interferes with "public" enjoyment of consumer spaces and (b) deconstructing the "status" of homelessness into its constitutionally regulable component "acts." The due-process revolution has thus spawned a cynical, eminently practical, and punitive version of the deconstruction of identity into the "conduct" and "behavior" for which the individual-as-chooser may be held responsible. In other words, the regulatory regime of prohibited acts does not, I argue, overcome the bare-life predicament; it is the point at which liberalism's willing, choosing, responsible "I" intersects with the politics of bare life, producing as a version of the responsible, choosing self one who is held responsible for choosing bare life—choosing to sleep in public, choosing to panhandle—and is thereby consigned to a subordinate legal and political status: the outlaw-citizen.[77]

The contemporary criminalization of the (conduct of the) homeless concerns neither exactly their idleness nor their offense against God for shirking productivity but their willful violation of the behavioral norms of public space. Mark Sidran, author and defender of the Seattle sidewalk-sitting ordinance, constructs citizenship as civility and attempts to convert sidewalk-sitting into a blatant act of impropriety. In an op-ed piece for the *Seattle Times* he discusses the case of David Todd, a homeless man who evinces (to Sidran at least) an utter lack of concern for his fellow citizenry by selfishly obstructing a busy sidewalk, "one of the busiest pedestrian intersections in the city": "Rather than sit or lie one block away in Westlake Park, he prefers 'his' corner without regard to the interests of pedestrians, including disabled, vision impaired or elderly, to whom he poses a safety hazard. Nor is he concerned about the impact of his behavior in undermining economic vitality by deterring people from using the sidewalk."[78] This is the new irresponsible street person: the one who insists on panhandling where pedestrians pass by, evincing no concern for the economic vitality of the consumptive public sphere.

In this model of citizenship, communitarian duties are heaped upon homeless people as a sign of respect. Personal responsibility and civility are equated with "standing," while the homeless "lounging on public sidewalks," profane outlaws of public space, defy communal norms and ignore the needs of upstanding citizens-in-motion. To become an upstanding member of this community requires literally "standing up." For those homeless people unwilling to adhere voluntarily to the duties of citizenship, the law will step in to provide an additional tug on the bootstraps.[79]

CRIMINOLOGICAL JUSTIFICATION OF THE NEW POLICIES: BROKEN WINDOWS, CITIZEN FEAR, AND FUTURE CRIMINALITY

The "broken-windows" theory of disorder and crime, and its order-maintenance prescriptions, have played a significant role in justifying the new public-space ordinances. For instance, in *Young v. New York City*, a case concerning a panhandling prohibition in New York City subways, a New York federal court heard testimony from George Kelling, one of the authors of *Fixing Broken Windows*, and cited that study approvingly in upholding the prohibition. Several other courts have discussed the broken-windows approach to "disorder" in public spaces in order to establish that a significant or compelling government interest is served by the statute under review. The broken-windows theory is, I argue, a modified version of the future-criminality justification for vagrancy law. Accompanying *both* the vagrancy/production and homelessness/consumption regimes is the criminological theory that seemingly innocuous behavior (loafing, begging, sitting, panhandling) breeds crime. There is also an important difference, however. Whereas the criminological theory underlying the vagrancy/production approach articulated a *direct* link between vagrancy and crime (vagrants turn into criminals without the discipline of forced labor), the contemporary anti-homeless approach articulates a *mediated* link: panhandlers present the appearance of disorder that signifies to others (criminals) that the space lacks the social controls needed to stop crime.

The broken-windows argument starts with a metaphor—a metaphor that brings to mind other metaphors, such as domino theories and slippery slopes, concerning the descent into disorder when an initial event is not prevented. The claim is that a single broken window left unrepaired signals to passersby that no one cares and therefore breaking more windows is cost free; likewise, disorderly conduct in public space, left uncorrected, signals that the mechanisms of social control are in abeyance and therefore criminal acts can flourish. Kelling and Coles state that "disorderly behavior unregulated and unchecked signals to citizens that the area is unsafe. Responding prudently, and fearfully, citizens will stay off the streets, avoid certain areas, and curtail their normal activities and associations." These prudent and fearful citizens, in withdrawing from public space, "also withdraw from roles of mutual support, . . . thereby relinquishing the social controls they formerly helped to maintain." The result is "increasing vulnerability to an influx of more disorderly behavior and serious crime."[80]

In the original *Atlantic Monthly* article on the broken-windows theory of crime, Kelling and James Q. Wilson seem to suggest that disorderly behavior such as public drinking, loitering by groups of youths, and panhandling (which appears to be their preoccupation) sends two distinct signals to two groups. To "citizens," the message is to stay away and be afraid. To "criminals," the message is to come and capitalize on the absence of informal social-control mechanisms: "Disorderly behavior unregulated and unchecked signals to citizens that the area is unsafe [while] muggers and robbers, whether opportunistic or professional, believe they reduce their chances of being caught . . . if they operate on streets where potential victims are already intimidated by prevailing conditions. If the neighborhood cannot keep a bothersome panhandler from annoying passersby, the thief may reason, it is even less likely to call the police to identify a potential mugger." In the broken-windows theory, panhandlers do not become criminals, but they are crimogenic. They frighten upstanding citizens, create a climate of fear and intimidation that is receptive to crime, and send signals to criminals that this climate exists: "Serious street crime flourishes in areas in which disorderly behavior goes unchecked. The unchecked panhandler is, in effect, the first broken window."[81] From vagrancy as a moral pestilence and the vagrant as the "chrysalis" to the panhandler as "the first broken window": both metaphors concern future criminality, but the broken-windows theory places citizen fear and withdrawal as the mediating link between panhandling and more serious crime.

This more complicated version of the future-criminality argument (an argument rejected by Justice Douglas in *Papachristou*) recasts the "moral disease" of vagrancy into a behavioral analysis of public spaces. Just as emphasis on "conduct" avoids overt criminalization of suspect identities, the broken-windows justification of conduct-based ordinances avoids any claims about the vagrant or panhandler's character and immorality; it is a new criminological vision or theory unmoored by the deep chains of pathology and criminal identity. Nevertheless, the broken-windows discourse succeeds in dividing the world into two groups: upstanding but fearful citizens who prudently avoid disordered public spaces, and homeless panhandlers who are the personification of broken windows. Although Kelling and Coles claim to have avoided the criminalization of status via a focus on behavior, their "text of behavior is in need of a subtext of identity," as Schram puts it in the context of welfare reform.[82] They find it in the irresponsible panhandler-as-broken window.

If the key mediator between disorder and crime is citizens' fear of disorder, one might ask whether their fear of panhandlers is justified. Does citizen fear of some kinds of disorder reflect prudence and citizen fear of other forms reflect prejudice? Such questions cannot be asked within the broken-windows theory, because citizen fear of disorder turns out to be its own justification. Kelling and Coles claim that it is "neither an unreasonable nor extreme reaction, since disorder does indeed precede or accompany serious crime and urban decay."[83] But disorder, they argue, leads to crime *because* citizens fear it and withdraw from public spaces. Thus they create an undifferentiated category of disorder and, in a circular argument, close off questions about the reasonableness of citizen fear.

That citizen fear of homeless persons and panhandlers is central in the creation of public-space restrictions can be seen in the lead-up to the passage of the Baltimore City Council's aggressive-solicitation ordinance: a "Security Task Force" made up of members of the Downtown Partnership (which administers a "special taxing district" and provides "supplementary security" as part of the blurring of private/public boundaries in urban spaces), city officials, police officers, and "community representatives" issued a report on "people causing anxiety" and concluded that "two discrete populations of people . . . cause much of the public anxiety downtown: aggressive beggars or panhandlers who intimidate and harass other individuals, and the hardcore homeless, whose situations are exacerbated by a range of economic, physical, or social problems."[84]

Even if we grant Kelling and Coles's claim that citizen fear of panhandlers and homeless persons leads to crime because fearful citizens withdraw from public spaces and create crimogenic conditions, our effective responses are not limited to the prohibition of panhandling and public sleeping. We might instead break out of the circularity of the argument, questioning whether such fear is justified, and whether a more appropriate response is for domiciled citizens to refuse sanctuary in their fear, and to remain engaged in public spaces with "social disorder."

This is the recommendation of Richard Sennett, who, in *The Uses of Disorder,* urges urban dwellers to overcome a desire for complete control and certainty and to become receptive to disorder, uncertainty, and difference. Urban planning and policy, according to Sennett, should be oriented toward fostering unplanned encounters between strangers to help them overcome their fears of disorder and difference. Such unplanned encounters would permit the experience of difference in a milieu that prevents those differences from being converted into otherness. Sennett claims that "what should emerge in city life is the occurrence of social relations, *and especially relations involving social conflict,* through face to face encounters." He argues that when day-to-day conflictual contact with strangers (who are the bearers of difference) is lacking, reified, purified identities will form. These purified selves, "unused to the daily shocks of confrontation and the expression of ineradicable conflict, react with . . . volatility to the disorders of oppressed groups in the city, and meet the hostility from below with an oppressive hand." Day-to-day contact with strangers prevents their becoming wholly "other"—not because one "sees past" the difference and "discovers" that these others are "really" no different from ourselves but, rather, because the demand for mutual survival, the reality of interdependence, the impossibility of withdrawal prevent the dynamics of identity/difference from taking an ugly turn: "Confronted with the need to act, to deal with human differences in order to survive, it seems plausible that the desire for a mythic solidarity would be defeated by this very necessity for survival."[85]

Sennett's reasoning suggests that even if broken-windows policing succeeds in excluding social disorder from the consumptive public sphere, domiciled citizens' fear of disorder will only increase as they become unused to face-to-face encounters with difference and, as Susan Bickford points out, they rely more exclusively on media stereotypes for representations of others who are "zoned out" of purified spaces. But Bickford also cautions against "demonizing fear as deeply undemocratic." It is no easy task to determine which citizen fears are justified and which are unjustified: "Sometimes . . . democratic politics requires citizens to act in certain ways in spite of fear and risk, and a political ethic of courage might help to revitalize democratic politics in an inegalitarian society. But surely public life cannot require of us that we never act on our fears. How do I know when to act against or in spite of my fears, and how do I know when my fear is discerning in a way that should guide my actions? These are challenging and disturbing judgments to make, and part of the uncertainty that enclosed spaces help us avoid is the uncertainty of how to act with respect to a disturbing stranger."[86]

It is important not to dismiss the fears of domiciled citizens in disorderly public spaces. But it is also important not to accept fear of disorder as an unquestioned basis of public policy, for the security that broken-windows policing and anti-homeless legislation create for the domiciled in public spaces is simultaneously the creation of insecurity for those who are excluded from the consumptive public sphere: "If the consuming white middle-class public comes to feel at risk in the presence of those who do not look or act like them, then purifying public space of risk for them means increasing danger, discomfort, or outright exclusion for those typed as alien or unknown."[87] The broken-windows argument closes off these lines of thought in a circular argument concerning citizen fear as both the (intermediary) cause of crime and the justification for the policing of disorder. Although Bickford is right to suggest that there is no easy answer to the question of when citizen fear of disorder is justified and reasonable and when it should be overcome, one way of getting a better handle on this question is to dis-aggregate the forms of disorder that Kelling and Coles consistently conflate. Indeed, a recent study of New York City panhandlers and sidewalk ven-dors suggests that the broken-windows theory may suffer from an unrig-orous definition of disorder. Mitchell Duneier, in *Sidewalk*, discovers a com-plex urban ecology of panhandlers, vendors of printed matter, and the housed citizens who support them. Frequently, according to Duneier, pan-handlers and vendors become the eyes and ears on the street that help to sustain social order. Some vendors and panhandlers do act abusively and seek to intimidate passersby, but for the most part, Duneier says, "their presence on the street enhances social order." Furthermore, their presence fosters the sorts of encounters across social and cultural boundaries that Sennett suggests can make citizens less fearful: the vendors' tables became "a site for the interaction that weakens the social barriers between persons otherwise separated by vast social and economic inequalities."[88]

Duneier suggests not that we abandon broken-windows approaches to policing but rather that they be better targeted so as to avoid the blanket harassment of street-dwellers, panhandlers, and sidewalk vendors. This requires us to refuse the easy identification of physical forms of disorder—literal bro-ken windows, graffiti, and other vandalism—with actual existing persons: "How do Wilson and Kelling know when they see instances of *social* bro-ken windows that tell potential criminals that they can break the law? 'Social disorder' is not the same as a public telephone that has been vandalized. The men working on Sixth Avenue may be viewed as broken windows, but this research shows that most of them have actually become public characters who create a set of expectations, for one another and strangers, . . . that 'someone cares.'"[89] Whereas Wilson and Kelling's assertion that "the pan-handler is the first broken window" offers a new version of the future-criminality defense of vagrancy law, Duneier's study suggests that such forms of "social disorder" may neither warrant fear and withdrawal on the part of domiciled citizens nor send encouraging messages to opportunistic criminals.

The transition from vagrancy law to anti-homeless legislation reveals both continuities and discontinuities. First, vagrancy law was centered upon the issues of labor and idleness, and prohibitions against vagrancy sought to shore up a productive public sphere by creating coercive mechanisms to ensure a stable laboring population. Those laws were discursively linked to sumptuary law—prohibitions against excessive consumption. Anti-homeless legislation centers on issues of consumption and appearance, promoting a zone of "friction-free" consumptive activity for middle-class users of the postindustrial city and constituting a vision of a normative public through the constitutive exclusion of homeless street-dwellers and their actions.

Second, vagrancy law involved a specification of suspect identities and states of being, often explaining precisely who "shall be deemed a vagrant." Anti-homeless law creates a typology of prohibited acts. This shift from identity and status to act and behavior is reflected in constitutional rulings such as *Papachristou,* which rejected broad, identity-based vagrancy law as unconstitutionally vague, and *Robinson v. California,* which rejected the criminalization of a status as cruel and unusual punishment in violation of the Eighth Amendment. This transition indicates not the abandonment of concern for a legal subjectivity but rather the constitution of new forms of subordinate legal subjectivity and the assignment of responsibility, achieved in part through the deconstruction of identity into its constitutionally criminalizable component acts.

Third, the new public-space restrictions are justified by a modified version of the future-criminality justification for vagrancy law. By mediating the link between "disorder" and "crime," this modified version avoids statements about the criminal nature of homeless persons as a suspect class and instead installs citizen fear as the mediating link between panhandling and more serious crime, a link that turns out to be self-legitimating in a circular logic that makes the fears of a normative public the basis of public policy and policing strategies.

When the Supreme Court rejected Jacksonville's vagrancy law as a historical anachronism, it did not entirely defeat a punitive approach to the displaced poor. Rather, it unwittingly shaped a new direction in punitive policy—act-based as opposed to identity-based, and oriented toward protecting the postindustrial consumptive spaces of redevloped urban centers. But act-based ordinances—regulating sidewalk-sitting, panhandling, and public sleeping and camping—have themselves been challenged in district and appellate courts. The next chapter examines some of the victories won and defeats suffered by litigators for homeless rights.

The Legal Construction of the Homeless as Bare Life

Court challenges to anti-homeless legislation and police practices—pan-handling restrictions, sidewalk-sitting ordinances, public-sleeping bans, police sweeps of homeless encampments, and the confiscation of street-dwellers' property—have had mixed results.[1] Without a Supreme Court ruling on the constitutionality of public-sleeping bans, for instance, lower-level federal courts remain in disagreement. In such cities as Miami, Chicago, Santa Ana, San Francisco, and Dallas a key issue has emerged: the extent to which homelessness is an involuntary status or a result of individual choice. Like the sociologists of disaffiliation discussed in the introduction, judges at the district and appellate court levels have grappled with issues of liberty and constraint, agency and incapacity, in their representations of homeless persons, and the issue of the state's coercive power over bare life hovers in the background of these debates. Courts that find homelessness to be involuntary will tend to strike down public-sleeping restrictions, making the particular argument that such restrictions punish the homeless for an involuntary status and thus constitute cruel and unusual punishment in violation of the Eighth Amendment.[2] Courts that find homelessness not to be an involuntary status contend that it is entirely legitimate for governments to ban public sleeping and camping.

The legal debate over voluntariness and status links court cases to wider social discourses about homelessness, and indeed court records frequently include social scientists' statements on the factors and forces that lead people to become homeless. A key part of this wider debate concerns the question of the causes of homelessness. Some analysts stress the contribution of "structural" factors (such as deindustrialization, rising unemployment, reductions in federal housing subsidies) to the rise of homelessness; others stress "individual" factors such as alcoholism, mental illness, personal failure, and the desire to "disaffiliate" from mainstream society.[3] The debate contrasts macro-social explanations that deemphasize individual agency, on the one hand, and micro-social explanations that emphasize individual agency and personal responsibility, on the other hand.

The judicial debate concerning whether or not homelessness is an involuntary status, however, is much more than a simple rehashing of the traditional ideological conflict between left liberals (who stress the structural and social determinants of such problems as crime and poverty) and neoconservatives (who embrace a discourse of individual responsibility and choice). It also involves both the specificities of homelessness and the specificities of legal power. The recurrent polarities that mark the politics and discourse of homelessness include the double image of the homeless as bearers of natural liberty and as persons socially constrained. Conflicting judicial opinions concerning the rights of the homeless reflect this polarity, developing legal representations of homelessness as marked either by helplessness and constraint or by freedom and choice. Furthermore, these specifically legal representations of the homeless play a fundamental role in constituting the bare-life predicament because, in constituting the homeless as either helpless victims or responsible agents, they are simultaneously authorizing and delineating the scope of state police power over biological life, upholding public-sleeping bans and the police confiscation of property or, in the more sympathetic legal opinions, authorizing the institution of the shelter as a space of confinement.

These legal opinions *appear* not to reduce the homeless to a subordinate political status (of bare life): the decisions upholding anti-homeless legislation claim to be targeting freely chosen conduct, not status; the decisions striking down anti-homeless legislation claim to be protecting those already confined by social forces to an involuntary status. Nevertheless, both carve out a subordinate legal status for the homeless. I argue that the judicial construction of homeless persons as choosers *and* the judicial construction of the homeless as helpless share a hidden foundation: both ways of imagining the homeless depend upon (and reinforce) the reduction of the homeless to the legal status of bare life. From the profane image of dirty, abject lifestyle choices to the sacralized vision of pure helplessness, these legal opinions express the dualities of political power's isolation of bare life.

The cases I examine in depth all concern public-sleeping bans, sweeps of homeless encampments, or confiscation of homeless persons' property. These cases constitute some of the main published opinions concerning the rights of the homeless and the constitutionality of what many term the war against the homeless.

I explore the background concepts, categories, rhetorical displacements, theoretical exclusions, and repressed imaginings that enable the discursive positioning of homeless persons as either willful agents responsible for their plight or helpless victims of necessity defined by the compulsions that mark their condition. Most secondary legal commentary in this area treats legal arguments instrumentally, as tools to be employed in a struggle either for the rights of the homeless or for the maintenance of public order.[4] By contrast, I read some of the key cases in this still-evolving body of precedents with less focus on strategy and doctrinal development and with greater attention to the production of meaning—to the constitutive dimension of legal argument and to the rhetorical devices at work. I do so not because I believe that judicial opinions (as opposed to decisions) have some certain causal impact on the material situation of the homeless but rather because they are potent sites of meaning—significant places where cultural constructions of the homeless get articulated and, furthermore, a set of texts in which the relationship between the abject realities of extreme poverty, displacement, and alienation and our political ideals of individual agency, freedom, and citizenship get worked out. As Judith Failer argues, "Images [of homeless people in legal discourse] point to implicit assumptions in the law about how homelessness renders people sufficiently different under the law to qualify them for a different bundle of civic obligations."[5] Thus I look to legal discourse as one area in which a dominant set of understandings of homelessness and its relation to political order are expressed, a realm in which citizenship and the political are constituted in opposition to the subordinate status of homeless bare life.

PROFANE FREEDOM: BARE LIFE, LAW'S AGENCY, AND THE (LIFESTYLE) CHOICE TO BE HOMELESS

Rather than asking whether homelessness is in reality an individual choice, I want to examine the political effects of judges' imagining homelessness as a choice within legal discourse, and the rhetorical displacements involved in the construction of homelessness as a voluntary condition. My argument is that the judicial attribution of agency and personal responsibility to the homeless carries considerable baggage. In *Joyce v. San Francisco* the district court rejects the argument that homelessness is an involuntary status, and by "finding agency" in homelessness it simultaneously recovers the agency of the state to *punish* the homeless, and recovers its own agency over and against the "compulsions" of legal and scientific arguments. In *Love v. City of Chicago* the district court opinion constructs homelessness as an expression of individualism, a lifestyle choice, and at the same time delegitimates the claims of the homeless to be secure in their possessions by trapping them in the double bind of a despatialized model of public and private. By conceiving of public and private as dimensions of agency and by forgetting the spatial preconditions of this agency, the court turns homelessness into a form of dispossessive individualism. In the legal imagination, the choice to be homeless becomes the choice not to possess and not to consume; in the legal imagination, to choose homelessness is to choose bare life, and this is why the legitimate choices of the homeless extend no further than the minimum necessities to sustain life itself.

In *Joyce v. San Francisco* (1994), the federal district court of Northern California rejected an Eighth Amendment challenge to a collection of ordinances and government policies toward the homeless known as the "Matrix Program." The court rejected the claim that homelessness is an involuntary status and, further, distinguished between conduct (which may be punished) and status (which cannot). In upholding a conception of voluntary homelessness, Judge D. Lowell Jensen denied the motion of Bobby Joyce and three other homeless plaintiffs for a preliminary injunction against elements of San Francisco's Matrix Program. The plaintiffs challenged in particular the law enforcement component of the program, which criminalized certain life-sustaining activities such as sleeping or camping in public. The district court later ruled in favor of the city in an unpublished opinion. After San Francisco's Mayor Willie Brown voluntarily suspended the Matrix Program in 1996, the plaintiffs' appeal of the ruling was declared moot, and the case was dismissed by the Ninth Circuit Court of Appeals.

While the court adopts a sensitive posture toward the degree of hardship and compulsion faced by homeless persons, Judge Jensen refuses to accord to homelessness the concept of "involuntary status." In rejecting the Eighth Amendment claim, he rejects the precedent of a Florida federal district court which, in *Pottinger v. City of Miami,* held that punishing the homeless for sleeping, sitting, and eating in public punished them for involuntary conduct that was inextricably linked to the involuntary status of homelessness.[6] According to the Florida court, laws punishing people for sleeping in public are in essence punishing people for being homeless; by punishing conduct inextricably linked to status, therefore, the Miami ordinance violated the Eighth Amendment's prohibition against cruel and unusual punishment. In *Joyce*, Jensen rejects the logic in *Pottinger* as a "dubious extension" of past Supreme Court rulings on "status crimes." He raises two related objections to the Eighth Amendment argument.

First, Jensen argues that status and conduct linked to status are two separate entities entirely: "On no occasion, moreover, has the Supreme Court invoked the Eighth Amendment in order to protect acts derivative of a person's status."[7] Citing *Robinson v. California*, the California district court notes that although the Supreme Court struck down a law that prohibited a person from being a drug addict, it upheld a law prohibiting the act of public drunkenness.[8]

Second, in addition to distinguishing between status and conduct derived from status, Jensen goes on to deny that homelessness is a status at all, arguing that it is instead a "condition." He distinguishes between a condition such as homelessness, and a status such as one's "age, race, gender, national origin and illness." Key to the determination of what is to count as a status is "the involuntariness of the acquisition of that quality (including the presence or not of that characteristic at birth) . . . and the degree to which an individual has control over that characteristic." The court goes on to assert that homelessness is not completely involuntary: "While homelessness can be thrust upon an unwilling recipient and while a person may be largely incapable of changing that condition, the distinction between the ability to eliminate one's drug addiction as compared to one's homelessness is a distinction in kind as much as degree." Jensen does not explain exactly how it is a distinction "in kind" but instead immediately proceeds to what might be the most important reason for denying that homelessness is an involuntary status: "To argue that homelessness is a status and not a condition, moreover, is to deny the efficacy of acts of social intervention to change the condition of those currently homeless." Here it appears as though the real reason for imbuing homelessness with some agentic dimension is to recover and reinstate the agency of the rest of us: to make homelessness involuntary and to deny to the homeless "control over that characteristic" is simultaneously to "deny the efficacy of acts of social intervention" by government services and concerned citizens.[9]

Further into the court's discussion of status, Judge Jensen is also concerned about the relationship between the "status" of homelessness and the "acts" of others, but here the logic is reversed—rather than seeking to recognize the power of agentic acts of social intervention to *end* homelessness, Jensen downplays the agentic acts of social intervention that *create* homelessness: "Plaintiffs argue that the failure of the City to provide sufficient housing compels the conclusion that homelessness on the streets of San Francisco is cognizable as a status. This argument is unavailing at least for the fundamental reason that *status cannot be defined as a function of the discretionary acts of others.*[10] The court seems to find itself in the contradictory position of both cautioning against underestimating "the efficacy of acts of social intervention" to end homelessness and cautioning against overestimating the agentic power of the government in creating homelessness. To call homelessness a status is *both* to attribute too little agentic power to government interventions designed to overcome homelessness and too much agentic power to government interventions (or the lack thereof) in the housing market which lead to homelessness. Furthermore, should the court accept the plaintiffs' argument, linking status back to the acts of state, it would then limit the discretion of state officials in dealing with the problem of homelessness (for instance, in banning the public performance of life-sustaining activities) by making unconstitutional any government efforts to prohibit conduct emanating from the status of homelessness that the government itself produced.

Beneath these contradictory gestures toward the social and governmental acts of creating and ending homelessness lies a deeper anxiety that motivates the rejection of the idea of a status resulting from political relations and "discretionary acts": tracing homeless status back to the discretionary acts of the state would threaten the figure of the voluntaristic, liberal agent as the foundation of liberal society and liberal government. If discretionary acts of the state (such as funding decisions about public housing and decisions about urban redevelopment projects) lead to making people involuntarily homeless, then the state, in punishing sleeping in public, would be punishing people for becoming what the state has made them. Although the realm of "biology" and "nature" can be grouped under status (race, gender, nationality, illness, in the court's reckoning), the recognition of a politically produced status would threaten the liberal promise that liberal society overcomes the compulsion of nature and the compulsions of an ascriptive society by liberating the individual from the bonds of nature and feudal categories—the promise of a state made by individual subjects instead of individual subjects made by the state. Thus the court develops an essentialist, prepolitical definition of status as what Janet Halley calls an "intrinsic, prelegal personality structure." The notion of "status" that appears to be at work in this opinion is not an account of a socially and legally mediated position, "constituted in relationship, interaction, or representation," but rather what Halley describes as "a type of personal character that inheres so deeply within a person that it constitutes a pervasive personal essence."[11] Indeed, the court goes to great rhetorical lengths to deny the possibility that status could be related to government decisions and social relations.

Finally, by finding that homelessness is not an involuntary status, the court is simultaneously able to free *itself* from compulsion. The court posits the plaintiffs as agents of compulsion, attempting to *force* the court into accepting homelessness as a status: "Plaintiffs argue that the failure of the City to provide sufficient housing *compels the conclusion* that homelessness on the streets . . . is cognizable as a status." And later on, Jensen asserts that "the Court must approach with hesitation any argument that science or statistics *compels a conclusion* that a certain condition be defined as a status."[12] By recovering the agency in homelessness from the jaws of determinism (the determinism of economic structures), the court recovers its own agency in refusing to be compelled (by social scientific arguments and evidence). The agency of the homeless and the agency of other citizens and government institutions are co-implicating. In the *Joyce* court's opinion, the granting of agency to the homeless is simultaneously an endorsement of the state's power to punish the homeless. Freedom and agency become accusations directed against an outlaw. The state grants agency to the homeless, refusing to recognize homelessness as an involuntary status, and in so doing it ironically helps to produce a political status subordinate to full citizenship: the homeless as outlawed bare life caught in the sovereign ban on public sleeping.

In the secondary legal literature justifying public-space ordinances, the willful, agentic characteristics of homeless persons and panhandlers are emphasized even more. The homeless "lounge" on public sidewalks; they seek to sleep in "any place of their choosing" and to beg "in any manner they see fit" (see chapter 1). These constructions of the homeless person as agent recall William Connolly's Nietzschean reading of modern versions of the free subject: "The subject is the agent of freedom; but when one is reminded, 'you *chose x*' or, worse, 'you *freely chose y,*' one is being accused, reminded, held responsible for the consequences of that action. . . . Thus, the subject is free, but many authoritative assertions of its freedom are accompanied by the announcement of a verdict or a warning that it will be treated institutionally as a non-subject if its conduct gets too far out of line."[13] It takes very little for the freely choosing homeless to get "too far out of line." This is profane freedom, the freedom of the outlaw caught in the ban on the public performance of life-sustaining activities.

A second case in which a vision of voluntary homelessness was upheld, *Love v. City of Chicago* (1996 and 1998), concerns the constitutionality of the Chicago police practice of confiscating the possessions of homeless persons. Two motions for injunctive relief by the plaintiffs in this case were denied. Although the federal district court acknowledged that the city of Chicago had violated its own policies in confiscating property placed in a designated safe area, it asserted that no *constitutional* violation occurred. Although this case does not concern constitutionality under the Eighth Amendment, as do the rest of the cases discussed in this chapter, it connects with those cases in making the issue of the voluntariness of homelessness central to its analysis.

A group of homeless persons living in the Lower Wacker Drive area of Chicago challenged the constitutionality of the city's practice of removing unattended belongings of the homeless and discarding them during street cleanings. In January 1996, three homeless persons filed suit on behalf of themselves and others similarly situated, alleging a city practice since 1993 of seizing and destroying homeless persons' property during street cleanings, in violation of the Fourth, Fifth, and Fourteenth Amendments. Between January and June 1996 the city voluntarily suspended off-street cleanings and, in June, instituted temporary procedures for safeguarding the belongings of homeless residents of Wacker Drive by providing advanced notice of street cleanings, but it continued to confiscate those items not moved to designated "safe areas." In October 1996 the plaintiffs' first motion for a preliminary injunction was denied. Then, on December 1, 1997, the city engaged in a street cleaning of Lower Wacker Drive during which some twenty residents lost almost all their belongings, including those stored in the safe areas that had been established by the temporary procedures. The plaintiffs filed a renewed motion for a preliminary injunction, and on February 5, 1998, this motion too was denied by the federal district court.

Rejecting the plaintiffs' demand for a preliminary injunction that would prevent the city from continuing its practices of dispossession and require new procedures to protect the property of the homeless, Judge Wayne Andersen's October 1996 opinion is significant for its rhetoric of voluntarism and individualism, and its palpable anxiety about consumption and accumulation by street dwellers.

The district court establishes the voluntary nature of homelessness from the very beginning in its finding of fact: "Most of the homeless individuals involved in this lawsuit, at least those who are not mentally ill, appear to be choosing homelessness." Although individualism and voluntarism are, for the normative public, the ideological counterparts of private property possession, Andersen turns these categories against the aspirations of street-dwellers to be secure in their possessions. The discovery of choice in the condition of homelessness paves the way for rejecting the demand for additional procedural safeguards around the property of homeless people in the Lower Wacker Drive area. Andersen asserts that "the city does not have an obligation to ensure the safety of property that people voluntarily leave on the City's property, or on the dock areas. . . . The City is not an insurer for the property of people who choose to live on city property rent-free, nor is the public required to accommodate totally the life-style choices made by homeless individuals. The choice of the homeless . . . includes the assumption of the risk that their property may be lost."[14] The government's role as guarantor and protector of the private property rights of everyone else is ignored, and the government is repositioned in the argument as simply another property owner. One need not be committed to a view of homelessness as an utterly involuntary condition to be troubled by Andersen's rhetoric of voluntarism and lifestyle choices, which deflects attention from the harsh and brutal conditions of a life lived entirely in public space and turns the public into the passive victim of an unrestrained, dedomesticated "possessive individualism."

The struggle between the city and the residents of Lower Wacker Drive continued through 1997, and in its February 1998 opinion again refusing the plaintiffs' demand for injunctive relief, the district court justified the city's confiscation of property by describing a scene of excessive consumption.[15] Although the court acknowledges that the city violated its own temporary procedures for safeguarding possessions placed in a designated safe area and that "as a result, most Lower Wacker Drive residents lost all of their possessions," the opinion describes the plaintiffs as accumulating *beyond necessity* and thereby losing their entitlement to protection: "Plaintiffs accumulated an unprecedented amount of possessions. . . . About twenty-eight charity groups brought food, clothing, and blankets. . . . Moreover, the residents collected many items beyond those necessary for life on Lower Wacker Drive such as chairs, boxes, sofas, computers, keyboards, potted plants, box springs, and extra mattresses." Citing public safety concerns, the court refuses to require city workers to sift through the items to separate "property" from "trash." Furthermore, "the city should not be compelled to reimburse plaintiffs for possessions that were intermingled with filthy or improper items that posed a hazard to pedestrians and vehicles."[16]

The opinion concludes with the articulation of what was assumed in the prior reasoning: property legitimately possessed by street-dwellers is restricted to those items essential for physical survival, reduced to that which sustains bare life: "My own view . . . is that some of the plaintiffs are entitled to compensation . . . provided that those belongings were attended to or relocated to safe areas, were not intermingled with unsafe or unsanitary items, and *were the basic items, such as a sleeping bag and several blankets, required to live on the sidewalk.*"[17] Andersen's claim legitimates the processes of compression and dispossession that mark the homeless condition in the postindustrial city, turning these processes into a lifestyle choice. The choice of homelessness, however, is the choice to live a lifestyle of perpetual insecurity and dispossession: "*dis*possessive individualism." As Kawash argues, "Through material, psychological, and emotional dispossession, the extension of the homeless body in the world is pressed closer and closer to the bodily boundary marked out by the skin."[18] It is this limitation on "extension" that the *Love* opinion endorses. For the lifestyle choice of homelessness to be a choice free of legally sanctioned state dispossession, one may possess only the absolute minimum of items required to sustain life itself—a sleeping bag and several blankets.

The *Love* opinions demonstrate how liberalism confronts the bare-life predicament. Within an individualistic framework of voluntarism, agency, and lifestyle choices, the court both "recognizes" the agency of the homeless and turns the homeless into bare life, identified with trash, dirt, and willful criminality. The court manages to imagine the homeless as completely free (lifestyle choosers) and completely profane (identified with dirt, with property as trash, with filthy overaccumulation that threatens public health). How is this accomplished? I argue that the *Love* court constructs homelessness as freely chosen bare life by rhetorically trapping the homeless within a liberal and despatialized model of public and private agency.

The federal district court's opinion in *Love v. Chicago* succeeds in appealing to anxieties about excessive consumption and property accumulation. But it is important to remember that possession of property and consumption are practices that enact the central values of liberal individualism—autonomy, self-representation, freedom-as-choice.[19] Therefore, it is by no means obvious or automatic that acts of consumption and accumulation by homeless persons would be recognized as deviant; the court's opinion must *work* to construct property accumulation as deviance. It does so in part by describing a scene in which property and trash are difficult to separate, a scene in which homeless persons themselves are implicitly imagined as "filthy or improper items." But the homeless are not just filthy outlaws in the court's opinion, they are also lifestyle choosers. The court manages this combination, I contend, by trapping the homeless within the double bind of a despatialized model of private and public.

At a fundmental level, public and private are, as Ted Kilian has noted, all about access and exclusion.[20] To the degree that something is public, it is made more accessible (to someone); to the degree that it is privatized, it becomes off limits. But what is this thing that is made accessible to others or held in exclusion? The classical construction of the public/private dichotomy, from Aristotle to Arendt, is the opposition between the household and the polis: that is, between different types of spaces. Public space is (ideally) a space of access and exposure; it is a world of multiplicity, of citizens gathered together engaged in speech. Private space, by contrast, is by its nature exclusive and exclusionary; it is where we reproduce ourselves, where we care for life's necessities, and where we are able to exclude unwanted others.

Public space in the classical model is also exclusive in the sense that the public sphere, though marked by access to others (other citizens), is also constituted by the exclusion of bare life. So, as the public (others) is excluded from one's household, bare life is excluded from the public sphere. This exclusion could entail the separation of aspects of one's life (biological necessity) from the domain of the public; in this case, exclusions and divisions occur within the self that navigates between such spaces. But it also entails the separation of whole groups of people (slaves, women), viewed as bearers of a disruptive bare life that threatens the purity, wholeness, and identity of a consuming, producing, or political public. Furthermore, as Agamben notes, the double exclusion of the bare life of the household from the political life of the polis is a *constitutive* exclusion. This double exclusion constitutes the public sphere as a space of citizenship and the private sphere as a space of bare life, its protection and reproduction.

The classical separation of household and polis is not the only version of the public/private dichotomy, however. A second, liberal form contrasts the public realm of the state to the private realm of the nonstate. Although similar to the household/polis distinction, it is different in a crucial way: in its most simple form the dichotomy separates not *spaces* but *areas of concern*. What is public is properly of concern to the government, and what is private is properly of concern to the individual and only the individual. This view reflects the rise of individualism and involves a certain kind of abstracting away from spaces to normative principles of jurisdiction and agency. The classical contrast is spatial; the liberal distinction is jurisdictional. But both involve relations of access and exclusion. When we talk about a matter of public health, or a matter of public safety, we tap into this sense of the public/private dichotomy. If I am purposely infecting other people with a deadly virus, I become a public health concern, and the state has "access" to me in restraining my liberty. It does not matter whether I am doing this in a public or a private space. Daniela Gobetti, pointing out that the transition from the classical to the liberal model involves a transition from a dichotomy based on institutional domains (spaces) to a dichotomy based on jurisdiction and "modalities of agency," says of the liberal model: "Private jurisdiction extends to all the activities in which an adult engages without harming or endangering others. . . . When harm is done, intrusion on the part of public authority into the person's private jurisdiction is legitimate."[21]

As Gobetti argues, in the liberal model it is the *consequences* of one's actions that determine whether the action is to be considered "public" or "private." In this despatialized version, privacy is crystallized less in the image of the closed door of the bedroom than in the statement "I was just minding my own business." Although privacy is still about excluding unwanted others (in this case, coercive state power), its referent is not a space but a properly acting individual. Furthermore, whereas publicity in the classical model is about exposure to strangers in a space of plurality and difference, publicity in the liberal version of the dichotomy is closely linked to harm and coercive state power: harmful actions that turn one into a "public enemy" or a threat to public safety are of proper concern to the state.

But it is not sufficient to say that the liberal model of public and private *replaces* the classical model. After all, we do not inhabit a despatialized world. Thus, the liberal model and the classical model coexist in thought and practice. Carole Pateman sees the transition from the classical model of household and polis to the liberal model actually superimposing the latter on the former.[22] The two forms intersect in complex and often unacknowledged ways.

In the *Love* opinion, the liberal model of public and private agency is applied to the homeless, who are described as making presumptively private "lifestyle" choices—agentic acts falling within the domain of personal autonomy. But the "choice" to live one's life entirely in public space turns private voluntary acts into matters falling under public jurisdiction: if excessive property accumulation by the homeless is potentially harmful to others, it becomes a public health concern. The liberal model of privacy (as the jurisdiction of individual choice) is applied to the homeless while the classical model of privacy that is its precondition (the private sphere as institutional domain 'housing' bare life) forms the invisible substratum that enables the conversion of homeless lifestyle choices into abject, deviant outlaw behavior. So the homeless are granted the status of the private individual-as-chooser, but by "choos[ing] to live on city property rent-free" they are seen as threatening the public-as-victim.[23] Yet the lack of a private space makes the homeless person's agency *by definition* a matter of public concern. Rather than acknowledging that the lack of a space of withdrawal makes the liberal model of public and private agency unworkable in the case of homelessness, the court sticks to the liberal model as if it had no spatial prerequisites, thereby turning the homeless into responsible, criminal, outlaw choosers and accumulators.

If homelessness is a condition of freedom, a lifestyle choice, but the legitimate exercise of this private agency extends no further than the most minimal possessions that maintain biological life, then the freedom of the homeless lifestyle chooser is profane freedom: the freedom of bare life that is already caught within the sovereign ban. To choose homelessness within the liberal model of public and private is to choose to approach the vanishing point of possessive individualism. In the *Love* court's despatialized approach to public and private, the homeless are caught in a trap: private individuals without private spaces making "lifestyle choices" that create public harms. To "choose homelessness" is to choose to renounce the enabling structures that render (private) choices legally recognizable in the first place. The very existence of homeless persons is legally suspect, and whatever personal property the homeless have is, in a sense, always already trash, to be confiscated.[24] So, although the *Love* court attributes agency to the homeless as lifestyle choosers, it turns this choice into the choice of outlawed bare life: the only way for the homeless to remain secure in themselves and in their possessions is to limit their extension into the world to an absolute bare minimum.

In the reasoning of the *Love* opinion the homeless, by choosing to live in public space, have chosen a life full of risks, including the risk that the public authority will confiscate their property. The homeless have chosen to be outlaws and as such—rhetorics of voluntarism and lifestyle notwithstanding—are caught within the sovereign ban and its reduction of the citizen to bare life. So the choice to live in public is the choice to have the bare minimum of personal property necessary for survival— the choice to possess only a sleeping bag and several blankets. The choice to be homeless, if it is to remain recognized as legitimately private and not entering the domain of public authority (by harming the public), is the choice to limit one's spatial extension into the world to the absolute bare minimum.

SACRED UNFREEDOM: INVOLUNTARY HOMELESSNESS, BARE LIFE, AND THE SHELTER AS A SPACE OF CONFINEMENT

Not all courts have adopted a view of homelessness as an agentic condition, a product of lifestyle choices; several have been receptive to the litigation efforts of advocates for the homeless. Challenges to the constitutionality of various public-space ordinances have met with limited success by claiming that homelessness is an involuntary status, and that laws against public sleeping and camping in effect punish people for their involuntary status, by punishing life-sustaining conduct (public sleeping) that is inextricably linked to status. Seeking an extension of the Supreme Court's decision in *Robinson* that deemed punishment of status (in the case of drug addiction) to be cruel and unusual punishment in violation of the Eighth Amendment, homeless-rights litigators have found three courts receptive to their claims. Two federal district courts and one state appellate court have struck down public-camping and public-sleeping ordinances on Eighth Amendment grounds.[25] In two of these cases the decisions were later overturned on procedural grounds, by a federal appeals court in *Johnson v. Dallas* and by the California Supreme Court in *Tobe v. Santa Ana*.[26] The case of *Pottinger v. Miami* remains as the first, landmark case adopting the Eighth Amendment challenge, and it has not been overturned. In *Pottinger* the court affirms the plaintiffs' claim of punishment for status (the status-crime challenge) and grounds it in the involuntariness of homelessness and the involuntariness of conduct directly linked to this status.

But the seeming victories for homeless-rights litigators are problematic because they share with the *Love* court opinion a discursive reduction of the homeless to the status of bare life. In emphasizing the *involuntariness* of homelessness, they appear to respect the homeless by refusing to demonize them as willful, profane outlaws; nevertheless, they identify the homeless with biological necessity, veering to the other pole of the freedom/unfreedom axis and refusing to accord respect to homeless persons as acting citizens. Constraint, compulsion, and necessity become the dominant themes in these cases. Denying that homelessness is a lifestyle choice, such courts end up identifying homelessness with an absolute helplessness that legitimates a person's confinement in the most minimal and degrading of emergency shelters— again, just enough shelter to maintain the physical life of its inhabitant.

The polarity between absolute freedom and absolute unfreedom in our understandings of homelessness is a sign of political power's isolation of bare life. Indeed, legal debates about the voluntariness or involuntariness of homelessness are structured by the reduction of the figure of the homeless person to bare biological life. It is this reduction that enabled the

Love court to invoke simultaneously the "lifestyle choice" to be homeless *and* the opinion that this choice gives one entitlement to no more than the bare necessities (a blanket) for sustaining bare life. And it is this reduction of the homeless to bare life that frames the legal logic in the Eighth Amendment cases as well—even those that present "victories" for the homeless and their legal advocates. Such victories, because they share the homeless-as-bare-life assumptions of the *Love* court, establish a right to exist in public space that is as precarious as the right to personal property. Just as only the most minimal provisions are legitimately possessed by street persons, according to *Love,* the most minimal space in a shelter is sufficient to turn street-dwelling back into a (constitutionally criminalizable) choice. Where a shelter floor is available, public sleeping is illegal, and the homeless shelter becomes a space of confinement.

The double-edged nature of these legal arguments becomes evident in certain surprising agreements between legal critics and defenders of punitive public-space laws. For instance, Edward Walters, a critic of blanket restrictions on camping and sleeping in public, proposes a "do or die" exception to criminalization of the homeless. Homeless persons who are faced with a forced choice (violate the law or die) are exposed to cruel and unusual punishment; homeless persons who are faced with a "difficult choice" (such as accepting shelter restrictions and dangers as opposed to criminalization) are not thereby exposed to cruel and unusual punishment: "If there were shelter available in a city, and a homeless person chose not to avail herself of that shelter, she would have to face the possible consequences of violating a prohibition on sleeping in the park." Walters's approach to Eighth Amendment protection for the homeless is redirected, away from the question of the voluntariness or involuntariness of the status of homelessness and toward the question of choice versus compulsion in performing particular acts: "The inquiry outlined above will involve difficult determinations of what decisions are actually 'choiceless,' especially where actions seem irresistible, but are not actually forced. For example, imagine a homeless person who has the choice to sleep in a shelter, but chooses not to because of a valid fear that the shelters are too dangerous; or consider a homeless husband and wife who choose to sleep in a park because the only shelters available are segregated by sex. Although there will be difficult cases, courts should be able to meaningfully distinguish between people faced with difficult choices and those with no choice at all."[27]

Walters says nothing more directly in relation to these examples, so it is not entirely clear where he personally would draw the line between punishable difficult choices and the unpunishable condition of no choice at all.

Nevertheless, the summary of his argument points to the view that any and all provision of shelter that can keep the homeless person physically alive offers a choice. The only time the homeless lack a choice (and are thus involuntarily dwelling on the street) is when the alternative is death: "A city may prohibit acts of the homeless only if it can show that homeless people have a lawful alternative (death does not count as an alternative)." Although "break the law or die" is not, according to Walters, a valid or real choice, the logic of his argument leads to the conclusion that any option that sustains physical life would count as a real (though "difficult") choice and thus enable the constitutional application of the (public-sleeping) ban.[28]

Strikingly, Robert Tier, who is an *advocate* of public sleeping and panhandling prohibitions (see chapter 1), makes exactly the same argument as Walters. Tier goes so far as to support a complete ban on panhandling: "In fact, in terms of communication, the beggar stands in the same position as the hold-up man with a gun." He opposes Eighth Amendment application to the homeless, but he argues that even the most expansive reading of the amendment warrants the criminalization of public camping where a "choice" to be on the street can be found: "To be covered by any Eighth Amendment necessity defense, one must be truly homeless. If someone has an option of a place to go, the essential element of involuntariness vanishes. Rejecting shelters because they demand sobriety, insist upon prayer, require nominal fees, require helping out in the kitchen, or impose a curfew should not count. The availability of such places makes it possible to obey the law. This is all the Eighth Amendment requires, even at its most expansive reading."[29]

To be "truly homeless," it appears, is to be reduced to bare (and helpless) life. To be "falsely homeless," one can infer, is to insist upon acting as a thinking, judging, coping person. To be falsely homeless is to "choose" homelessness; the voluntarily homeless are those who have "someplace else to go." Tier posits what he considers reasonable restrictions that shelters may place on their temporary residents. But the underlying logic of the argument is that the "availability of such places makes it possible to obey the law." That is, the availability of shelter space—whatever its condition, whatever the degree of spatial compression, whatever the degree of degradation, and whatever the disciplinary strings attached—turns public sleeping or camping into a legitimately punishable, voluntary act.

The isolation of bare life by the law is evident not only in legal scholars' commentaries but also in judicial opinions upholding homeless plaintiffs' status-crime challenges to the ban. In *Pottinger v. Miami* the court, in declaring unconstitutional the Miami police practice of arresting and harassing homeless persons, under a variety of ordinances, for eating and sleeping in public space, concludes that these police actions constitute cruel and unusual punishment of an involuntary status. The court's claim that the plaintiffs are involuntarily homeless is, as Wes Daniels notes, "a predicate for its favorable rulings on each of the constitutional counts. This is most explicitly true with respect to the Eighth Amendment cruel and unusual punishment claim."[30] Indeed, Judge Clyde Atkins, writing for the district court, establishes the involuntariness of homelessness via a chain of compulsions. First, the court establishes that sleeping in public is involuntary for the homeless because their condition (homelessness) compels the act: "The record in the present case amply supports plaintiffs' claim that their homeless condition compels them to perform certain life-sustaining activities in public." In the next sentence, the court says, "As a number of expert witnesses testified, people rarely choose to be homeless. Rather, homelessness is due to various economic, physical or psychological factors that are beyond the homeless individual's control." Here the chain of compulsion is extended back one step: the condition that compels the conduct is itself unchosen. Furthermore, the court establishes the extreme difficulty of overcoming the condition of homelessness, pointing out that the Miami area has some seven-hundred shelter beds for an estimated six-thousand homeless: "The lack of adequate housing alternatives cannot be overstated. The homeless have truly no place to go."[31]

The court asserts, then, that the condition of homelessness is unchosen, that this condition compels the performance of life-sustaining activities in public, and that this condition cannot be easily overcome by an individual absent outside assistance:

> In sum, class members rarely choose to be homeless. They become homeless due to a variety of factors that are beyond their control. In addition, plaintiffs do not have the choice, much less the luxury, of being in the privacy of their own homes. Because of the unavailability of low-income housing or alternative shelter, plaintiffs have no choice but to conduct involuntary, life-sustaining activities in public places. The harmless conduct for which they are arrested is inseparable from their involuntary condition of being homeless. Consequently, arresting homeless people for harmless acts they are forced to perform in public effectively punishes them for being homeless.[32]

The homeless, in this passage, are defined by compulsion: their condition is involuntary; the conduct for which they are punished is involuntary; and it is the involuntary condition that compels the performance of the involuntary conduct.

The court concludes that because homelessness is generally an involuntary condition, then so long as the city fails to provide adequate shelter,
sleeping in public is not a voluntary act: "An individual who loses his home
as a result of economic hard times or physical or mental illness exercises no
more control over these events than he would over a natural disaster.
Furthermore, as it was established at trial, the City does not have enough
shelter to house Miami's homeless residents. Consequently, the City cannot argue persuasively that the homeless have made a deliberate choice to
live in public places or that their decision to sleep in the park as opposed
to some other exposed place is a volitional act."[33]

What would it take to turn sleeping in public into a volitional, and hence
punishable, act? The court does not make this clear, but the logic of the
argument is that the provision of shelter that enables the performance of
life-sustaining activities in an unexposed space would turn sleeping in public into a legitimate target of state power. Such an interpretation is consonant with comments by Judge Atkins indicating a refusal to evaluate the
adequacy of shelter provisions if and when the city claimed to be providing emergency shelter for all homeless persons, thus making sleeping in
public a choice and enabling the renewal of punitive efforts. In a later opinion remanding the case, Atkins says that "while the court is concerned that
homeless people receive appropriate services and are treated with dignity,
it is not for the court to judge the efficacy of the [Dade County Homeless]
Trust's efforts."[34]

A second Eighth Amendment ruling on a public-sleeping ban (a ruling
later overturned on procedural grounds) makes the logic of power, choice,
compulsion, and bare life more explicit. In *Johnson v. City of Dallas,*
plaintiffs attacked the city's ordinance prohibiting public sleeping and its
proposed eviction of a homeless encampment. The *Johnson* court claims
that the ordinance targeted conduct, not status; nevertheless, "maintaining human life requires certain acts, among them being the consuming of
nourishment, breathing, and sleeping." After establishing that the conduct
being regulated is that which sustains physical life, the court goes on to
establish that the homeless plaintiffs are homeless involuntarily: "At any
given time there are persons in Dallas who have no place to go, who could
not find shelter even if they wanted to—and many of them do want to—
and who would be turned away from shelters for a variety of reasons. There
are not enough beds available at the area shelter to accommodate the
demand. Some persons do not meet particular shelter's eligibility requirements." The court reasons that since life requires sleeping, and since the
homeless are involuntarily confined to public space, the homeless must sleep

in public space. Therefore, punishing public sleeping in essence criminalizes the involuntary status of homelessness: "They have no place to go other than the public lands they live on. In other words, they must be in public. And it is also clear that they must sleep. Although sleeping is an act rather than a status, the status of being could clearly not be criminalized under *Robinson*. Because being does not exist without sleeping, criminalizing the latter necessarily punishes the homeless for their status as homeless, a status forcing them to be in public."[35]

The *Johnson* court, like the court in *Pottinger,* establishes a chain of compulsions: a temporal claim about involuntariness, stretching back into the past (the condition of homelessness was involuntary in its acquisition); a claim stretching into the future (the condition is "irremediable"); a claim about human necessity (homeless people, like all people, must sleep); and a claim of logical or definitional compulsion (if homeless people must sleep, then they must sleep in public, because to be homeless is by definition to be confined to public space). All these claims lead inescapably to the conclusion that a public-sleeping ban is punishment for status.

But then, after establishing such an elaborate rhetorical weight of compulsion (it is as if the goal of the repetition of this "being forced" in all its permutations is finally to compel the agreement of the audience), the court remarkably explains what would be required to make public sleeping no longer an involuntary act committed by necessity by people who are involuntarily homeless: "For many of those homeless in Dallas, the unavailability of shelter is not a function of choice; it is not an issue of choosing to remain outdoors rather than sleep on a shelter's floor because the shelter could not provide a bed that one found suitable enough. The evidence demonstrates that for a number of Dallas homeless at this time homelessness is involuntary and irremediable."[36] The court here makes explicit what it would take to turn the compulsion to sleep in public into the choice to sleep in public: the presence of space on the floor of a shelter.[37] The legal legitimation of space on a shelter's floor as an adequate response to the predicament of homelessness manifests what Kawash describes as the "strategies of containment and constricton brought to bear on the homeless body."[38] The *Johnson* opinion, though, displays a specifically legal strategy of constriction and containment: discursively reducing homeless persons to the compulsions of life's necessities, and then authorizing their confinement in the most minimal form of shelter.

A corollary of the reduction of homelessness to compulsion is a reduction of the homeless to bare life, as in the *Johnson* decision, where the involuntariness of homelessness is tied to the absence of any alternative method of sustaining bare life. But paradoxically, the reduction of the homeless persons' requirements to eating, sleeping, and breathing reinstates and criminalizes the agency of the homeless. Because the homeless are bare life, their saying no to a shelter space that keeps that bare life alive is interpreted by the court as a willful, volitional, and therefore punishable act. Because the homeless are legally constricted to the status of bare, biological life, the barriers to legally established agency are lowered as well. (It is worth considering at this point whether a natural disaster victim would be similarly viewed as making a punishable choice in sleeping outdoors in order to avoid an overcrowded, noisy, and potentially dangerous shelter. Or would this option be viewed as "no real choice at all," given that the natural disaster victim retains the status of citizen—is not reduced to bare life—whereas for the urban street-dweller, any space that sustains bare life counts as an option?)[39] Once the homeless have been reduced to bare life in the legal imagination, the shelter becomes a legitimized space of confinement, and resistance to it becomes constitutionally punishable via the ban.

To the extent that court decisions such as *Pottinger* push cities to abandon criminalization efforts, the real nature of such a victory needs to be acknowledged. If Eighth Amendment status-crime lawsuits prompt new directions in homelessness policy, then these should be recognized. As Daniels argues, "Even seriously inadequate programmatic responses to homelessness may provide some meaningful, if ultimately shortterm, relief to the immediate suffering of some homeless individuals. If litigation can evoke a pain-mitigating response, criticism of those efforts should proceed with caution."[40] The *Pottinger v. Miami* decision, which, unlike the district court's opinion in *Johnson v. Dallas,* was not overturned, has resulted in limited but meaningful change. As the NLCHP reports, the final settlement of the lawsuit barred the arrest of homeless persons for engaging in life-sustaining activities and enjoined the police to transport them to shelters.[41] To be sure, the overturning or restricting of public-sleeping bans and police practices of harassment, displacement, eviction, and property confiscation may ameliorate the condition of homelessness.

Still, it is important to understand the logic of the legal opinion and how the shelter as a particular space is constituted within the law. If there is one thing that legal advocates for the homeless and "broken-windows" supporters seem to agree on, it is this: if a city provides sufficient shelter space for its homeless citizens, however minimal and structured by disciplinary rules, then sleeping in public is constitutionally punishable. (And the corollary, I suggest, is that this voluntarily homeless person may be coerced into the shelter.) Indeed, the *Pottinger* settlement includes the policy that homeless people may still be arrested for sleeping in public *if* there is shelter space available and it is refused.[42] The legal logic here turns the shelter into a space of confinement.

The very limited nature of the homeless-rights victories in *Johnson* and *Pottinger* can be seen clearly in the way these cases have been interpreted as precedents. In *Joel v. Orlando* (2000), the Eleventh Circuit Appeals Court upheld Orlando's public-camping ban, while also affirming the logic of the district court opinions in *Johnson* and *Pottinger* which struck down public-sleeping bans. Distinguishing the facts under review in the Orlando case from the situations in Dallas and Miami, the court says:

> In concluding that the ordinances in those cases violated the Eighth Amend-ment rights of the homeless, the district courts in *Pottinger* and *Johnson* explic-itly relied on the lack of sufficient homeless shelter space in those cases, which the courts reasoned made sleeping in public involuntary conduct for those who could not get in a shelter. . . . By contrast, here the City has presented unrefuted evidence that the Coalition, a large homeless shelter, has never reached its maximum capacity and that no individual has been turned away because there was no space available or for failure to pay the one dollar nightly fee. Consequently, even if we followed the reasoning of the district courts in *Pottinger* and *Johnson* this case is clearly distinguishable. The ordinance in question here does not criminalize involuntary behavior.[43]

The legal constitution of the "involuntarily homeless," though promis-ing that it offers to provide a space of protection from criminalization, simultaneously makes "voluntary homelessness" fully punishable. Fur-thermore, the involuntarily homeless are, in the legal imagination, again reduced to a bare life in the limbo of (potentially minimal and degrading) shelter space.

The construction in legal discourse of homeless persons as agents, as choosers, and the construction of homeless persons as victims, marked by a condition of compulsion, constitute a double bind. On the one hand, where homeless persons are deemed agents, that agency is converted into a form of blame: not only are they held responsible for their own plight, but their choices are viewed, as in the *Love* decision, as victimizing the pub-lic. The homeless gain agency only at the moment of their transgression of the law. Their legitimate choices extend no further than the accumulation, consumption, and occupation of that which is absolutely and minimally necessary to stay alive. Anything beyond that constitutes the choices of an outlaw, an excessive consumer who has become a threat to public health. On the other hand, where homelessness is figured as an involuntarily acquired condition, a consequence of forces beyond the individual's control, the homeless are reduced to utterly helpless victims defined by biological necessity. As involuntarily homeless, compelled to perform life-sustaining activities in public space, they are granted protection from the criminal law, but the fact that only the bare minimum of provision (the floor of a shelter) is regarded as necessary reintroduces agency into homelessness and legitimates the criminalization of that agency. In short, the involuntarily homeless regain agency-as-transgression when the minimal conditions for the protection of bare life are introduced.

Thus, the *Love* decision and the *Johnson* decision, which seem so different—the *Love* court upholds a vision of homelessness as choice and rejects claims for protection of homeless persons' property; the Johnson court upholds a vision of homelessness as involuntary and accepts the plaintiffs' claim to strike down punitive measures—share a hidden and fundamental logic: that the legitimate extension of the lifestyle choice to be homeless goes no further than a sleeping bag and a few blankets (*Love*) and that the city need do no more than provide room on a shelter's floor to turn sleeping in public into a (criminalizable) choice (*Johnson*). Anything beyond a sleeping bag is legally confiscatable, and every place outside of the shelter is legally uninhabitable. It is the vision of the homeless as bare life that underwrites both the legal confiscation of all property but some blankets in *Love* and the judicially approved prohibition of public sleeping and camping where the most minimal shelter space is available in *Johnson*. Agamben's critique of the "secret solidarity" between state power and humanitarian organizations in the context of refugee crises can be appropriately applied to this context as well: "punitive" and "compassionate" legal approaches maintain a similar "secret solidarity" in isolating bare life, to be either punished by the ban or confined to minimal and perhaps degrading shelter.

RETHINKING AGENCY AND VICTIMHOOD BEYOND BARE LIFE

What this reading of cases concerning the rights of the homeless suggests is that their agency and victimization need to be rethought in ways that do not trap them in the double bind of bare life that is either punished or confined. In the conclusion I suggest one way in which such a rethinking can occur: by thinking through the ways in which we *all* inhabit public space and are as a result *all* potential outlaws in the context of public-space bans. Here, however, I want to explore possible ways of respecting and enabling the agency of homeless persons within the law: that is to say, resisting the reduction of the homeless to helplessness and physical necessity (as in *Johnson*) without construing their agency as the agency of an outlaw (as in *Love*). Examples of such an alternative way of thinking include Jeremy Waldron's exploration of homelessness as an issue of freedom. Waldron wants to redescribe basic needs in terms of the freedom (and the spatial preconditions of freedom) to fulfill those needs precisely so as to redirect us from a fixation on necessity that reduces the homeless citizen to passivity, as in the *Johnson* case. "When a person is needy," Waldron says, "he does not cease to be preoccupied with freedom; rather, his preoccupation tends to focus on freedom to perform certain actions in particular." By thinking of freedom and need together, Waldron avoids the trap of thinking of homeless agency either as an outlaw lifestyle choice or as Thomas Dumm's romanticized spiritual freedom of the open road. A respect for homeless agency should entail respect for the agency of a *citizen*, not the agency of either a profane or a spiritual outlaw.[44]

The case of Joyce Brown indicates the ways in which the law might be able to respect the agency of the homeless as citizens, as opposed to reducing them to some subordinate legal status, whether sheltered or outlawed. The trial in this case, concerning the involuntary confinement of Joyce Brown (also known as Billie Boggs) in a psychiatric hospital, received a great deal of media attention in the late 1980s. A New York state judge released Brown from a mental institution to which she had been involuntarily committed as part of Mayor Ed Koch's effort to sweep the "mentally ill homeless" from public space in order to "protect" them from the public and from themselves. Although the trial court's decision was overturned by an appeals court and the case was later rendered moot and dismissed, the opinion of the trial court judge offers a mode of reasoning that does recognize homeless persons as citizens and not as outlawed or sheltered bare life.[45]

In *In the Matter of Billie Boggs, Petitioner,* Judge Robert Lippmann finds Joyce Brown to be sane and, warning against conflating mental illness with homelessness, makes a real effort to imagine what rationality might entail, given the insanity of the hostile spaces and citizens that Joyce Brown has encountered. Considering her seemingly insane practice of ripping up the paper money occasionally thrown at her by passersby, Judge Lippmann notes that Joyce Brown mocked those who gave her money just so that "they could feel good" and refused those who gave in a condescending or insulting manner; if they insisted, she tore the bills up or burned them: "Her explanation for destroying paper currency . . . may not satisfy a society increasingly oriented to profit making and bottom-line pragmatism, but it is consonant with safe conduct on the street and consistent with the independence and privacy she vehemently insists on asserting. Apparently, beggars can be choosers."[46] Judge Lippmann attributes agency to Joyce Brown without resentment or accusation; rather than seeing deviance as cause for criminalization, confinement, or diagnosis of irrationality, he interprets it as a strange but comprehensible assertion of dignity.

Noting that Brown has successfully navigated life on the streets, retaining her physical health, he seeks both to illuminate the boundary of experience that separates the housed public from the homeless and to break it down through imaginative projection and careful listening to Joyce Brown's story: "To the passerby seeing her lying on the street or defecating publicly she may seem deranged. 'Bitter poverty,' Juvenal wrote, 'has no harder pang than it makes men ridiculous.' But how can anyone living in security and comfort even begin to imagine what is required to survive on the street? It cannot be reasoned that because Joyce Brown is homeless she is mentally ill."[47]

Finally, Judge Lippmann rhetorically links together the shelter and the mental institution, both resisted by Joyce Brown, as spaces of confinement: "She refuses to be housed in a shelter. That may reveal more about conditions in shelters than about Joyce Brown's mental state. It might, in fact, prove that she's quite sane. She refuses confinement in Bellevue's psychiatric facilities, preferring freedom on the street with all its attendant risks. Freedom, constitutionally guaranteed, is the right of all."[48] The judge manages to attribute agency to Joyce Brown without turning agency into an accusation. Furthermore, his exploration of the hardships, cruelties, violence, and insecurity of life on the street is not prefigured by a degrading reduction of Joyce Brown to bare life—a form of life that may be confined or punished by the sovereign power that holds it in its ban.

One can detect traces of the romantic sacralization of homelessness (as a form of spiritual freedom) here. When Lippmann turns Joyce Brown's burning of money from a symptom of insanity to a critique of "a society increasingly oriented to profit making and bottom-line pragmatism," he falls prey to the romanticizing and exoticizing impulse whereby the homeless person becomes the sacred outsider, offering spiritual guidance to a profane and materialistic society. Such an approach does little to resist the construction of homeless persons as outlaws; it simply sacralizes that outlaw status. When Lippmann asserts that "beggars can be choosers," however, and when he argues that there may be good reasons for a person to resist or refuse confinement in shelters and psychiatric hospitals, homeless agency is not so much romanticized as understood to be a thinking and acting citizen's reasonable, eminently understandable response to institutional injustices.

The next chapter considers a concrete micropolitics that enables the political agency of homeless persons in resisting the bare-life predicament: politicized homeless encampments. Dominant policy discourses stigmatize claims for legal recognition and the legalization of homeless encampments as a counterproductive "identity politics," but I argue that they should be understood as a pluralizing response to political injustices of exclusion. This claim is controversial: according to some, *any* legal recognition of the homeless and of homeless encampments is counterproductive, interfering with efforts to end homelessness. Although such a position is attractive to the extent that it affirms a vision of a future without the hardships and injustices of homelessness, I argue that it works ideologically to mask and legitimate unjust operations of state punitive power.

CHAPTER 3

Redistribution, Recognition, and the Sovereign Ban

Because some, though not all, bans on public sleeping and camping have run into trouble in the courts, cities through the late 1990s and early 2000s became increasingly more careful. They hoped to avoid the pitfalls confronted by the Santa Ana City Council, whose paper trail of documented hostility toward the homeless influenced a state court to strike down its public-sleeping ban.[1] City governments have since developed more finely tuned ordinances and more carefully crafted justifications for them. These new justifications are not explicitly about the need to protect valued consumer spaces from intrusions by a homeless other, about panhandlers "lounging" on busy sidewalks, the "lifestyle choice" to be homeless, or the intrinsic purpose of public space. The new justifications—call them "compassionate conservatism" or "tough love"—claim that a punitive approach is really about *helping* the homeless. Furthermore, cities are crafting "holistic" policies that combine the criminalization of conduct such as sleeping in public with referrals to shelters and outreach efforts by social workers.[2]

Defenders of public-space laws manage to present criminalization and compassion as *one coherent policy*. Their ability to do so should not be a surprise, given that punitive "civility" laws and shelter services both reflect sovereign power's constitution of the homeless as bare life. These "holistic" policies and their public justification indicate the easy shift from criminalization to compassion (as mirror-image policy responses), reflecting and reinforcing the exclusion of the homeless from the category of citizenship. But advocates of "compassionate" homeless criminalization *defend* this connection by suggesting that criminalization laws are part of a coherent and compassionate welfare state policy designed to end homelessness. Legal challenges to criminalization, they claim, are nothing more than a counter-productive identity politics for the homeless. Thus, it is necessary to go further than simply asserting the punitive and exclusionary (as opposed to compassionate and inclusive) link between public-sleeping bans and emergency shelters. It is necessary to dissect the argument against legal recognition itself.

Advocates of punitive policies suggest that restrictions on public sleeping and camping are one element of a broader policy that combines legal prohibitions with social service outreach, emergency shelter provision, drug treatment programs, and mental health referrals—the "tough love" needed to end homelessness. They claim that when homeless-rights activists argue for legal recognition of the right to be homeless (or the right of homeless persons to exist in public spaces free of legal harassment), they are undermining efforts to ameliorate the condition of homelessness. For instance, in response to an Oregon state court's striking down of Portland's ban on public sleeping, Mayor Vera Katz said, "I can't see spending millions of dollars to make sure the homeless are housed and at the same time see them camp in our streets. Our preference is to see the homeless have roofs over their heads."[3] In other words, the entire effort to win legal recognition for the homeless is regarded as counter-productive—not just for home-dwelling citizens but for the homeless themselves. Legal recognition of, and city support for, homeless persons and homeless encampments is seen as existing in opposition to therapeutic interventions by social service agencies.

Among other examples of this critique of legal recognition for the homeless, a *New York Times* article concerning a proposed amendment to Santa Cruz's public-sleeping ban, which would provide for certain safe areas where it would be legal to sleep, articulates the dilemma as follows: "Santa Cruz, which is at least as politically left-wing as Berkeley, has agonized over its public sleeping ban for years. Time and again, the City Council has discussed the idea of softening the law. Each time, people have objected. . . . [Some] objected on philosophical grounds. Shouldn't Santa Cruz be helping people off the streets rather than helping them stay on them?"[4]

Kelling and Coles, in developing their broken-windows argument for policing to maintain order, offer advice to cities seeking to crack down on aggressive panhandling and public camping: when coming up with ordinances restricting public sleeping, sitting and camping, and aggressive panhandling, cities should anticipate a legal challenge by homeless advocates and should therefore demonstrate a record of helping the homeless with various services. "Evidence of the city's intent will be provided as well in a consistent record of having met its respnsibilities to the poor and indigent by attempting to offer social services, job training, counseling, housing and other resources. . . . [A]s an independent element in the city's record, their existence will serve to dispel the notion that the city intended in any fashion to discriminate against indigent, homeless, or otherwise disadvantaged persons through its order-maintenance efforts." Documented efforts to redistribute goods, provide shelter, and offer services can help to forestall any litigation aimed at legal recognition of homeless persons; conversely, a lack of such efforts, combined with a paper trail indicating anti-homeless bias, may produce legal victories for homeless-rights activists. Where cities make a redistributive effort, they can craft public-space restrictions that pass constitutional muster and nip recognition efforts in the bud. Such was the case, Kelling and Coles write, when Seattle's sidewalk-sitting ban was upheld by two courts: "Clearly [Seattle city attorney] Sidran's careful attention to creating a record of Seattle's treatment of the homeless through measures reflecting integrity, concern and the provision of concrete services was effective."[5]

There are two important points to make about Kelling and Coles's arguments. First, cities are crafting policy "in the shadow of the law," developing ordinances in *anticipation* of a constitutional challenge.[6] Homeless-rights ligitators, then, may succeed in curtailing some of the most egregious practices of harassment, such as police sweeps and mass arrests, through the threat of litigation and past victories in other cities. Second, the "redistribution not recognition" argument is part of a broader strategy aimed at demonstrating an absence of hostility towards the homeless, despite the fact that homeless persons are the key targets of order-maintenance policing and public-space "civility" laws.

Whether it is simply a strategic gloss or a genuine argument, "redistribution not recognition" merits further exploration. This is a more nuanced, qualified, and compelling defense of homeless criminalization policies than those justifications that simply mobilized public hostility toward homeless bare life and the right of upstanding, home-dwelling citizens to be free to occupy the consumptive public sphere of urban America.

But *does* a politics aimed at legal recognition of the rights of the homeless to exist in public space (expressed in such constitutional language as the right to be free of cruel and unusual punishment, the right to travel, and the right to equal protection of the laws) work to enable homelessness? Does it give support to this identity and at the same time undercut efforts to end homelessness through redistributive policies providing more affordable housing, more job training, more transitional housing, and, at a minimum, more shelter beds? If cities allow homeless encampments to exist, and if cities develop policy to support homeless subsistence efforts, is there a danger that homelessness will become accepted as a normal part of the urban landscape and that the economic injustice of homelessness will be effaced by an expanding multicultural pantheon that includes homelessness as a revalued minority identity? If so, there would indeed appear to be a conflict between redistribution programs for the homeless and recognition efforts for the homeless. Critics of legal rights to sleep and camp in public space would then be getting at a significant tension or problem, and not just providing a compassionate gloss to their punitive ambitions. Homeless-rights activists would find themselves in what Nancy Fraser calls the "redistribution/recognition" dilemma, faced with a politics of economic redistribution that runs at cross-purposes with a politics of cultural recognition.[7] This is the more theoretically sophisticated way of expressing the very same claims made by the Santa Cruz citizen and the mayor of Portland: the redistribution of shelter resources is needed to get people off of the streets, whereas legal recognition will only help them to stay on the streets.

My argument is that this tension is greatly overdrawn in the case of homelessness. Homeless activism—including politicized homeless encampments that challenge public-sleeping bans, the paucity of shelter resources, and the stigmatizing effects of shelter policies—is not a counterproductive form of identity politics but a potentially pluralizing movement challenging the multiple injustices of homelessness. Furthermore, I suggest that policy discussions of "redistribution not recognition" in the case of homelessness evince a neglect of the political, of state power and a specifically political dimension of injustice. Indeed, it is this "displacement of politics"[8] that *underlies* and *enables* the very assertion of a conflict between helping the homeless off the street and recognizing their legal right to exist in public space. I develop and amend Fraser's framework for analyzing (in)justice issues, tacking back and forth between the theory and the case of homelessness. Her framework is useful because it directs our attention to the multiple injustices in the phenomenon of homelessness; however, its failure to thematize a specifically political form of injustice—political exclusion—limits its ability to make sense of justice struggles and is reflected in a similar blindness to the specificities of state power in the claims made by advocates of homeless-criminalization policies. Pragmatic, empirically grounded, and theoretically incisive analyses of contemporary forms of injustice are best developed within a "trivalent" framework. Hence, I develop a

threefold theory of injustice that brings into view the interrelated yet ana-
lytically distinguishable dynamics of maldistribution, misrecognition, and
political exclusion.

An exploration of specifically political forms of injustice can help orient a response to those advocates of homeless-criminalization policies who
claim that legal recognition of the homeless runs at cross-purposes to the
redistributive goal of ending homelessness. Homeless-criminalization policies are best understood not as the tough love needed to end homelessness
but as a specifically political form of injustice: political exclusion. I return
to Agamben's discussion of the sovereign ban on bare life, and I explore
Hannah Arendt's penetrating analysis of the status of the refugee to illuminate this dynamic of injustice. Where a "recognition" politics is aimed
against a set of punitive policies that seek to deny homeless persons the very
right to exist, "legal recognition" is not identity politics run amok but rather
the struggle for political inclusion in response to the ban on bare life. The
fundamental and necessary first step in combatting the injustices of homelessness is establishing citizenship.

REDISTRIBUTION AND RECOGNITION

Nancy Fraser diagnoses the problem with contemporary progressive politics as the "decoupling of cultural politics from social politics, and the
relative eclipse of the latter by the former."[9] She maintains an analytical
separation between economic politics (redistribution) and cultural politics (recognition), but this not the same distinction as the old left's account
of legitimate class-based politics and illegitimate "identity" politics (of
race, gender, sexuality, etc.). Fraser says, "In my diagnosis, . . . the split
in the Left is not between class struggles, on the one hand, and gender,
'race,' and sex struggles, on the other. Rather, it cuts across those movements, each of which is internally divided between cultural currents and
social currents."[10] Collectivities such as those formed on the basis of gender and race classification and oppression face both economic injustice
and cultural injustice. These are social groups constituted by, and enmeshed
in, practices and institutions that both maldistribute resources and stigmatize persons. These "bivalent collectivities" find themselves in a
bind: the attempt to combat cultural injustice by, for instance, revaluing
femininity comes into conflict with the attempt to eliminate economic
injustice by, for instance, eliminating the gendered division of labor.
For bivalent collectivities, cultural politics often interfere with progressive economic restructuring.

Not all recognition politics impede progressive economic transformation, though. Indeed, Fraser goes on to complicate her model by delineating two forms of recognition politics and two forms of redistributive politics: in each domain there is a surface politics of affirmation and a deeper politics of transformation. The liberal welfare state represents the affirmative politics of distribution; its cultural counterpart is "mainstream multiculturalism" with its celebration of previously stigmatized identities. Socialism or some form of social democracy represents the transformative politics of economic distribution; its cultural counterpart is deconstruction, which transforms cultural binary oppositions by destabilizing them.

With this complication of the redistribution/recognition model, Fraser focuses her critique on affirmative remedies for both economic and cultural injustice. First of all, a politics of identity that celebrates and revalues a previously stigmatized identity—what Fraser terms mainstream multiculturalism—undercuts transformative efforts at economic redistribution. Transformative efforts to achieve economic justice involve seeking to eliminate the social group's exploited or marginalized place in the economic structure; mainstream multiculturalism involves affirming the group's identity in the face of patterns of cultural stigma. Such forms of cultural politics as cultural feminism's revaluing of the feminine, a celebration of black pride, and the construction of a gay identity on the ethnic group model of American pluralism do not combine well with a "social politics of equality." Thus, there is a significant tension between certain forms of recognition (especially mainstream multiculturalism) and socialist efforts to overcome economic injustice: "The transformative redistribution politics of socialism seems at odds with the affirmative recognition politics of mainstream multiculturalism; whereas the first tends to undermine group differentiation, the second tends rather to promote it."[11]

In addition to critiquing affirmative cultural politics of recognition, Fraser explores the inadequacies of affirmative economic politics of redistribution propounded by the liberal welfare state, which fails for three reasons to redress economic injustice adequately. First, its "surface reallocations" of consumptive shares leaves the deeper structure of class inequalities and the capitalist system of production intact. Second, the two tracks of government provision—social security for employed workers and stingy "welfare" benefits to the unemployed poor—work, ultimately, to enhance group differentiation, dividing the "employed and nonemployed fractions of the working class" and stigmatizing the recipients of welfare. Third, by marking out a class of poor people as morally deficient, the liberal welfare state contradicts its own commitments to universalism.[12]

The redistribution/recognition dilemma can be finessed, however. Not all forms of cultural recognition impede progressive efforts to restructure economic relations. Fraser ends up endorsing the twin projects of economic socialism and cultural deconstruction over their deficient counterparts: the liberal welfare state and mainstream multiculturalism. The affirmative economic remedies of the welfare state and multiculturalist cultural remedies can exacerbate identitarian conflicts and resentments, reinforcing the stigmatization of despised groups and, in their "surface reallocations," fail to transform the "deep structures" of economic and cultural injustice. On the other hand, a "transformative" politics of economic redistribution (socialism) and a transformative politics of cultural recognition (deconstruction) both engage the deep structures of injustice, avoid reinforcing the flows of resentment, and undermine group differentiation by transforming exploitative relations of production and deconstructing the hierarchical binary oppositions that sustain practices of cultural misrecognition.[13]

The claim that there is a significant tension between (transformative) redistribution and (multicultural) recognition has been explored by other theorists on the left, some of whom even reference homelessness as a kind of limit case pointing to the problematic nature of some kinds of identity politics.[14] For instance, David Harvey explores the tension between an identity politics for the homeless and a deeper politics oriented toward restructuring social relations and transforming unjust social processes. He argues that "if respect for the condition of the homeless . . . does not imply respect for the social processes creating homelessness, . . . then identity politics must operate at a dual level. A politics which seeks to eliminate the processes which give rise to a problem looks very different from a politics which merely seeks to give full play to differentiated identities once they have arisen." In other words, an "affirmative" politics of recognition would seek respect for "differentiated identities once they have arisen" and do nothing to confront, in a transformative way, "the social processes creating homelessness." Here, homelessness figures as the absurd outer limit to a politics of identity recognition. Recognition of the identity "homeless" signifies a cultural politics run amok, because that recognition on its own would do nothing to challenge or change the socioeconomic processes that create homelessness. Progressive politics must not get so attached to identities and the attendant requirements of recognition that they become unwilling to engage in political action to eliminate the unjust processes that gave rise to those identities. Harvey says, "There are subtle ways in which identity, once acquired, can precisely by virtue of its relative durability seek out the social conditions (including the oppressions) necessary for its own sustenance"; therefore, "the mere pursuit of identity politics as an end in itself (rather than as a fundamental struggle to break with an identity which internalizes oppression) may serve to perpetuate rather than to challenge the persistence of those processes which gave rise to those identities in the first place."[15] As Edward Said puts it, "Marginality and homelessness are not, in my opinion, to be gloried in; they are to be brought to an end, so that more, not fewer, people can enjoy the benefits of what has for centuries been denied the victims of race, class, or gender."[16] If ever there was a case of tension between multiculturalist recognition and transformative redistribution, homelessness would seem to be that case.

HOMELESSNESS AND MISRECOGNITION

According to the logic of the "redistribution not recognition" argument, attempts to redistribute housing and shelter resources—and thereby put the homeless "out of business as a group"[17]—are undermined by efforts to win legal and cultural recognition for the homeless. Indeed, if they are not a "bivalent collectivity" like those formed on the basis of race and gender but rather victims of economic injustice pure and simple, then there is not just a tension between redistribution and recognition (as there is for bivalent collectivities), but rather, *all* homeless identity politics would prove counterproductive. If the causes of homelessness are rooted in the economic structure, then the solution to the injustice of homelessness is economic redistribution. What Fraser says of the (ideal-type, as opposed to real-world) proletariat, we might say about the homeless population: "The last thing it needs is recognition of its difference."[18] Rather, the remedy for this injustice is to put everyone into homes: a resource that is currently exclusive should be transformed into an inclusive good. A corollary to this argument is the belief that homelessness does not implicate, in a central, nontrivial, nonderivative way, questions of cultural injustice and misrecognition.

On the left, the primary argument locates the causes of homelessness in the economic structure of society. Indeed, it appears to be imperative to do so as a way of resisting (a) the location of homelessness as a product of individual irresponsibility, (b) its identification with mental illness, drug abuse, and alcoholism, or (c) its equation with a cultural lifestyle choice. As Talmadge Wright puts it, "Thinking of homelessness as primarily an individual problem, to be solved by clinically based therapies, displaces the concern over structural social inequalities onto concerns over 'proper' comportment and individual responsibility."[19] Left-progressive scholars, those who make the economic-structure argument, downplay the prevalence of mental illness (and the corresponding role of deinstitutionalization as cause) and emphasize the socioeconomic/structural causes of homelessness: economic recession in the 1980s, deindustrialization, rapid transformations in technologies rendering many job skills obsolete, federal cutbacks for housing subsidies, and rising rents due to urban gentrification. If ever there was a collectivity differentiated "by virtue of the economic structure," the homeless would seem to be it.

Peter Marcuse provides one example of the approach to homelessness as centrally a problem of maldistribution: "Homelessness has three related causes: the profit structure of housing, the distribution of income, and government policy. Briefly, housing is supplied for profit, as a commodity. . . . Changes in the economy have deprived many people of the income with which to pay for housing. The government only acts to provide housing for persons unable to pay the market price when the economy may need such people in the future or when those people threaten the status quo." Thus, for Marcuse, the injustice of homelessness is tied to three problems of distribution: the market approach to the distribution of housing, economic marginalization of workers as a result of deindustrialization, and governmental retrenchments or cutbacks in redistributive policies as well as subsidies and tax breaks to developers who "redevelop" cheap housing. Given these problems, Marcuse suggests three corresponding answers: "uncouple the housing system from the rest of the private market and make it respond to need; change the economic system so that all have a decent living wage; or provide government subsidies to provide housing for those who cannot get it through the private market."[20]

The first two of Marcuse's solutions are, in Fraser's terminology, transformative: they transform economic structures, the first by decommodifying housing for everyone, and the second (somewhat underspecified) through a massive redistribution of income. The third proposal is more of a surface reallocation—targeted housing subsidies to the poor, a common approach of the liberal ("affirmative") welfare state. Section 8 vouchers (rental subsidies funded by the federal government) are one kind of subsidy, and they may, like other surface reallocations, further differentiate the homeless and the precariously housed from other renters (and owners) by ghettoizing them either in stigmatized public housing or in only those private accommodations where the landlords accept the government subsidies.

Not only do the causes of homelessness appear to many scholars to be economic, but the resulting injustices would appear to be socioeconomic. The homeless do not generally suffer from exploitation.[21] Nevertheless, homelessness as a condition is marked by economic marginalization and the deprivation of certain essential goods: shelter, privacy, warmth, withdrawal and a protected domestic space for the performance of such life-sustaining bodily functions as eating, sleeping, and defecating, a space within which one is granted the (socially recognized and enforced) right to exclude others—in short, the multitude of basic and not-so-basic goods sustained collectively under the signifier and institution "home."[22]

I argue, however, that the homeless, deprived of basic and essential goods and subject to economic marginalization, also face misrecognition through stigmatization and invisibility. The extent to which homelessness is an injustice of both distribution and recognition is manifest strikingly in the double meaning attached to the word "address," which indicates both a spatial location and a mode of intersubjective recognition. To have an address means to have a place of residence, and to be addressed means to be spoken to, recognized as a human subject in dialogue. To be homeless is to risk being addressless in both senses. First, it is to lack a socially recognized and legally protected place in the world from which one has the right to exclude others. Second, in media discourse, in legal discourse, and in encounters on the street, the homeless are often simply not addressed but ignored, treated as objects blocking the free movement of the proper public citizen, denied identification in media reports.

I do not directly reject the leftist position that homelessness is caused by the economic structure of society. One can argue with Fraser that cultural injustices, "far from being rooted directly in an autonomously unjust cultural structure, . . . derive from the political economy."[23] One can take the first version of the redistribution/recognition model and, considering the homeless as a collectivity formed directly by the economic structure of capitalist society, treat the cultural injustices as derivative—an ideological gloss for economic dislocations. I do not find this position ultimately compelling, however, for cultural norms concerning what constitutes a proper home are deeply implicated in the phenomenon of homelessness. Housing policies that work to materialize these norms in the built environment produce a reduction in housing options and the emergence of street-and-shelter homelessness. To treat homelessness as a problem solely of maldistribution is to displace attention from the materialized values and norms that polarize society into home-dwelling citizens and homeless bare life. Thus, I believe that Fraser's more recent argument that virtually all real-world collectivities are bivalent—experiencing injustice traceable to both economy and culture—is persuasive in the context of homelessness.[24] And what Fraser says about class is thus also appropriate to the situation of the homeless

more particularly: "Cultural harms that originated as byproducts of economic structure may have developed a life of their own. Today the misrecognition dimensions of class may be sufficiently autonomous . . . to
require independent remedies of recognition."[25] Of course, positioning
the homeless as a bivalent collectivity does not resolve the issue of what
kind of recognition politics is needed, and certain forms of recognition
may indeed impede needed economic transformations. I take up this issue
below, but first I want to explore the forms of cultural injustice faced by
the homeless.

I trace out four prevailing themes in the misrecognition of the homeless.[26] The first is a form of complete nonrecognition—the homeless as *nonpersons* whom domiciled citizens "see right through" and seek to remove
from valued urban spaces. The homeless here are separated out from the
categories of personhood and citizenship and aligned with the abject—dirt,
feces, smell, disheveled clothes. The second is a conservative individualist
image of *disruptive subjects* responsible for their plight—unconstrained, profane outlaws of public space. This form of misrecognition involves greater
attention to the causes and consequences of homelessness and includes the
analogy between the panhandler and the broken window of an abandoned
building (see chapter 1). The third is a "compassionate" yet ultimately
degrading construal of the homeless as *helpless victims*—in what Hannah
Arendt referred to as the "abstract nakedness of humanity"—to be sheltered and kept alive with a bed, a blanket, and some soup. The homeless
are unfree, noncitizens, but also sacralized in their suffering; although full
personhood is denied them, charity in the face of their suffering is
emphasized. The fourth is a therapeutic vision of *clients with pathologies,*
who, through appropriate classification, surveillance, and intervention, can
be reintegrated into society. This vision treats the homeless not as nonpersons but as "persons in the making" who must be isolated from their pathol-
ogizing circumstances in order to achieve the status of the normal(ized),
home-dwelling citizen-subjects.[27]

Following Patchen Markell, I consider these practices of nonrecognition
and stigmatization to be "misrecognition" in two senses. First, misrecognition is, cognitively, a kind of mistake; an injustice that involves the failure to respect a person "as he or she really is." Second, misrecognition is,
constructively, the production of stigma, actively constituting a class of persons subordinate to the category of the normal citizen.[28] Furthermore, misrecognition operates on two levels. First, stereotypical and degrading
portrayals of the homeless in the news media and in fictional presentations
may shape domiciled citizens' views and appropriate policy responses.[29]

Second, certain practices of misrecognition—particularly the face-to-face reactions or nonreactions of domiciled citizens, the manner of treatment by agents of the welfare state and charitable groups, and the institutionalized patterns of meaning and value embedded in the rules governing shelters, job-training programs, and housing programs—may negatively shape the self-conceptions of homeless persons. All the forms of nonrecognition and stigmatization outlined above are present in a series of contexts, institutions, and spaces—in media and legal discourses about homelessness, in day-to-day encounters between homeless and non-homeless citizens in public space, and in welfare state policies of shelter provision.

The misrecognition of the homeless as nonpersons, with neither a name, nor an identity as a person, was evident in television portrayals of the crisis of homelessness in the 1980s, even before the onset of supposed compassion fatigue. As Richard Campbell and Jimmie Reeves argue in their analysis of the media coverage of Joyce Brown (the homeless woman forced against her will to confinement in a psychiatric institution), news reporters "sort out the homeless from the domain of 'people' . . . suggest[ing] that the homeless reside outside the bounds of what it means to be a person in our society."[30] In network news reports about the Joyce Brown controversy, while experts articulated views about the social problem of homelessness, the homeless themselves were "rarely identified and [spoke] nonsense." Whereas most "person-on-the-street" interviews perform the function of giving a voice to "common sense," interviews with homeless street persons perform different functions: the identification of homelessness with madness, and the refusal to recognize the personal identity of the homeless subject. One television report discussed by Campbell and Reeves began with the following voice-over: "Sometimes he calls himself John. Sometimes Henry. This man is homeless. He's also mentally ill. There are 20,000 like him in New York City."[31] The homeless, in such media coverage, suffer from perhaps the most basic form of nonrecognition: the denial of one's individual, personal identity, the refusal to recognize one's proper name.

The view of the homeless as nonpersons manifests itself not only in media discourses but also in face-to-face encounters between homeless citizens and domiciled citizens in public spaces. In his phenomenologically informed ethnography of residents of a Boston homeless shelter, Robert Desjarlais finds that shelter residents describe their life on the streets as diminishing their sense of self. Reduced contacts with other persons, exhausting survival struggles, and a "raw state of anxiety" turn "the street" into the edge of civil society: "In effect, the streets could come close to effecting a civil death . . . in which people ceased to be fully social

human beings. . . . The personhood of those staying on the streets of
Boston could often be disconfirmed and denied." This reduction in personhood is attributable not just to the physical, material conditions of the
street but also to an intersubjective misrecognition by home-dwellers: "In
trying to skirt any engagement, people often disregard panhandlers or
street dwellers, treating them as shadowy untouchables to be overlooked.
The inattention, which often comes close to a lasting, ritualized excommunication, can add to a dweller's sense of being a ghostly nonperson,
absent and silent in the world of others."[32]

The significance of misrecognition by other citizens is made clear in
Stephen VanderStaay's *Street Lives,* an oral history of homeless persons. Joe,
from Philadelphia, discusses the stigma of being homeless, which is exacerbated for him as a man, he claims, because of the male breadwinner norm:

> You a human being, but you not treated like one. You go in the train station
> and the cops chase you out. It's rainin,' it's cold, you gotta go someplace.
> You can't stay on the street. . . . This especially true of the single male. Peo-
> ple have no sympathy for the male, he the one society really hate and reject.
> 'Cause they've always had a stigma in this country that any man that's not
> out liftin' 200 pounds per load is a bum. So they treat you that way. And if
> you treated that way for long enough, you start to act like one.[33]

Differing from *non*recognition—in which homeless persons are simply
invisible and ignored—media discourses often *mis*recognize the homeless
by stigmatizing them as disorderly, out-of-place subjects. In a certain
conservative individualist view, the homeless are responsible for their own
plight, and disruptive figures in public spaces rightly occupied by upstanding (domiciled) citizens. Kelling and Coles's *Fixing Broken Windows* stig-
matizes the homeless panhandler as a willfully insubordinate disrupter of
civility. Mark Sidran justified Seattle's no-sitting-on-the-sidewalk ordinance
with a similar claim: "Rather than sit or lie one block away in Westlake Park,
he prefers 'his' corner without regard to the interests of pedestrians, including disabled, vision impaired or elderly, to whom he poses a safety hazard. Nor is he concerned about the impact of his behavior in undermining
economic vitality by deterring people from using the sidewalk."[34] In this
vision, homeless panhandlers are neither invisible, nor reduced to needi-
ness and helplessness, nor simply seen as "dirt" or "matter out of place";
rather, they are willfully and irresponsibly out of place. Not simply "material blockage" that prevents the public from achieving a fantasized wholeness, they are also freely choosing subjects—homeless outlaws embody-
ing a dangerous and profane freedom.[35]

Street Lives documents how the various forms of stigma reinforce each other. Joe articulates perceptions of the homeless both as helpless victims to be kept alive and as individuals to be held responsible for their own plight: "In the new world you in society but you not really a part of it no more. And the society you live in it really don't try to help. . . . They keep you alive, that's the name of the game, they keep you alive and say, 'if you wasn't so lazy everything would be all right.' . . . The society we live in treat you like dogs."[36] In a situation of cultural hostility, charity means maintaining life itself but also holding the homeless responsible for failure to go beyond survival.

The main institution for keeping the homeless alive is the shelter. The institution of the homeless shelter ought to be analyzed, as Fraser would argue, not simply in terms of its adequacy as a form of housing redistribution but also for the cultural subtexts it embodies and institutionalizes. Injustices of misrecognition, she writes, are not confined to some "separate sphere" of symbolic value. Rather, all institutions and practices must be investigated if we are to understand the submerged and not-so-submerged cultural values and meanings they express.[37] Evaluating homeless shelters solely in terms of the degree to which they redistribute the needed good of shelter is to miss their (mis)recognition effects. As Doug Timmer, Stanley Eitzen, and Kathryn Talley put it, "We often ask what shelters do *for* the homeless; perhaps we should ask, what do shelters do *to* the homeless?"[38]

Many analysts observe that shelters have developed along two tracks: large dormitory-style, "emergency" shelters that provide minimal privacy and allow temporary stays, and smaller "designer" or "program" transitional shelters that allow longer stays and tend to treat a homogeneous subgroup of homeless persons classified by a particular vulnerability or pathology.[39] There is no bright-line distinction between forms, however. In both emergency and program shelters, homeless persons are classified according to personal pathologies, supervised by case managers, and directed toward appropriate treatments: alcohol or drug rehabilitation programs, job training, life skills classes. A disciplinary institution, the shelter involves "the accounting of comings and goings, lack of privacy, and regimented daily schedules."[40]

The difference lies in each shelter's specific misrecognition effects. Emergency (temporary) shelters tend to treat their clients as dependent bare life—to be sheltered from the elements by the most minimal provisions, "kept alive." Designer (transitional) shelters treat their clients as subjects-in-the-making—persons with pathologies and dependencies who, through appropriate therapeutic intervention, can reenter the housing market as autonomous, domiciled citizens.

Degrading conditions, extensive rules, lack of privacy, and surveillance by emergency shelter staff demonstrate certain values and conceptions. Minimal provisions (a cot and a blanket) and minimal privacy (rows of cots in large undivided warehouse spaces) express a vision of the homeless as bare life, as beings stripped of human personhood and individual identity; they are to be kept alive but not given the resources and privacy for individuation.[41] Furthermore, write Charles Hoch and Robert Slayton, "the spatial exclusion and high visibility of these shelters highlights the social stigma of failure, reinforcing the social distance between the homeless and those farther up the shelter hierarchy."[42] Such a hierarchy, Kathleen Arnold suggests, can be manifest even in a single shelter, where those who have proved themselves to be drug- and alcohol-free are given the privacy of a cubicle, while the rest are massed together in one large room filled with cots.[43] Emergency shelters foster what some critics term "shelterization": a process of institutionalization that maintains dependency and passivity.[44]

The more specialized designer or program shelters for homeless families and for homeless persons categorized by a particular need or dependency, such as drug addiction or mental illness, often provide more privacy and more "homelike" arrangements. Nevertheless, their extensive rules and surveillance practices express a conception of the homeless as damaged subjects to be reformed through appropriate monitoring and therapeutic intervention, and their classificatory practices produce stigma by treating a particular personal deficiency as the cause of a person's homelessness. As Hoch and Slayton argue, "Caretakers use the vulnerabilities and pathologies of the homeless street people not only to inspire public concern and support for shelters but to assign the homeless to specialized shelters organized to meet particular needs."[45] Although program shelters and transitional housing are publicly justified as a step toward full political inclusion (the damaged homeless subject becoming gradually reintegrated into the realm of home-dwelling citizens after becoming sober, gaining coping skills, and receiving job training), these shelters in fact work to enclose and intern.[46] According to Foucault, such "dividing practices" separate normal from deviant subjects—regulating subjects on both sides of the divide—and then separate deviant subjects along the lines of various pathologies: "The subject is either divided inside himself or divided from others. This process objectivizes him. Examples are the mad and the sane, the sick and the healthy, the criminals and the 'good boys.'"[47]

I believe that such dividing practices constitute an injustice of misrecognition in the sense that they result in the production of stigma and the construction of a deviant "homeless" subject against which the "normal" subject stands. As Timmer, Eitzen, and Talley write, "Homeless persons tend to be regarded as the culture of poverty in action." Their normalization becomes then the institutional role of the shelter: "The individual or family traits, characteristics, values and the 'deviant' behaviors based on them that have made the homeless homeless must be changed; that is an important, if not the most important role for the shelter."[48] One example is the linking of access to housing and jobs with continued drug testing and maintaining a "drug-free" body. A National Institute for Drug Abuse (NIDA) report demonstrates how "home" can function as a mechanism through which homeless persons' bodies are monitored and normalized: "This therapeutic approach, in which rules and consequences are applied to help people change their behavior, is called contingency management. . . . [A]ccess to housing and employment is contingent on following the rules, which homeless participants soon learn: stay clean of drugs and alcohol, and you can live in a furnished apartment and enter work therapy. Test positive for drugs or alcohol and you go back into a shelter and lose your job until you are drug free."[49]

As the contingency management case reveals, institutional responses to homelessness frequently stress disciplinary normalization as the means of reintegrating "damaged subjects" into the world of housed citizens. Homelessness is explained as a consequence of personal pathologies and irresponsibility, and the answer is "the overt control exerted over every aspect of life, including the scheduling of waking, sleeping, eating, and showering, restrictions on personal habits, and demands to be enrolled in required programs to continue to receive shelter." In interviews, homeless persons frequently compare shelters to prisons and juvenile detention centers.[50] And with good reason—the shelter *is* a disciplinary institution. An egregious example of the similarity between a shelter and a prison (and the corresponding stigmatization of the homeless) is an Indianapolis facility that requires its occupants to give up their clothing and wear orange jumpsuits.[51]

The shelter complex misrecognizes the homeless in another but related, way: by casting them either as bare life to be "kept alive" or as disaffiliated and damaged subjects to be reformed and reintegrated, shelters neglect the community affiliations and networks that exist among homeless persons and, indeed, actively break these down—both by the individualizing logic of case managment and needs assessment and by the grouping of homeless persons according to shared disability or dependency. The multiple and complex connections to diverse others that existed in older residential hotel neighborhoods and in contemporary homeless encampments are invisible to well-intentioned social workers, psychologists, and shelter managers, who replace these civil society attachments with the single and hierarchical professional-to-client relationship.[52] The individual intake exam with a "case manager" is followed by the assignment of a homeless person to a "group identity" and a corresponding program on the basis of a particularized pathology, deficiency, or need. Foucault understood the logic of individualization as disciplinary power: "Each individual has his own place; and each place its individual. Avoid distributions in groups; break up collective dispositions; analyse confused, massive or transient pluralities."[53]

But Foucault's account of disciplinary and normalizing power makes only partial sense of the injustices of homeless shelters. For one thing, emergency shelters tend not to individualize their clients in any systematic way. Sheltered subjects at the bottom of the hierarchy are warehoused in dormitory spaces with no privacy at all—warehousing that may reflect a form of power in a *post*disciplinary society, where, as Desjarlais argues, not all bodies need to be incorporated into a regime of industrial productivity. For another thing, that shelters rely on a threat of expulsion as the ultimate sanction distinguishes them from disciplinary institutions, where the ultimate threat is not expulsion but further, more rigorous confinement and isolation.[54]

Both Foucault's concept of disciplinary power and the redistribution/ recognition framework, each in its own way, miss a key dynamic in homeless politics: the role of state power over bare life.[55] Within Fraser's framework, the shelter's threat of expulsion is not exactly an economic injustice, nor is it exactly a cultural injustice; it is the threat of abandonment. The homeless subject who resists disciplinary normalization may be expelled, abandoned, and returned to a shadowy outlaw existence on the streets. The threat of abandonment links the shelter, then, to the fundamental ban on bare life. The categories of culture and economy cannot fully capture the processes that produce this injustice.

The shelter, an institution having both economic effects (the redistribution of a resource) and cultural effects (the production of stigma), is also a form of power. Fraser uses the redistribution/recognition framework to generate many important critical insights into the injustices, both cultural and economic, of the contemporary U.S. welfare state, understood as a "central nexus of interpenetration of economy and culture."[56] But what is significant for my purposes is that the state as a state vanishes from view; it becomes a kind of medium through which cultural and economic processes develop.[57] The welfare state as a bureaucracy, the welfare state as a form of political power that classifies and indeed produces subjects, mixing therapeutic aid with punitive exercises of political power—these elements get sidelined in the redistribution/recognition model. As Wendy Brown argues, "The state does not simply handle clients or employ staff but produces state subjects, as bureaucratized, dependent, disciplined, and gendered." Brown cautions against the temptation for progressive political actors and theorists to leave the state undertheorized as a site of power and injustice, to turn to it uncritically "for adjudication of social injury."[58]

HOMELESSNESS AS POLITICAL EXCLUSION

While establishing in that the homeless face both maldistribution and misrecognition, the previous section did not establish that recognition efforts on behalf of the homeless are congruent with a politics of redistribution. Fraser's redistribution/recognition dilemma might still be there. However, the analysis of the shelter also aimed at showing that before this issue can be resolved, specific attention needs to be paid to fundamental issues of political power, exclusion, and abandonment. Indeed, in "Rethinking Recognition," Fraser says in a footnote that maldistribution and misrecognition may not exhaust the dimensions of social justice comprehended by her framework: "I have in mind specifically a possible third class of obstacles to participatory parity that could be called *political*, as opposed to economic or cultural. Such obstacles would include decision-making procedures that systematically marginalize some people even in the absence of maldistribution and misrecognition . . . [and] might be called *political marginalization or exclusion*." Fraser leaves this dynamic of injustice undeveloped.[59] But an expansion of the theory of justice to include a third dimension of the political is vital, I argue, to critically examining the state, to appreciating specifically political dynamics of injustice, and to compensating for the depoliticizing thrust of the language of cultural and economic injustice.[60] The redistribution/recognition framework does not simply sideline issues of state power but also performs its own kind of misrecognition: it renders invisible such forms of state power as the ban on bare life. And so it is necessary not just to add a third dimension, political exclusion, to the theory but to understand how the language of redistribution versus recognition works in policy discourse to misrecognize the *state*.

In the asserted instance of a counterproductive politics of recognition for the homeless, a redistribution/recognition conflict is described in order to legitimate certain state actions (prohibition, arrest, displacement, dispossession) and to undercut movements—such as collectively organized homeless encampments—that challenge these political exclusions. In other words, the assertion of a conflict between economic redistribution and cultural/legal recognition for homeless persons and homeless encampments is not politically innocent; it enables punitive state policies to slip in the back door under the guise of a compassionate politics of state-sponsored and -funded redistribution.

Take a look at another version of the argument, this time justifying a legal ban on a homeless encampment in Seattle. A *Seattle Post-Intelligencer* editorial, "Tent City Not the Answer, but Real Solution Coming," opposed the efforts of SHARE/WHEEL, a Seattle-based homeless-advocacy group organizing a tent city. Despite the fact that the "Real Solution" was still only in the design phase, the editorial used it as justification for maintaining the prohibition against tent camps on city property and private property. The editorial contrasted the plight of "a rag-tag band of homeless people . . . being shepherded around the city by SHARE/WHEEL, an advocacy group determined to legalize tent cities no matter what the price in cost and public safety," to the city government's proposed "Safe Harbors" program, which planned to "use a computerized intake and referral system to help move homeless people towards self-sufficiency." Exactly what the "cost" and threat to "public safety" might be in allowing a homeless encampment to exist legally was never specified. But the future redistribution program—transitional housing and job training—is offered as the right way "to help the county's 5,500 homeless receive the services they need to permanently get off the streets," in contrast to the misguided efforts of an advocacy group, "shepherding" a "peripatetic group of five dozen people" from one campsite to another.[61]

The *Post-Intelligencer* editorial manages to prioritize (potential) welfare redistribution over and against legal recognition by displacing attention from the forms of coercive state power that make legal recognition necessary. For instance, it completely neglects the obvious question: What is forcing this "peripatetic" group to wander from place to place? Ignoring the political and legal dynamics of injustice allows the editorial writer to stigmatize the "wanderings" of a homeless tent camp and to attribute the placelessness of the homeless to the homeless themselves, avoiding acknowledgment of the role of law and police in producing their "nomadic lifestyle." Indeed, the asserted conflict between redistribution and recognition is a dilemma faced by a normative public in relation to an already marginalized other: Do we recognize them, or do we get them off the street? The prioritization of redistribution over recognition has been structured by the underlying political exclusion of the homeless, by their status as dependent subjects of an alternately punitive and therapeutic state.

To be sure, laws regulating sidewalk sitting, public sleeping, camping, and panhandling are not independent of economic and cultural processes. Business improvement districts and owners of downtown stores, the driving forces behind such laws, are interested in maintaining the attractiveness of their shopping areas for middle-class consumers. And these regulations draw support from, and in turn reinforce, both stigmatizing images of homeless persons and panhandlers as disorderly, out-of-place subjects and naturalizing images of public space as serving the particular purposes of commerce, consumption, and transportation. But the end goal of these laws (whether or not the goal is realized in the complex practices of enforcement) is to turn the homeless into outlaws. Neither the category of cultural stigma nor the category of economic deprivation can adequately encompass this legal abandonment of the homeless. Such a process of exclusion is not adequately captured by the category of misrecognition; it is better understood as a form of political exclusion.

The overall effect of these laws *is* to turn the homeless into outlaws, noncitizens whose everyday coping strategies place them outside the law. Ordinances banning public sleeping place a ban on homeless persons themselves. Returning to Agamben's notion of bare life and its capture by the sovereign ban, the idea of the ban is closely linked to the idea of abandonment. Because the bare life that is held in the sovereign ban is both included and excluded, to be an "out-law" is to be both outside the law's protection (exclusion) and subject to law's punishment (inclusion). Agamben therefore argues that "he who has been banned is not . . . simply set outside the law . . . but rather abandoned by it. . . . exposed and threatened on the threshold in which life and law . . . become indistinguishable."[62]

Like the shelter's power of expulsion, police confiscations of homeless persons' property, bans on public sleeping and camping, and prohibitions of other life-sustaining activities manifest this relationship of abandonment. That the law, in turning street-dwellers into outlaws and reducing them to bare life, is abandoning the homeless is strikingly demonstrated by Mark Sidran, in his response to the question "where can a homeless person sleep without breaking the law?" Given that Seattle's city parks are closed at night, that a well-enforced parks' exclusion law allows the police to ban homeless people from open spaces at all times for various misdemeanor violations, and that the city has destroyed most homeless encampments and forced the latest one into perpetual movement, the question, asked by a provider of services to the homeless, brought to light the essential ban that homeless people are subject to in Seattle. Sidran responded by saying, "I don't think there is an answer to your question."[63] Here the abandonment of the homeless by the law is made completely explicit: not only are the homeless subject to various prohibitions, but the frank admission that there is "no answer" performs, in one simple sentence, their abandonment by law.

It is this abandonment about which Hannah Arendt also writes, in the context of refugees: "Their plight is not that they are not equal before the law, but that no law exists for them." That political exclusion is a fundamental dynamic of injustice, not reducible to "economy" or "culture," is evident in the situation of refugees. As Arendt goes on to argue in *The Origins of Totalitarianism*, the deprivation of legal status underlies more particular deprivations. The stateless are deprived of legality as such. Such a condition of rightlessness is not the denial of specific rights (such as voting rights) or a particular cultural stigma but a fundamental exclusion from political community. Economic and cultural injustices, in such a stark situation, are consequences of that rightlessness. Deprived of legality, refugees are deprived "of a place in the world which makes opinions significant and actions effective."[64] Arendt's analysis points to the inadequacy of a framework that emphasizes economic and cultural injustice but makes the state—the political and legal institutions—subsidiary, reduced to playing a role in cultural injustice and economic injustice. In discussing Nazi persecution of the Jews, Arendt makes a claim about the temporal priority of political exclusion: disenfranchisement came first, before the deprivation of life. But there is also, I think, an ontological claim here—that the political domain is in some sense the ground of other domains and, at the very least, more than a handmaiden of economic and cultural processes. To be excluded from the political community—a civil death—is to be deprived of the right of action and of opinion. It is not easy for someone deprived of legality to challenge more particular deprivations, economic or cultural.

The homeless, subject to punitive policies and police confiscation of property, are not deprived of legality as such, not excluded from political community altogether, as are stateless persons such as refugees. My claim is that political exclusion is a dynamic of injustice and not an either/or condition. Anti-homeless laws do not convert the homeless into nonmembers of the political community; indeed, homeless persons retain voting rights in almost all states, including the right to register by listing a shelter or public space as residence.[65] The de facto criminalization of a person's existence, however, through public-sleeping bans and police sweeps of homeless encampments, turns the homeless into persons who are simultaneously community members and outlaws. In short, they have a legal status, but one that marks them as different from the unmarked norm of home-dwelling citizen. As Judith Failer argues, "Even though members who are accorded different civil rights and capacities . . . might still be full citizens in the sense of nationality . . . their different bundle of powers as citizens affects the way in which they stand before the other members of the polity."[66] It is this dynamic—that the homeless are citizens reduced to an outlaw status—which constitutes an injustice of political exclusion.

HOMELESS ENCAMPMENTS: MAKING SPACE FOR CITIZENSHIP

If public-sleeping bans are an injustice of political exclusion, a form of the sovereign ban on bare life, what, if anything, constitutes political *inclusion* for the homeless? Shelters, I have argued, are not promising in this regard; they persist in isolating and containing the homeless as bare life, to be kept alive, while stigmatizing them as helpless victims and damaged subjects. In response partly to state actions that turn the homeless into outlaws, however, homeless encampments have sometimes managed to politicize issues of housing and poverty, with resulting changes in the misrecognition effects of some shelter policies, and (albeit modest) improvements in the availability of needed resources. Scholarly research on homeless encampments points to their key role in resisting the recognition and redistribution injustices of homelessness. But more fundamentally, these encampments have enabled homeless persons to contest their outlaw status and to remake themselves as citizens. Only by contesting political exclusion—by establishing, as Arendt puts it, "a place in the world which makes . . . action effective"—can homeless persons challenge as citizens the injustices of maldistribution and misrecognition.

Encampments in places as far apart as Portland, Maine, and Portland, Oregon, have succeeded in asserting (temporary) control over a public space. Establishing a space relatively free of police harassment and nonstate violence, homeless persons resisted the political exclusion of the ban and engaged in "placemaking" that fostered nonstigmatized identities and paved the way for collective action. In other words, having established (precarious) control of physical spaces and resignified those spaces as dwelling spaces, they moved beyond the defense of the camp to make demands as citizens concerning the cultural and economic injustices of homelessness more broadly.

Such encampments have succeeded partially and temporarily in nourishing relations of reciprocity and solidarity among homeless persons and between the homeless and the housed in creating a sense of place and thereby helping to construct a nonstigmatized collective identity. They also provided the basis for collective action—including demands for housing and reform of shelter policies, the politicization of urban development policy, the occupation of abandoned buildings—and for forging links between homeless activists and church groups, students, and community organizers. For instance, homeless encampments such as those in San Jose studied by Talmadge Wright in *Out of Place* broke down the opposition between home-dwellers and the homeless, allowing them to forge alliances and journey into each other's worlds.

Working together, occupants of homeless encampments can protest the injustices of maldistribution and misrecognition experienced in emergency shelters. The anthropologist David Wagner reports that in 1987 a tent-city protest emerged in Portland, Maine (which he calls North City in the text), against "the lack of adequate shelter space and the humiliating, degrading conditions that were imposed on shelter users." The forms of cultural injustice under protest included a requirement that persons seeking shelter identify themselves as members of a particular shelter-eligible category, such as the mentally ill or substance abusers; the tent city effort succeeded in eliminating this method of bed distribution. Significant in this protest, Wagner says, was the dual nature of grievances oriented toward both the "paucity of services" and "the nature of the 'service.'"[67] In other words, the tent city was able to assert grievances concerning both the distribution of shelter and the recognition effects of the manner in which shelter was distributed.

Even persistent critics have been forced to concede some of the benefits of well-run, politically oriented encampments. For instance, an editorial in the *Oregonian* pointed to some of the benefits of a homeless encampment in Portland, Oregon, acknowledging the arguments in favor of the "Dignity Village" camp, especially compared with a demeaning and stigmatizing shelter system: "You can argue that Dignity has been an effective political statement. You can argue that it has educated us. Dignity Village has made the point that homeless people need more privacy than the shelter system affords, more ability to forge relationships, to stow possessions, and to keep pets. Dignity offers an intangible, autonomy, that some individuals prize more highly than any tangible comfort. That's important to know." Despite recognizing these benefits, the editorial nevertheless maintains that shelter services are preferable to the privacy, autonomy, and relationships fostered by homeless encampments, which it calls an ineffective policy in "helping move people up and out of homelessness."[68]

In Chicago the "Tranquility City" encampment, according to Wright, provided a safe haven for homeless persons and the basis for establishing relations of mutuality and trust. In contesting the proper purpose of public space and establishing a claim to public space, homeless residents engaged in resistant forms of placemaking and thereby developed new, nonstigmatized collective identities. Wright describes a pluralizing form of placemaking that succeeds in altering the significations of spaces, "replac[ing] authoritative meanings of social-physical space with their own meanings." And in the San Jose homeless encampment that developed in the early 1990s, camp dwellers "redefined their space not simply as 'an area under a bridge,' . . . but as a home . . . a 'collective' home with embedded meanings of family and community."[69]

Wright describes a process of placemaking that nurtures both homeless identities and collective action and that challenges misrecognition injustices in two ways. First, these encampments help foster relations of mutual recognition among their homeless occupants and overcome internalized stigmas. Wayne, a resident of Tranquility City, described to Wright the group meetings that fostered solidarity and personal confidence: "We had our little group sit downs. You know, nice day, get under the trees, sit down and discuss it. You know a lot of people would tell what happened to them. How they was doing, what they had, what they lost—and we even had some of the people crying while they was talking about it. And they would get up and want to go away, and we would tell them we support what you are doing. Man, you got friends here." Second, homeless encampments can alter the ways in which the housed public views the homeless, by providing greater visibility of homelessness and, more significantly, by forging links through affinity groups to non-homeless citizens. As an organized, self-managed collectivity, a homeless encampment may win positive recognition from other citizens. Wayne also described these positive relations of recognition: "We got respect from the Metra police, the city police. We got respect from the community business people. They helped us out. . . . When people seen the way we was keeping the whole area clean, I mean we didn't have to be out there on the railroad tracks chopping weeds down, they got people that do that, they get paid for that."[70] Wright's interviews reveal the role of homeless encampments in nurturing positive self-conceptions among their residents, relations of trust and solidarity within the camp, and widening relations of recognition between homeless and housed as camp-dwellers speak to church groups and student activists become involved in homeless advocacy.

Although Chicago confiscated the Tranquility City huts in 1992, the encampment and the resulting publicity helped to achieve some modest distributive change: after negotiations with the city, all the camp-dwellers received apartments in public housing projects. The San Jose encampment did not lead to such clear distributive changes, but did nurture forms of collective action that went beyond demanding recognition of the camp and self-defense against police sweeps: "SHA [Student Homeless Alliance] struggles ranged from defending homeless encampments from arbitrary police sweeps to challenging the very context of city redevelopment policies."[71] What Wright's study of homeless encampments reveals is that recognition and redistribution politics are often combined. One might argue that the redistribution/recognition framework is sufficient for comprehending the dynamics of homeless encampments. Although a potential conflict between recognition and redistribution was identified (as articulated by defenders of public-space restrictions: recognizing the homeless in encampments versus "getting them off the streets"), ethnographic research and analysis led to the conclusion that in this case redistribution and recognition need not conflict but tend to go together successfully. Homeless encampments turn out to be not a redistribution-impeding form of identity politics for its own sake but rather a form of transitional group solidarity that is necessary, in Fraser's words, "to get a politics of redistribution off the ground."

This analysis makes sense to me, but I would argue that these ethnographies of homeless encampments also point to a deeper political dynamic that precedes questions of distribution and recognition. Homeless activists contest their political exclusion, their reduction to the status of outlawed bare life, and in so doing remake themselves as *citizens*. In other words, the camps provide a base from which homeless persons may contest their political exclusion, asserting their right to dwell in a particular space and thereby challenging the logic of exclusion manifest in anti-homeless ordinances and routine police practices of harassment and property confiscation. By resisting the logic of placelessness and creating a space of dwelling, homeless persons in the encampments have challenged legal and political exclusion, establishing "a place in the world which makes opinions significant and actions effective." Only by contesting political exclusion have homeless citizens challenged particular injustices of misrecognition (by shelter agencies and housed publics) and maldistribution (of housing resources).

In making this claim about a fundamental political dynamic, I do not mean to suggest that struggles over distribution and recognition are not political. Rather, I am using the term "political" in several senses. First, the fundamental political injustice of exclusion links the political to the capacity of official state institutions and practices to draw boundaries of inclusion and exclusion. Public-sleeping bans, to the extent that they turn homeless persons into outlaws, are an example. A second and related sense of the political involves oppositional action in contesting these exclusions— one might call this a *fundamental* politicization, since what is being contested is the very boundary between citizen and noncitizen, between political actor and outlawed bare life. A third sense of the political could be called *secondary* politicization—contestation of economic and cultural norms and practices, naming these as injustices, and demanding redistribution and recognition.[72]

Of course, my defense of homeless encampments as a pluralizing force, challenging the political, economic, and cultural injustices of homelessness, is vulnerable to the charge of romanticism that I leveled at Thomas Dumm's embrace of the homeless as resisting the containment fields of modernity. Perhaps this account embraces the very same romanticized vision of the homeless as free and sacred outlaws of public space, a vision that I've argued is not a challenge to but rather a symptom of the ban on bare life. If what I have suggested about the structuring force of the sovereign ban on bare life is correct, it would be naive to suggest that my own analysis and the practices it embraces are somehow unmarked by that dynamic. Nevertheless, it is significant, I think, that politicized homeless encampments have the potential to contest the position of sacred outsiderhood by fostering links between homeless and housed, engaging in collective action, politicizing housing and shelter policy, and breaking down the strict separations between public and private that produce the bare-life predicament.

THE TRIVALENT APPROACH TO JUSTICE AND INJUSTICE: IMPLICATIONS FOR DEMOCRATIC THEORY

Consider the following two arguments concerning the relationship between justice (as redistribution and recognition) and democracy (as citizen participation in collective decision-making):

> I assume that to be a radical democrat today is to appreciate—and to seek to eliminate—two different kinds of impediments to democratic participation. One such impediment is social inequality; the other is the misrecognition of difference. Radical democracy, on this interpretation, is the view that democracy today requires both economic redistribution and multicultural recognition.[73]

> Rather than concentrating primarily on the goals of these struggles (specific forms of distribution or recognition) and the theories of justice which could adjudicate their claims fairly, as has been the dominant orientation

among political theorists, one should look on the struggles themselves as
the primary thing. . . . The aim of such an aspectival political philosophy
and corresponding political practice would not be to discover and consti-
tutionalize the just and definitive form of recognition and distribution, but
to ensure that ineliminable, agonic democratic games over recognition and
distribution, with their rival theories of distribution and recognition, can
be played freely.[74]

The first claim, made by Nancy Fraser, privileges the substantive goals
of redistribution and recognition as preconditions of democratic participation (Fraser also calls these "conditions for participatory parity"). The
second claim, made by James Tully, privileges democratic political practice as the open field in which rival justice claims are put forth. Read
together, I think they illustrate the difficulty in bringing together claims
about the cultural and economic goals of justice, on the one hand, and
dynamics of political inclusion and exclusion, on the other hand. Either
substantive goals of justice are posited as preconditions of political inclusion and participation, with the emphasis on achieving those preconditions, or an open political process is posited as the necessary precondition
for the articulation of justice claims, with the emphasis on maintaining the
openness and inclusiveness of that process. The first move has two problematic tendencies: making an end run around democratic politics and
contestation by turning debatable principles of substantive justice into
"preconditions" rather than outcomes of democratic politics; and envisioning the state as the neutral medium through which these preconditions are realized. The second move has the tendency of abdicating critical scrutiny of the substantive aims of movements for redistribution and
recognition in favor of "the struggles themselves." [75]

To be sure, concerns about the theorist's role in articulating the substantive goals of movements for justice invoke the traditional tension between
philosophy and (democratic) politics. But on the perspective he advances.
Tully is overdrawing the tension between a political philosophy oriented
toward an examination of the goals of justice struggles and a political philosophy oriented toward preserving the openness of the democratic contest. Within the trivalent approach to justice sketched out above, the question of political inclusion and exclusion is explicitly thematized as itself a
key dimension of justice struggles, irreducible to "culture" or "economy."
The openness of the democratic contest is itself frequently one of the goals
of the political struggles under examination, and in a trivalent approach
(economic, cultural and political) to justice and injustice, the question of
the inclusiveness of the political process is fundamental.

This chapter has explored the dynamic of political inclusion and exclusion in the context of policy responses to homelessness. When policies are analyzed with respect to specifically political forms of injustice, the new compassionate conservative defense of homeless criminalization begins to seem less compelling. Furthermore, when policies are analyzed with respect to specifically political forms of injustice, the supposed tension between redistribution and recognition begins to look like a false antithesis. What had seemed like a counterproductive struggle for "cultural" recognition might actually be a pluralizing movement, an attempt to shift the issue of homelessness from its place caught in the sovereign ban on bare life to the register of citizenship, justice/injustice, and democratic politics. Homeless encampments may sometimes work to assist the homeless in crossing that "critical threshold,"[76] to establish themselves as citizens with "the right to have rights," entitled to justice in the first place.

In looking at dynamics of political inclusion and exclusion, this chapter has also pointed a skeptical eye toward homeless shelters that both isolate people and deny them privacy, reinforce cultural stigmas, and enforce petty humiliations. The next chapter continues an examination of the shelter as an institution by placing its current ubiquity in the historical and ideological context of alternatives that have been squeezed out. The story of their disappearance is in part a story of political theory.

CHAPTER 4

Housing Diversity and Democratic Pluralism

At 3:00 A.M. on August 4, 1977, 330 police officers descended upon the International Hotel in San Francisco, a single-room-occupancy residential hotel, to evict the forty remaining residents, mostly poor, elderly Filipinos. The police move on the residential hotel was the culmination of eight and one-half years of a political struggle involving residents, developers, city officials, and activists from a range of organizations (including the International Hotel Tenants Association) and various left-wing groups. The evictions, defended by the original property owner as "slum clearance," were claimed by protesters to represent the "Manhattanization" of San Francisco: an imperialistic destruction of a struggling ethnic minority community, and the continued elimination of low-cost housing for the elderly. As protesters looked on, the evictions took place with the sheriff in charge even using a sledgehammer to break down some of the doors. Immediately after, the building that housed the hotel and a basement nightclub was torn down by the Hong Kong–based Four Seas Corporation, the new owners of the property. Although various rumors circulated as to what would be built in its place—perhaps an office tower that would extend the reach of the financial district, or a "flashy" Chinese shopping center that would extend the reach of Chinatown—nothing in fact was built in its place, and the site remained vacant. Well, not completely vacant: observers noted as late as 1992 that the abandoned walls and archways of the basement portion were being used by homeless people seeking refuge from the wind and cold.[1]

Many stories could be told around this example, about redevelopment, transnational capital, and the restructuring of American cities; about
the possibilities and limitations of social movements and protests defending the rights of the poor; about the ways in which protest movements seize
upon an event as a symbol of larger processes and thereby forget the people they were originally trying to help; about how discourses of the
nation and the foreign play out in struggles over particular spaces (in this
case, the discourse of "foreign capital" invading "our city" combined in
complex ways with a discourse of protecting an embattled "Third World
community" from imperialistic capitalist development).

For my purposes, the story is a vivid example of, and metaphor for, not
only the loss of affordable housing in American cities but also the reduction of housing options in urban settings. For those without the money,
know-how, or social connections to secure an apartment or to double up
with friends or relatives, this reduction of options is severe; street and shelter become the alternatives. And those alternatives have had real consequences for the ways in which people imagine the homeless, and homelessness policy gets constructed. As the emergency shelter has become a
central institution for dealing with street homelessness, appeals to "do
more" for the homeless have often essentially come down to the call to
build more shelters or to make more beds available in armories, ware-
houses, and interstitial spaces such as the hallways and foyers of government buildings. Implicit in the demand for more shelters is the assumption of what is being sheltered: in Agamben's words, bare life.[2] In other
words, coeval with the emergence of the shelter is the constitution of
the sheltered subject as bare, needy life, stripped of all privacy, kept warm
by some blankets and a sleeping mat. A reduction in housing options,
including the loss of single-room-occupancy (SRO) hotels, has reduced
the ability of some in society to establish the necessary conditions for privacy, autonomy, and civic involvement. Only recently have homeless encampments and tent cities (see chapter 3) emerged in many cities to protest the
inadequacies and injustices of shelter programs.

The existence of housing options, particularly options *between* the degrading conditions of warehouse-like shelters and the normatively established
private houses and apartments of mainstream middle-class life, is crucial for
the promotion of democratic citizenship. Yet, as several commentators have
noted, there has been a steady loss of such options.[3] Whereas there once
was a complex array of housing forms, institutions, and practices—boardinghouses, rooming houses, guest lodgings, flophouses, residential hotels—
housing practices and policies since the Progressive Era have tended to

consolidate around a monolithic home ideal: the fully detached, single-family home in a low-density, single-function residential neighborhood.[4]

The ideal of homeownership is hegemonic and closely connected to our deepest and often unarticulated understandings of what it means to be a successful, normal person and an upstanding citizen. As Samira Kawash argues, "In what can only be called a contemporary mythology, home-ownership is held up as the supreme achievement of American adulthood. This mythology is underpinned by an array of subsidies, preferences, and prejudices that are granted additional force by the intense cultural identi-fication of happiness, normalcy, and success with the detached single fam-ily house." Homeownership, as Nancy Rosenblum documents, has become prized above health and rewarding work. April Veness says that in the 1960s, "so certain were Americans of the basic values embedded in the home ideal and the possibilities of its universality that alternative, less home-like, accommodations were gradually eliminated. Boarding and rooming houses were closed, state hospitals were emptied, and residential hotels and inner-city apartments were demolished for urban renewal." And in the 1980s, when homelessness as a phenomenon was "rediscovered," "undesirable and illegal accommodation alternatives were reduced [and] people fell further and further from the home ideal."[5] The loss of residen-tial or SRO hotels is especially significant, considering their prominence historically, the anxieties and criticisms they aroused in Progressive Era reformers, and the production of homelessness that is partly a result of their destruction and conversion.

The history of housing in the United States is in part a history of the antipathy of certain well-intentioned reformers to alternative forms of dwelling that did not conform to conventional notions of privacy, normalcy and family. Frequently, such well-intentioned reformers described the peo-ple living in nonconventional dwellings as homeless because, after all, *how could anyone really live like that?* But calling occupants of residential hotels homeless is perhaps one of the more perverse forms of the performative speech act: it was in part by misrecognizing the viability of alternative habits of dwelling, by misrecognizing the residents as homeless, and thus by aiding in the destruction of what they confidently termed "substandard housing" that reformers helped to create more homelessness.

My goal here, both critical and constructive, is to survey a discursive landscape of home. It includes a particular set of values connected with home, such as privacy, individualism, and community; a particular articu-lation of the linkages and separations between the home space and other social spaces; and a stigmatizing vocabulary directed at forms of dwelling that fail to conform to the home ideal. Certain normative idealizations of home undercut housing reformers' capacities to imagine viable alternatives to the single-family homeownership ideal, and these normative idealizations were implicated in the reduction of housing options in U.S. cities, encouraging the polarization of society into home-dwelling citizens, on the one hand, and the displaced poor, on the other.

My constructive alternative emerges from this critique, starting with the suggestion that the promotion of housing options and, by extension, the pluralization of our cultural ideal of "home" are crucial in opening up new possibilities, not just to ameliorate the condition of homelessness but further, to promote a more robust form of democratic pluralism generally. Given the multiple and sometimes crosscutting values embodied in home, and given the multiple ways people have of interpreting, prioritizing, and acting upon those values, housing pluralism is essential for democratic pluralism.

My argument connects me to two literatures in contemporary political theory. First, in privileging a conception of democratic pluralization in my analysis of housing options and idealizations of home, I draw on the work of contemporary "agonistic democrats" such as Bonnie Honig, Chantal Mouffe, William Connolly, and others who see human plurality, value plurality and political conflict as inescapable (and perhaps desirable) features of the contemporary world. Bonnie Honig explicitly links agonistic democracy to the problematization of the home ideal: "To take difference—and not just identity—seriously in democratic theory is to affirm the inescapability of conflict and the ineradicability of resistance to the political and moral projects of ordering subjects, institutions, and values. . . . It is to give up on the dream of a place called home, a place free of power, conflict, and struggle."[6] The literature in democratic pluralization also draws attention to the various depoliticizing moves in both theory and practice that attempt to obscure value conflicts, competing interpretations, and contestations of social norms through rhetorics of normalcy, rational consensus, and objective standards. My effort to critique certain normative idealizations of home and certain confident invocations of such categories as "substandard housing" draws upon these insights.

Second, my application of pluralization to the household realm draws inspiration from feminist investigations that have critiqued traditional idealizations of family life and explored the politics of the domestic sphere.[7] Feminist theorists argue that normative idealizations of the family as a sphere of affective unity have masked and legitimated domestic inequalities in power, forms of violence, and injustice; I argue that normative idealizations of the domestic sphere have worked also to produce homelessness and undermine the variety of dwelling options necessary for a robust democratic pluralism. Furthermore, feminist theorists argue that the assumption of a unity of interests obscures the plurality of perspectives and interests within the family unit; I argue that the assumption of a single value manifest in the household form obscures the value of pluralism connected to housing, and the essentially contested nature of the home ideal itself.

THE RISE AND FALL AND RISE AGAIN OF RESIDENTIAL HOTELS IN THE UNITED STATES

Residential or SRO hotels have been criticized for almost as long as they have been around, and often for good reason. Reformers and journalists at the turn of the century documented slumlike conditions, overcrowding, poor ventilation, and poor sanitation, and such criticisms continue to be voiced today. But recent historical revisionists have begun to question the wholesale dismissal of residential hotels. While acknowledging that many of these problems did exist, housing and homelessness scholars are pointing to the positive values that were supported by this dwelling form, such as individualism, autonomy, and community.

At the turn of the century, residential hotels helped constitute a thriving subculture in cities across the United States. While often providing little more than a bedroom and access to shared bathing facilities, they offered cheap housing to middle-class single migrants to urban centers and poorer working-class urban residents. Residential hotels—which gradually came to replace boardinghouses and the common practice of guest lodging in private homes—were a housing form geared predominantly to single people, not families. As Groth in *Living Downtown* and Hoch and Slayton in *New Homeless and Old* demonstrate, however, residential hotels spanned the class spectrum, from luxury accommodations for wealthy individuals and families to basic single rooms for poor workingmen; from simple but well-maintained lodging for middle-class single office and retail workers to poorly managed, poorly ventilated, and unclean flophouses and "cage hotels."

Residential hotels catering to middle-class and working-class singles offered the possibility of individual autonomy and community that may have been unavailable in other housing situations. Unlike the older boardinghouses, the hotels had a general absence of social control mechanisms. Front desk clerks and managers did not monitor the comings and goings of residents and guests, on the whole, and the generally market-based transactions enabled single men and women to explore urban life without the moral constraints of family and traditional household. As Paul Groth puts it, "Hotel life can be virtually untouched by the social contracts and tacit supervision of life found in a family house or apartment unit shared with a group."[8] Another difference between residential hotels and older boardinghouses was the absence of common meals: Usually lacking kitchens (although some had community cooking facilities), hotel residents ate at inexpensive local restaurants, and districts with residential hotels also offered plentiful services, entertainments, and shopping. For instance, in turn-of-the-century Boston, the main residential hotel district contained "87 cafes, 65 basement dining rooms, 41 saloons, 24 liquor stores, 27 drug stores, 112 pool rooms, 78 laundries, and 70 tailor shops."[9]

Pete Yamamoto, an occupant of the International Hotel in San Francisco before its destruction in 1977, described the values of individualism and community that persisted in hotel life through the 1970s:

> All these single men who had immigrated here lived there. They had lonely, solitary lives. They had themselves as their families. . . . There was a beauty to living there. There were all these eating places, the barbershops, the pool hall. There were so many good things there, like Kearny Street Workshop, which provided a place for Asian-American artists to participate, and Everybody's Bookstore downstairs. There was a smell, an ambience, a humidity level of the I Hotel. You could cut the air like a knife. . . . The [tenants] formed a community amongst themselves. There was a lot of kidding and joking in the hallways and in the community kitchen. Someone would have a pot of rice cooking on one, another guy would have a stir-fry going, and they were all sitting around, smoking their pipes, in their slippers. I can't emphasize enough the feeling of extended family there.[10]

Yamamoto's testimony demonstrates the complexity of hotel living: on the one hand, single men lived "solitary lives," having only themselves as family; on the other hand, the communal spaces of the hotel and the dense texture of the urban public sphere nurtured a "feeling of extended family."

If the new interpretations of residential hotel life point to the positive values supported by this dwelling form, one must also be clear that the individual autonomy and community enabled by SRO districts did not fit the type of individualism and community that became articulated through the modern home ideal, which, as Veness argues, crystallized during the same time that residential hotels were flourishing. The individualism encouraged by residential hotels was not linked to "the anchor of private property," and the community created was not connected to the sanctified sphere of the family. Rather, SRO hotels encouraged what might be called a nonpossessive form of individualism and a community created in the commodified spaces of urban cafes, bars, pool halls, and restaurants and in the spaces of communal hallways and kitchens of the hotels themselves.

Reformers justified their campaigns against residential hotels, guest lodgers in homes, and tenement overcrowding, both in the Progressive Era and later, principally as the removal of substandard housing.[11] Progressives decried what they saw as the personal immorality of hotel life and its threat to the proper institution of the household—the nuclear family. Stereotypes of skid row "derelicts," visions of gender-norm-defying young women gaining independence in the city, and images of an urban jungle of pleasures and bodies intermingling in unhealthy ways formed the basic stock of reform discourse. Although at first, according to Groth, the housing reformers accomplished little more than a shift in rhetoric, by the 1920s this rhetoric had worked its way into housing codes and zoning laws. Progressives, though resisting the importation of a European model of state-funded and built housing for the working class, did win important battles for restrictive legislation, housing codes, and slum clearance.

Much of their work ought, I think, to be viewed as a much needed push for some state regulation of speculative housing builders who were constructing unsafe, unhealthy tenements and hotels and as an attempt to do something about severe overcrowding. An 1894 New York City Tenement House Committee headed by Lawrence Veiller heard testimony about a three-room apartment housing fourteen people, including two separate families and four male lodgers. But two points are worth making here. First, Progressives tended to view minimum housing standards in moral terms—not a "right" so much as a key to social control of the immigrant underclass and the elimination of various vices such as drunkenness, idleness, and prostitution. Second, in urging legislation to battle overcrowding, housing reformers were inspired more by visions of slum clearance and notions of proper family privacy than by a nuanced and textured understanding of the effect of reforms on people's lives. The 1894 committee, for instance, was more concerned to pass legislation limiting overcrowding than it was to consider the consequences to struggling immigrant families who had taken on guest lodgers in order to be able to afford the rent. As Roy Lubove writes, "Such institutions as the boarder . . . had become integral features of the social and economic structure of the immigrant community," but the tenement committee condemned "the boarder's intrusion upon familial privacy."[12]

Residential hotels came under sustained attack in the 1920s and continued to be slated for demolition under various redevelopment and urban renewal programs throughout the 1960s and 1970s. In the main skid row neighborhood of Chicago, estimates are that 80 percent of the SRO units were lost between 1960 and 1980, and in New York City, 87 percent of the stock of cheap residential hotel rooms were lost between 1970 and 1982.[13] These losses were, according to Groth, not simply the result of unplanned processes of market-sorting and profit-seeking; rather, they resulted in part from zoning regulations, policy decisions, and government subsidies provided to particular forms of redevelopment: "Housing officials began a one hundred year campaign to write hotels out of public policy because hotel life undermined middle and upper class cultural ideals and hotel land-use mixtures threatened professional hopes for a new, specialized city." Hoch and Slayton agree, arguing that "SRO hotels are being lost in Chicago, and in other cities, not because they are bad investments . . . but because of public policy."[14]

Underlying this policy shift was a new vision of the rationalized city, where functions and uses would be carefully zoned apart, and where the new vision of the home sphere was a dwelling that could provide space for family community and guarantee sufficient privacy for each of the family members. The home ideal constituted one element in a set of sensibilities and values orienting the zoning laws, public subsidies, and urban renewal programs that targeted residential hotels and the complex urban ecology in which they were embedded. (I have more to say about the housing reformers' critiques below).

The resulting loss of residential hotel units constituted both a reduction in the array of housing options for the poor and the necessary condition for what might be termed the street-and-shelter homelessness that emerged in the 1980s. As Hoch and Slayton argue, "Poverty is a necessary but not sufficient condition to account for homelessness. It is the lack of cheap SRO-type housing that turns urban poverty into homelessness." Thus, revisionist scholars of residential or SRO hotels want to resist attempts to imagine the "new homeless" as a distinct social type—either a new sort of victim or a new sort of pathological character. "The unexpected rise in the number of homeless people and their persistent dependence," Hoch and Slayton assert, "has more to do with the nearly wholesale destruction of the SRO hotels . . . than either the changing social composition or personal vulnerabilities of the urban poor." Indeed, demographic studies indicate that the street homeless and shelter clients of the 1980s and 1990s have social characteristics closely matching the residents of SRO hotels in earlier periods.[15]

With the elimination of residential hotels, an institution that had provided limited privacy, freedom from social control, and the possibility of constituting individual identity and relations of urban sociability was replaced by public spaces, homeless shelters, and a network of social services, counselors, and police officers. Where there had existed a market-based institution for providing limited autonomy and community to the very poor and the precariously housed, the new institutions trapped the precariously housed and the homeless in an expanded web of both punitive and protective social-control mechanisms: "Shelterization offers a poor substitute for the low rent SRO-type housing."[16] Both emergency shelters and specialized designer shelters organized around particular (professionally identified) client pathologies and vulnerabilities according to many observers, actually foster the forms of dependency they are designed to overcome. These dependency-producing effects should give pause to liberals and conservatives alike before they accept shelterization as the key to ameliorating the condition of homelessness.

None of this is to say that residential hotels were a space of simple happiness, or that opposition to such hotels was motivated only by biased middle-class norms of propriety. There *were* a lot of slums and horrible conditions. But the Progressive vision of home and city prevented appreciation of even the potential virtues of alternative forms of dwelling that did not conform to the single-family, homeownership ideal. The renewed appreciation of residential hotels is not limited to historians and sociologists. In cities such as New York, Portland, and San Diego, public/private partnerships and nonprofit organizations have worked to preserve residential hotels, build new ones, and revamp old tourist hotels. But these precarious achievements are always under pressure from other redevelopment interests, zoning laws, and the continued stigmatization of residential hotels that is due to their simultaneous distance from the modern home ideal and from the social control of the shelter as a disciplinary institution. Thus, it is worthwhile to explore the discursive landscape of home that surrounds opposition to residential hotels and to consider an alternative vision that might provide a more solid justification for housing pluralism.

HOME, DEMOCRACY, AND PLURALISM

I turn to political theory discussions of home for two reasons. First, theoretical articulations of the relationship between household and public sphere may help to illuminate some of the underarticulated concepts and values that inflect housing reformers' discourse and contemporary thought and action concerning housing and homelessness. Second, bringing political theory models into a kind of dialogue with contemporary housing issues can point beyond certain impasses in the theories themselves and aid in developing a more pluralistic understanding of the relationship between household and public sphere. Political-theoretical reflection, then, may illuminate the problem and point toward some solutions.

Two conceptual maps—a *classical republican* model of the relationship between household and polis and a *modern pluralist* model of the separate spheres of home, market, and politics—both promise a commitment to pluralism, yet both reinforce a nonpluralistic conception of home. Indeed, variants of both models were voiced in Progressive Era critiques of residential hotel life, forming the basis of arguments for zoning exclusions, building codes, and government policies that undermined the array of housing options in twentieth-century U.S. cities.[17]

The classical republican model, as developed by Hannah Arendt in her "recovery" of the ancient political experience, posits the household as the realm of necessity and unfreedom, a foundation of and precondition for the plurality of speaking and acting selves in the public sphere. Pluralism does not extend in the Arendtian model to household forms themselves, or to the relation between private and public; pluralism is a feature of the public sphere itself, not a feature of the relationship between private and public.[18] Furthermore, in the context of an administrative state performing precisely the sort of "housekeeping functions" of which Arendt is so critical, the household-polis relationship becomes one of integration, not participation.[19]

The modern pluralist model, as developed by Michael Walzer, sees the home as one sphere with its own distributive logic and social goods, and pluralism is maintained when the "walls" between spheres are preserved. This model too tends to slide into a more integrationist vision when the underlying assumptions about the shared understandings of the political community and the comforts of home are revealed as anchors of a very domesticated form of pluralism. Twentieth-century urban planning drew upon a spatialized version of the "separate-spheres" argument in rationalizing "disorderly" cities and eliminating substandard housing.

In *The Human Condition*, Hannah Arendt turns to ancient Greece to retrieve a vision of political experience that has been lost in modernity. Human plurality is a central concern for Arendt, who sees the modern bureaucratic state, the rise of what she calls the social, and uprootedness as leading to a condition of worldlessness—a loss of a sense of reality which, she argues in *The Origins of Totalitarianism*, makes individuals vulnerable to totalitarian propaganda with its reassuring explanations and its fantasy of nationalist unity. What preserves a sense of the world is, on the other hand, the existence of a public sphere, where human beings with their diverse perspectives, coming from diverse standpoints, are brought together but at the same time distinguished from one another. The public realm is the site of plurality, whereas the household is marked by the singularity of our animality: the biological processes of bare life. Even the elements of the domestic, household sphere that are not reducible to biological necessities are, nevertheless, marked by a singularity that stands in stark contrast to the plurality of acting and spectating citizens in the public sphere: "Being seen and being heard by others derive their significance from the fact that everybody sees and hears from a different position. This is the meaning of public life, compared to which even the richest and most satisfying family life can offer only the prolongation or multiplication of one's own position." A life spent exclusively in the household is deprived.[20]

Although Arendt's contrasts between public and private indicate a certain disparagement of the household sphere, she also argues that the household is a necessary foundation for the political activities of the public realm. Arendt makes three interrelated points here. First, the household is the arena in which the necessities of life are mastered—it houses bare life. Before exercising our higher capacities as citizens, we must attend to the life-sustaining activities that define our animality: "The mastering of the necessities of life in the household was the condition for freedom of the *polis.*" Arendt's argument, then, is precisely the reverse of Thomas Hobbes's: the purpose of politics is not to enable life to be sustained; rather, the purpose of life-sustaining activities is to enable politics. "Without mastering the necessities of life in the household," she writes, "neither life nor the 'good life' is possible, but politics is never for the sake of life. . . . [H]ousehold life exists for the sake of the 'good life' in the *polis.*" Second, the household provides a necessary shelter from the glare of the public realm; it is a shadowy place to which we may withdraw. A life lived fully in public, Arendt says at one point, would be shallow; in fact, "to have no private place of one's own . . . meant to be no longer human." Third, the household provides the head of household with a political and spatial location and orients him as a citizen in the public sphere: "Without owning a house a man could not participate in the affairs of the world because he had no location in it which was properly his own."[21]

It is precisely the absence of a location in the world which Arendt points to as the fundamental feature of the plight of refugees, whose loss of a home has destroyed their "right to action": "The first loss which the rightless suffered was the loss of their homes, and this meant the loss of the entire social texture into which they were born and in which they established for themselves a distinct place in the world." Arendt considers this placelessness to be a "fundamental deprivation" which prevents not freedom of thought but the ability to act in the world. Without a location in the world from which to develop one's standpoint, the refugee, rightless and displaced, falls beneath the protection even of those "human rights" which are supposedly guaranteed to all.[22]

Arendt's project of retrieval serves the critical function of illuminating dimensions of political experience that have been lost in modernity with the rise of "the social." The modern bureaucratic welfare state has taken on "housekeeping functions," while the public sphere of the polis and the private sphere of the household have been supplanted by the modern categories of the social and the intimate.

Nevertheless, Arendt's description of the public and private spheres in ancient Greece does not appear completely alien to us moderns, and a certain form of the distinction between them remains in what Arendt would consider a highly debased form. In other words, the discourse of public and private, of the household and its relationship to citizenship, has remained, but it has been transformed in and by the context of modern bureaucratic governance and by the investment of meaning and intimacy in a private sphere of "home." The idea of a household and homeownership, as the necessary foundation for the practices of citizenship, remains; indeed, this argument is the basis for much of U.S. federal policy encouraging homeownership, and a version of the argument formed the basis of Progressive Era campaigns against substandard housing such as rooming houses and residential hotels. For instance, Senator Charles Percy of Illinois, in pushing for government subsidies to extend homeownership to the poor, argued in 1966 that "a man who owns his own home acquires with it a new dignity. . . . He becomes more self-confident and self-reliant. . . . It gives him roots, a sense of belonging, a true stake in his community and its well-being."[23]

This integrationist version of the classical republican model has been articulated most fully by Progressive Era housing reformer and hotel critic Lawrence Veiller. Concerned with the physical, moral, and spiritual effects of overcrowding in urban America, and particularly concerned with these effects in relation to immigrant populations, Veiller stressed the benefits of homeownership. Writing in the *Annals of the Academy of Social and Political Science,* he invoked the then familiar metaphor of the body to describe the city. Veiller saw clogged streets, overcrowded tenements, and residential hotels as the equivalent of blocked arteries and gangrenous extremities: the growth of what he termed "a vile slum" required "the offending portions . . . to be cut out with the surgeon's knife." Such non-ideal forms of dwelling contributed to moral degeneration: "In place of the home and the church, are the street, the dance hall, and the saloon."[24]

Veiller joined his reformist vision of more sanitary housing, with better lighting and less crowding, to an argument for the conservative benefits of extending homeownership to the poor, the dispossessed, the urban immigrants, on the grounds that homeownership could turn the rootless into stakeholders in society: "When a man has a home and owns it, he has an incentive to work industriously, to be economical and thrifty, to take an interest in public affairs; every tendency makes him conservative. But where a man's home is three or four rooms in some huge building in which dwell from twenty to thirty other families and this home is only month to month, what incentive is there to economy? What is there to develop a sense of civic responsibility or patriotism?" He went on to claim that the citizenship-undermining effects of dwellings that do not conform to the homeownership ideal were exacerbated in the context of European immigrants accustomed to rural, peasant life. But he did not confine his criticisms to the dwelling practices of the immigrant poor; native-born and wealthy occupants of fancy residential hotels also made for poor citizens: "The bad effect upon community of a congregate form of dwelling is by no means limited to the poorer people. Waldorf-Astorias at one end of the town and 'Big Flats' at the other end are equally bad in their destruction of civic spirit and the responsibilities of citizenship."[25]

Although his linking of homeownership to citizenship resonates with Arendt's discussion, Veiller's argument differs in the way it figures the citizenship enabled by homeownership. Homeowners do not transcend the realm of necessity to participate in the sphere of freedom, equality, and plurality; it is not the way homeownership enables entry into a public sphere of deliberation and action that he stresses. Rather, homeowners become integrated into a social order as stakeholders through contact with precisely the sort of "housekeeping" state that Arendt criticizes. Homeownership is valued because it puts the individual into direct contact with a bureaucratic state. Apartment renters and residential hotel dwellers, in stark contrast, are alienated from government, their political relations with state agencies replaced by market relations with a landlord. A renter or hotel resident, "no longer being a householder, no longer comes into contact with the different branches of the municipal government and no longer has the same interest in the affairs of the community. . . . [H]e no longer has to deal with the city's water department; . . . [or] with its department of street cleaning."[26] In other words, not only does the household form the foundation of citizenship, but also the *concerns* of the household (concerns that were prepolitical for Arendt) form the substance of one's exercise of citizenship. Homeownership not only enables citizenship but integrates the head of household into a social order and its housekeeping state. Heads of household do not transcend the realm of the private to enter a sphere of freedom; rather, they bring the household into the public.

Veiller's defense of homeownership, stressing the integration of the citizen-stakeholder into the political community, updates the classical civic tradition by reinterpreting the household/polis model as one of social integration into a housekeeping state. Veiller's vision is not the only modern defense of home, however. As modernization processes separated work from home and as people navigated a multiplicity of functionally separated spaces in daily life, home came to be understood as a space of intimacy, withdrawal, and meaning-making. Arendt, and scholars such as Richard Sennett, working in a similar vein, *criticize* the rise of modern intimacy (along with the rise of the "social" state) for its dangerously antipolitical character. Whereas the household, according to Arendt, shielded bare biological life and enabled a public sphere of acting citizens, modern intimacy has a tendency to overwhelm other areas of life, creating fantasies of national unity that destroy the distinctions between persons.[27] But modern (private sphere) intimacy can also be understood as something worth *defending*, particularly if it is kept in its proper place.

The modern private sphere as a space of intimacy and affection forms one of the many spheres of life that make for a complex existence, according to the political theorist Michael Walzer. His liberal pluralism complicates the simpler liberal model of public and private (discussed in chapter 2) in which the state is contrasted to the nonstate. Walzer affirms modern social complexity: the fact that we play multiple roles in different institutional settings such as families, factories, universities, churches, civil society, and so forth, is not just a sociologically interesting phenomenon, but also the foundation of a political theory of justice. Walzer develops an interpretation of our cultural understandings—the sort of understandings that guide our behavior in these roles and institutions and make it obvious that, for instance, as a family member I do not sell my love and nurturance to whichever sibling bids the highest, but as a businessperson I *do* sell my services to the highest bidder.

As family members we "distribute" love and affection; as market actors we exchange commodities. Walzer, in *Spheres of Justice,* discovers a plurality of social goods, each with its own set of shared meanings attached, and each operating according to a particular distributive principle. Justice demands that the boundaries around each sphere remain intact, the autonomy of the sphere be respected, and the convertibility of one social good into another be prevented. For instance, prohibitions against political bribery reflect the plurality of distributive spheres in modern society: the sphere of commodities is separated from the sphere of political power and influence, and the autonomy of each sphere is thereby protected. (Indeed, as Walzer points out, the very *notion* of bribery contains within it the sense of a taboo or "blocked" exchange of money for political influence.)[28] For Walzer, the sphere of "kinship and love," roughly corresponding to the domestic sphere, constitutes one such protected realm. What is crucial for him is not maintaining the *connections* between spheres but rather preserving the *boundaries* between them. This, he says, is the best way to prevent "domination," which occurs when a social group, after legitimately gaining privilege in one sphere (economic wealth, for instance), tries to convert that good illegitimately into another (such as political power, love, or religious salvation). In other words, a just society might very well contain significant inequalities in wealth, but such a society would also build walls around economic wealth to prevent its conversion into other social goods.

In "Liberalism and the Art of Separation," Walzer says, "Society enjoys both freedom and equality when success in one institutional setting isn't convertible into success into another, that is, when the separations hold." He also develops a more concrete spatial metaphor to describe this process of boundary-making. Liberalism, he argues, "is a world of walls." Against the premodern "undifferentiated land mass," the spatial mapping that produced an "organic and integrated" society, liberal pluralists practice "an art of separation," drawing boundaries around social goods such as kinship and love, commodities, and education, and their corresponding institutional settings—the family, the market, and the university. Legal walls around our social institutions create liberties—such as freedom of conscience—and "complex" equality: "Though there will be many small inequalities, inequality will not be multiplied through the conversion process."[29]

In *Spheres of Justice,* Walzer talks about the realm of "kinship and love" as an autonomous sphere. He points out that in ancient Greece (source of the Arendtian model) the household was the fundamental "economic unit," and the fundamental distinction was between the household and the political community of which it was a part. Modern sphere differentiation, however, has produced a tripartite distinction: home, market, and politics. Thus "the opposition of kinship and politics is very old," whereas the distinction between the economy and the household is more recent. But once this distinction developed, it had significant consequences for the way we understand the good of "home": "Whenever the economy takes on an independent character and makes for the company not of relatives but of strangers, whenever the market replaces the self-subsistent household, our understanding of kinship sets limits on the reach of exchange, establishing a space within which market norms don't apply."[30] If this home space is walled off from the market as Walzer suggests, how is the economy of the home organized?

Anthropological analyses of the meaning of home help fill out Walzer's argument. For instance, Mary Douglas makes clear this separation of home from market principles of distribution and exchange, and she articulates the contrast with reference to the distinction between a home and a hotel: both "plan for the future, but the planning of the hotel follows criteria of cost efficiency. The reason why the home cannot use market reasoning is . . . that it is a virtual community." A household *could* be structured on a logic of strangers who bargain and exchange as rationally calculating individuals; the experience of group houses where rent is shared among relative strangers fits such a model. But a home constitutes a different structure of exchange: "Not a money economy, the home is the typical gift economy described by Marcel Mauss." Home is not a space where precise accounts are kept of who owes what to whom; it involves a complex set of exchanges, debts and transfers, but "the transactions never look like exchanges because the gesture of reciprocity is delayed and disguised." Homes are "often cruel," "absurd," and controlling (even when they operate successfully), and the complex rules of exchange are sometimes subverted by "free-riders." Still, Douglas sees home as a community, a form of solidarity, deeply structured by a set of unarticulated rules and principles governing time and space. Her contrast between a home and a hotel is designed to crystallize the non-market structure of the exchanges that go on inside the home, and the more complex constructions of privacy that homes provide: "The idea of the hotel is a perfect opposite of the home, not only because it uses market principles for its transactions, but because it allows its clients to buy privacy as a right of exclusion. This offends doubly the principle of the home whose rules and separations provide some limited privacy for each member." The contrast between home and hotel is, fundamentally, the contrast between "a virtual community and a virtual market."[31]

In Walzer's theory, the sphere of home, family, and kinship is one among many; justice is the practice of maintaining this multiplicity of social spheres against the ambitions of those who are successful in a single sphere. Therefore, Walzer contends his theory is pluralistic: "The principles of justice are themselves pluralistic in form. . . . Different social goods ought to be distributed for different reasons, in accordance with different procedures, by different agents; and . . . all these differences derive from different understandings of the social goods themselves."[32] The repetition of difference in this passage suggests a multiplicity of differences to be endorsed and protected.

Yet these rhetorics of pluralism and difference are marked by a fundamental ambivalence: who or what is the site of plurality and difference? "Differing understandings of the social goods" would seem to point to differences between social actors: the conflicting interpretations of individuals, groups, and collectivities. However, the referents of "differing understandings" are in fact the different goods themselves. For instance, "bribery" is not one among many competing social actors' interpretations of the meaning of exchanging money for political influence. Rather, bribery expresses a common understanding of the proper bounds of commodity exchange and of politics. We, as a political community, *share* a plural set of interpretations that attach to a plural set of social goods. "Social goods have social meanings, and we find our way to distributive justice through an interpretation of those meanings."[33] Thus, Walzer's pluralism is anchored by unity—our shared understandings—and interpretive conflict is willed away. While his account of the autonomous distributional spheres and institutional settings—families, markets, universities, churches, politics—respects the plurality of social goods and social spheres, his theory does not respect the conflictual pluralism of contested goods, of conflicting interpretations and valuations of the goods being distributed. That is, Walzer's pluralism does not extend to conflicting interpretations of the goods themselves. For instance, what makes Walzer's theory pluralistic is not that a good such as home is subject to conflicting interpretations which a just society is bound to accommodate; what makes it pluralistic is that the walls between home, market, church and state are fortified, preventing the emergence of that "undifferentiated land mass" of premodernity, or a new geography of domination.

The pluralism of spheres is anchored by the unity of social interpretation, and this unity is made clear by the metaphorical distinctions that Walzer uses to distinguish his preferred "path" of moral philosophy, interpretation, from the path of "moral invention," which is his term for much recent social-contract theory. He illustrates the distinction between moral invention and moral interpretation by invoking, like Douglas, the contrast between hotel and home, only this time the contrast serves as a metaphor for rival methods of political theorizing. To the invention of moral rules and principles that occurs, for instance, behind a "veil of ignorance" in John Rawls's original position, Walzer contrasts the work of the connected social critic who interprets the dense and complex web of meanings and values that constitute an actually existing culture. Although the Rawlsian path of "invention" (where particular visions of the good, particular habits and practices, and particular identities are cast aside) may be necessary to a group of absolute strangers in figuring out a way to get along, it is a mistake, according to Walzer, to insist that members of a particular political community, with its shared traditions and habits, adopt such a perspective in considering the morality of their own practices: "Why should newly invented principles govern the lives of people who already share a moral culture and speak a natural language?"[34]

Moral inventors such as Rawls, Bruce Ackerman, and Jürgen Habermas have made a mistake: "It is as if we were to take a hotel room or an accommodation apartment or a safe house as the ideal model of a human home." Walzer argues that the subject of the Rawlsian original position probably *would* create a hotel room because, stripped of all self-understandings about what differentiates one from others (social position, tastes, habits, values), such a thin self would create a thin space: "Deprived of all knowledge of what our own home was like, . . . required to design rooms that any one of us might live in, we would probably come up with something like, but not quite so culturally specific as, the Hilton Hotel." We, as inventors of such a hotel, would no doubt "long for the homes we knew we once had but could no longer remember."[35]

Walzer's discussion of the metaphor of home and hotel concludes with what he calls "one telling dissent": a statement by Franz Kafka indicating a preference for hotels over homes. Walzer quotes from Kafka's journal: "I like hotel rooms. I always feel immediately at home in hotel rooms, more than at home, really."[36] This is Walzer's gloss on that passage:

> Note the irony: there is no other way to convey the sense of being in one's own place except to say "at home." It is a hard thing to suggest to men and women that they give up the moral comfort that those words evoke. But what if they do not share that comfort? What if their lives are like that of Kafka's K., or of any twentieth-century exile, outcast, refugee, or stateless person? For such people, hotels are very important. They need the protection of the rooms, decent (if bare) human accommodation. They need a universal (if minimal) morality. . . . What they commonly *want*, however, is not to be permanently registered in a hotel but to be established in a new home, a dense moral culture within which they can feel some sense of belonging.[37]

Walzer reads Kafka's irony weakly, suggesting that the conjunction of "feeling at home" and "hotel" reveals the *strength* of our normative idealization of home ("There is no other way to convey the sense of being in one's own place.") and not its *contestation*. The rhetorical power of a reversal of values gets lost here, and the ironic juxtaposition reveals not the author's subversion of the value of home but rather the inescapability of the ideal. But what if providing something *thicker* than "bare human accommodation" requires something other than pluralism's world of walls and its fortification of a shared understanding of home? What if it requires active pluralization that troubles the boundaries surrounding home in order to foster *multiple* "dense moral cultures"?

The power of Walzer's metaphor and his invocation of home as a singular moral culture stem in part from the slippage in the concept of home between the idea of a domestic dwelling and the idea of a national community ("homeland"). It is this slippage that is involved in moving from Kafka's contestation of home to the situation of those who are displaced from their homelands. Those "at home" possess (or are possessed by) a "dense moral culture." This easy slide from home as a domestic space to home as a national community of shared meanings—the invocation of home both as a comfortable and secure space of domestic rituals, sealed off from market pressures and calculations, *and* as a national homeland with its dense moral culture—suggests the ways in which an integrative version of "home" and "homeland" anchors and domesticates the pluralism of separate spheres. Home is both one of the realms whose distributive logic needs to be protected from domination (home as separate sphere) and a metaphor for the overall interpretive artifact (home as moral landscape) *and* the broader political location of this interpretive product (home as national homeland). This might suggest that the concept of home is not so much a metaphor for Walzer's theory of moral interpretation as an essential component: an idealized vision of the national homeland that anchors the shared understandings of its citizens. Walzer's citizens desire the comforts of home, and they find these comforts in the shared understandings and dense moral culture of the homeland.[38]

Walzer's map of the social world and his (implicit) map of the self suggest a particular model of the city: the zoned city, where things have their proper uses, and spaces are protected against infringement. Walzer states that the key question for a pluralist politics is this: "How do we draw the map of the social world so that churches and schools, states and markets, bureaucracies and families each find their proper place?"[39]

Walzer's question invites a spatial answer and receives one in the theory of single-function urban development. As Richard Sennett explains this vision, "Each space in the city does a particular job, and the city itself is atomized. . . . [H]ouses were built en bloc in vast numbers, with the services for families in those houses located somewhere else: a 'community center,' an 'educational park,' a shopping center, a hospital 'campus.'"[40] A model of the zoned city first developed at the turn of the twentieth century in Germany, where residential, industrial, and commercial functions began to be separated through zoning law.[41] This is the vision of the city that oriented early twentieth-century reformers in their campaigns against SRO hotels. As Groth argues, this ideology of "separate and single-purpose spaces" had no room for mixed uses, shared facilities, and "the old city of social and commercial mixture, pedestrian convenience, and shared kitchens and baths."[42] Preventing the contamination of the home sphere required a campaign against residential hotel life, which failed to ensure proper degrees of privacy (there was no private bathroom and kitchen), proper degrees of individualism (not even owning their own furniture, hotel dwellers were seen as suspect citizens for not possessing property), and proper degrees of community (residential hotel life disrupted the family by undermining traditional gender roles and such community-building rituals as the family dinner). In contrast to the mixed-use, high-density spaces of urban centers where people lived, worked, and shopped, Progressive reformers sought a rationalized city in which each function would have its proper place.

The Progressive reformer Lawrence Veiller, in addition to trumpeting the civic virtues of the homeowner/stakeholder-citizen, developed an argument about the physical and moral security of the home sphere. His writings manifest a concern for the relationship between spaces and the human subjects who inhabit them. For him, as a result, architecture takes on an irreducibly moral dimension. Just as homeownership is to be valued because it produces responsible citizenship, particular kinds of home spaces are to be prized for the sorts of responsible individuals they generate. A particularly telling example is the development of private bathroom facilities in rental apartment units to replace shared bathing facilities for a whole floor of apartments: "In multiple dwellings each family should have its own separate water-closet. The use of such conveniences in common leads to serious social evils and should not be tolerated in future buildings. In addition, such conveniences should be entirely within the control of the individual family and should not be located in public parts of the house."[43]

The reason that such facilities should be within the control of the family is not so much the convenience for tenants as the convenience of landlords: common spaces "are apt to be frequently abused," whereas private provisions are "advantageous to the owner as it enables him to center responsibility for sanitary abuses."[44] Veiller was clearly interested in the normalizing benefits of having an increasing number of spaces fall within the responsibility of the nuclear family. It was not just that the spaces become better maintained when responsibility is assigned for them; in addition, responsible tenants were created when spaces are cônstructed so as to enable accountability at the level of the nuclear family as opposed to the entire collection of tenants. Veiller's claims for the privatization of common spaces in the separate sphere of the home reflected his assumption, in one historian's words, "that housing influenced character" and that "better housing was a key to social control." Indeed, one might say (though Veiller would not) that such spaces worked to create the modern nuclear family. Proper spaces for familial privacy (alongside the norm of homeownership discussed previously) were central, for Progressives, in the "Americanization" of the immigrant poor.[45] As home spaces created good citizens and subjects, the Walzerian link between "home" and "homeland" started to become clear in the contours of a nation-building project of spatial rationalization.

The physical arts of separation—walls between families, walls between individual family members, walls between functions, and walls between types of persons—would all produce moral benefits in terms of the responsible, normalized individuals and the families they produce. In his proposal for housing reform, Veiller argued that it should "be made illegal to carry on a common lodging house in a tenement house. The mingling of the ordinary lodging house patron with the tenement house dweller is not a good thing for the community."[46] Within an ontological and epistemological horizon that placed physical and moral dangers together, operating according to the logic of contamination, mixture, and impurity, Veiller's attempt to rationalize housing helped to install the modern single-family home as an ideal and push out alternative forms of dwelling.

Just as the pluralist cartographer draws walls around each social institution, the pluralist urban planner builds spatial boundaries between spheres, and the sphere that is to receive the most special protection is the sphere of home. The theorist, the citizen, and the urban planner all practice this art of separation, and they all erect these walls in the name of avoiding or repressing disorder and contestation. To return to Walzer, I am suggesting not that his theory somehow requires this particular form of spatial arrangements, or that his metaphors should be taken literally, but that the deployment of these metaphors of home and wall reveal the striking absence of conflictual pluralism in his theory. Walzer's metaphor of home to describe the moral universe that socially connected interpretation elaborates makes sense in this context, because the language of home, and the contrast between home and hotel, emerge not out of an innocent context but out of the politically contested development of the modern American home ideal. This home ideal,

I suggest, emerges alongside the urban planning of the "zoned city" that so strikingly matches Walzer's version of justice-as-separate-spheres.

Progressive reformers fought multiple forms of contamination, mixture, and violations of spatial integrity: families' practice of renting out rooms to strangers (an intrusion of the market into the sphere of the home); the combination of activities such as eating, sleeping and cooking in a single room; and the mixture of uses such as consumption, production, residence, and entertainment in one neighborhood. For reformers, according to Groth, zoning out commerce and hotels from residential neighborhoods was of a piece with establishing the uses to which domestic spaces might be put. "In reformers' eyes, lodgers blighted home interiors just as mixed land uses . . . blighted residential streets."[47]

In a similar way, Walzer's liberal pluralism builds a world of walls, metaphorically, to prevent domination and contamination (of politics by money, of intimacy by political power, and the like). Walzer's pluralism prevents the uncontested domain of home from being contaminated from the outside by the logic of other spheres—commodification, for instance. Walzer's logic of separate spheres might not *compel* an argument against mixed-use, high-density, and diverse urban development, but it would strongly suggest a conclusion that the residential boarder, the stranger who pays his rent and lives with the family, does violate the integrity of the domestic sphere. And it is this spirit of protecting the integrity of spheres that animated the desire in the Progressive Era (and beyond) to eliminate diverse housing options in order to protect the modern nuclear family and its home from the contaminations of a disorderly, impure culture of urban diversity, individuality, and subcultural sociability.

Although there may be no necessary relationship between Walzer's justice-as-separate-spheres argument (along with its spatial metaphors) and the vision of urban planners and reformers in creating rationalized cities and households, both do seem to be animated by a desire to deepen and protect the modern processes of sphere differentiation. For Walzer, the operative contrast is between such sphere differentiation with its world of walls, on the one hand, and the "undifferentiated land mass" of premodernity, on the other. Setting up the contrast this way sublimates the possibilities for a conflictual, democratic pluralization—in which the entanglements and border skirmishes between social spheres are seen as opportunities for democratic engagement—in the practice of wall-building and sphere-separating, anchored by the shared understandings of the home/homeland. As Michael Shapiro concludes: "One can, in short, render boundaries innocuous by speaking unproblematically about 'public' and 'private' spheres, the 'workplace,' 'recreational space,' and so on. What is left of the political process in this model is primarily a policing function that consists in the prevention of intrusions from one institutional setting to another."[48] The promise of Walzerian pluralism, with its multiple roles, multiple spheres, and multiple distributive logics quickly lapses into the more integrative language of homeland and home. An integrative national political community serves as the basis of the interpretive enterprise that uncovers our shared understandings. And the integrative language of home functions both as a metaphor for Walzerian interpretation and as one of the primary institutional settings of an all too domesticated form of pluralism.

Progressive anti-hotel reformers drew upon the integrationist versions of both the classical republican and modern pluralist models of the place of home in a democratic society. Veiller, developing themes from what I have termed the classical republican model, saw homeownership as essential for citizenship, turning rootless immigrants into possessive individualists and integrating the head of household into the political community by tying him to an administrative state and its multiple bureaucracies. Homeownership was key to forming a proper individualism and a proper attachment to the political community.

Progressive reformers, including Veiller, also drew upon notions of separate spheres, the idea of the home as a rationalized and noncommodified space for intimacy and reciprocity, affective relations, and nurturance. Residential hotel life was a problem because such a household, absent property possession (residential hotel dwellers rented not only their rooms but also their furniture), encouraged a rootless nomadism as opposed to a stakeholder mentality and proper possessive individualism. It was also a problem because it encouraged the weakening of the gender roles that were seen as proper to the sphere of family life, encouraged the mixture of functions in a particular space and the mixture of persons outside the institution of the family, and encouraged a selfish individualism and a pathological isolation. Progressive Era reformers invoked an "integrity of the spheres" argument to oppose the mixture of uses, inadequate privacy, and commercialization found in hotel dwelling.

As Groth notes, there is an apparent contradiction in their critique. Drawing implicitly on the classical republican model, it sees residential hotels as *undermining* the possessive individualism needed for good citizenship, yet drawing implicitly on the separate-spheres model, it sees residential hotels as fostering *too much* individualism, replacing the community of the family with the selfishness of urban individualistic lifestyles: "Hotel housing was pathologically isolating, yet it was not sufficiently private. . . . [It] did not provide proper individuality and personal expression, yet it fostered selfish individualism."[49]

The modern home ideal, then, articulated through a critique of residential hotels, involves the careful management of a subjectivity that is individualistic in certain contexts and communitarian in others. "Home" both integrates the head of household, as a property-possessing individual, into the political order and provides a sphere of noncommodified relations of nurturance and reciprocity. This contradiction may have something to do with a wider contradiction that many historians have noted in American cultural history: the household and family become, in the late nineteenth century, repositories of a communitarian ideology that was expelled from the public sphere and promoted through the virtuous ministrations of proper wives and mothers. In other words, this seeming contradiction at the heart of the home norm was reconciled through a gendered division in which the head of household, male, pursued a masculine, individualistic posture toward the world, while the virtuous wife and mother made the home sphere itself a kind of communitarian haven.[50] Nevertheless, this seeming reconciliation could not suture over the basic fissure in the home ideal, a contradiction that exposed itself in the criticisms of residential hotel life.

Residential hotel life also involved, at least potentially, both forms of individualism and forms of communitarian connectedness, but it scrambled the home ideal's complex articulation of these values. Rather than connecting individualism to property possession and material extension into the world, residential hotels enabled a nonmaterialistic, nonpossessive form of individualism. And furthermore, whereas the home ideal posited community as achieved in a noncommodified sphere of home, residential hotel dwellers achieved community connections precisely through the commercial spaces of bars, dance halls, cafes, and the like.[51] The articulation of the home ideal through critiques of residential hotel life is revealed as a complex balancing of individualism and community, constructed through contingent relations to private property and (non)commodification.

This analysis of a purified home ideal brings us full circle to Chapter 1's account of a purified consumptive public sphere. I do not want to leave the impression that the constellations of meanings associated with the public and private spheres, respectively, are unrelated. Two ways in which these developments are related concern issues of consumption and security. First, if it is the public sphere that is to be secured *for* consumption *from* the threat of panhandlers and public sleepers, it is the home that is frequently the setting in which those consumer goods are enjoyed, the "dream home" that is the telos of public consumption.[52] Second, the anti-homeless laws that are instituted to make people less afraid in urban public spaces are designed for the person whose ideal of security has been formed through attachment to a mythic ideal of what Samira Kawash calls "the 1990s domestication of security in the form of the suburban safe house." The fearful subject who is to be reassured by broken-windows policing is a *domesticated* subject—the self who dwells in a secure and detached home, safely located in a residential neighborhood where commerce and disorder have been zoned out. As Kawash argues, "The fortified enclosure of domestic space is mirrored in the move towards the enclosure and privatization of commercial and previously public spaces."[53] My examination of the home ideal through political theory reflection on "household" and "home" has placed less emphasis on the themes of consumption and security than on the link between homeownership and citizenship and the separation of home from the spheres of market and politics. Yet, home is also a commodity, successfully sold as a fantasized site of protection from precisely the sort of public-space disorders targeted by anti-homeless legislation and broken-windows policing.

FROM PLURALISM TO PLURALIZATION

The reduction in housing options, the polarization of society into home-dwelling citizens and sheltered bare life, and the deep imbrication of the home ideal in our conceptions of citizenship, success, and normalcy are all signs of the limits of democratic pluralism in contemporary American culture. Responding to the widening gap between the home ideal and sheltered bare life requires moving from pluralism to what William Connolly calls pluralization. Pluralization is not a rejection of contemporary pluralism but an effort to radicalize it, with less wall-building and more cross-boundary experimentation. Indeed, my model of democratic pluralization does not reject Arendt's conception of plurality or Walzer's defense of pluralism but rather takes insights from both. From Arendt, I take the emphasis on the linkages between the household and the public sphere and the commitment to human plurality as the multiplicity of perspectives. From Walzer, I take a recognition of the more complex spatiality of modern sphere differentiation.

Neither Arendt nor Walzer, however, extend plurality back to the sphere of the household itself. Home became either the prepolitical foundation for political plurality or one of a plurality of distributive/institutional spheres whose walls must be defended. Neither model allows for contestations over the meaning and value of home itself, and by promoting a mythic vision of a singular home/household ideal, a combination of these models became justification for the narrowing of housing options. The Arendtian vision, concerned with preserving a plurality of perspectives, does not see the household form as sustaining such multiplicity. The Walzerian vision, concerned with preserving the plurality of distributive spheres, institutional settings, and social goods, does not sufficiently appreciate the conflictual pluralization of competing perspectives on those social goods; it treats pluralism rather as a pattern of existing understandings that needs defending.

Such defensive postures, William Connolly argues, stand in contrast to a spirit of "active pluralization." Active pluralization is nourished by an "ethos of critical responsiveness" to new movements and boundary crossings that operate at a murky level below our settled conventions concerning justice and injustice. This attitude of care for difference helps to maintain "the constitutive tension between pluralism and pluralization." Without this ethos and the movement toward active pluralization, "the demand to freeze temporarily defined limits into a set of fixed criteria all too readily inflicts the sort of injuries it purports to insure against."[54] The "cramped" and defensive pluralism of which Connolly speaks is evident in the contemporary shelter system.[55] There is a kind of pluralism within the shelter system—a pluralism based on classificatory regimes of homeless subpopulations—but this is not pluralization; it is a managerial practice of dividing and normalizing. Self-governing and politicized homeless encampments, an example of new drives to pluralization, are frequently represented as a threat to a pluralism that needs protection. Connolly's argument suggests that democracy would be better served by an "ethos of critical responsiveness" toward such a movement than by an anxious defense of traditional definitions of public and private.

A robust politics frequently emerges from precisely the sort of boundary crossings and boundary disputes that the practice of wall-building is designed to prevent. An agonistic approach to democratic pluralization presents the entanglements and crossings between social spheres as *opportunities for democratic engagement,* rather than as *violations to be policed.* Indeed, only when a particular distributive sphere's autonomy and integrity are "threatened" do social critics and citizens have the opportunity to articulate a vision of the supposedly shared social values that are being undermined. Conflicting interpretations of a good such as home and entanglements between home, market, and public spheres form the substance of the dialogue and debate so crucial to democratic politics.

How might a vision of *conflictual* democratic pluralization inflect our normative judgments about housing options? First, no single and uncontested conception of the value of home and no single conception of how that value is developed through the connections and boundaries between home, market, and political community can suffice for a robust theory of democracy. Not only are the values associated with home and household pluralistic, but the mechanisms for their realization are also pluralistic. For instance, the fact that part of the function of a home, a private sphere, is to nurture individualistic identities does not resolve the question of whether the individualism is fostered through property possession or through rented dwellings that are marked by the absence of social-control mechanisms. Similarly, although "home" connotes relations of reciprocity, care, and affection, a democratic pluralism leaves open the question of how these forms of community may be realized: by creating a noncommodified sphere of affection walled off from the market, or by creating forms of dwelling that are nested in larger spaces of urban sociability and friendship.

Second, by arguing that the pluralization of household forms should be encouraged, this vision of democratic pluralism resists the polarization of society into citizen-homeowners on the one hand, and dependent clients of a shelter system, on the other. From the perspective of agonistic democracy, housing options should be developed in order to resist such a polarization; multiple dwelling forms should be promoted that enable different, and indeed conflicting, forms of individual identity construction and communitarian connectedness. Residential hotels have made a comeback, thanks to policy changes, and public-private partnerships as well. These developments ought to be encouraged, not simply because they provide shelter to needy bodies, but also because they resist the building of social walls between citizen-homeowners and bare life.

Third, although having a household does form the basis of civic involvement, democratic pluralization nurtures multiple, differing connections between home and politics: not only those of Veiller's citizen-stakeholder (whose domestic preoccupations integrate him into the housekeeping state) but also renters' rights movements and campaigns to protect SROs (in which people develop a posture of critical citizenship towards housing policies as a result of their domestic situations). And homeless encampments provide a direct link between home-dwelling and civic involvement not only by making dwelling spaces into an experiment in collective self-governance but also by making this form of housing a very public act of witnessing, a dramatization of housing inequalities in American society.

Making housing diversity central to democratic pluralization does not, however, mean that "anything goes," that whatever someone is willing to call "home" should receive societal recognition, or that any attempt to call certain housing forms inadequate should be considered an imperialistic projection of a middle-class home ideal.[56] This is an important caution, but it misses the central point (worth repeating) that a *non-pluralistic* conception of home, far from providing homes to all, has worked rather to polarize society into normative home-dwellers, on the one hand, and the needy, dependent bare life of urban shelters and public spaces, on the other hand. As emergency shelters attempt to fill the gap left by the destruction of residential hotels, dependent shelterized subjects—objects of either pity or scorn—replace the less visible individuals and communities of residential hotels. As networks of caregivers, professional social workers, and substance-abuse counselors draw the street homeless and the shelter homeless into an increasingly thick web of social control and relations of dependency, the possibility that values such as autonomy, privacy, nonpossessive individualism and urban sociability can be realized in nonnormative forms of dwelling should not be forgotten.

Robert Frost, in his poem "Mending Wall" writes, "Before I built a wall I'd ask to know / What I was walling in or walling out."[57] Those lines bring to mind the multiple layers of wall-building that surround home and homelessness: how we construct the material spaces of our homes; how the differentiated spheres of modern social life are fortified by political and cultural boundaries; how our discursive landscape of home brings certain possibilities into view while excluding alternative possibilities as unthinkable; how our normative idealizations of home become symbolic barriers, walling some people in and walling some people out; and how the homeless, though confined to public space ("walled in") as a result of their lack of a private space, are also excluded as bare life from the public status of citizenship ("walled out") as a result of punitive legal barriers and cultural stigmas. I would add that political-theoretical reflection can help provide an answer to Frost's question, help us examine what is getting walled in and what is getting walled out before we build more walls. My conclusion reflects more generally on the role of the state in building walls through the creation of differential legal statuses (such as those of the housed citizen and the homeless), and explores the possibilities for breaking down such walls through an ethic of dwelling.

The Empty Tent of Citizenship

The bare-life predicament is strikingly illustrated by two federal court cases read side by side. The cases are both about activists who protested housing policy outside a political executive's home. Both concern public sleeping as a form of protest, and both concern homelessness—either current or impending. In one, *Clark v. Community for Creative Nonviolence,* the Supreme Court ruled against homeless activists in Washington, D.C., upholding a Parks Department regulation against camping and its application to homeless demonstrators. The activists were allowed to erect two "symbolic campsites" in Lafayette Park and on the Mall near the White House but were not allowed to occupy them. According to the Supreme Court, the Parks Department was acting constitutionally in allowing the tent cities to stand, while also "den[ying] CCNV's request that demonstrators be permitted to sleep in the symbolic tents."[1] In the other case, *Metropolitan Council, Inc. v. Safir,* a federal district court ruled in favor of a group of activists for tenants' rights who were protesting a proposed rent increase in rent-controlled apartments in New York City. The court issued a preliminary injunction that allowed a sidewalk-sleeping protest to occur near Gracie Mansion, ruling that in this case a police ban on sleeping on sidewalks was "overbroad."

According to the Supreme Court in *Clark,* the government has an interest in preventing damage to parkland and preserving its accessibility to other members of the public; this interest is served by preventing people from occupying the symbolic tent camp.[2] In *Metropolitan Council,* the district court distinguishes the facts of the rent-control protest from those of *Clark* in terms of the *absence* of a significant governmental interest that would be served by enforcing a public-sleeping prohibition; the court asserts that the overnight vigil is a form of conduct that "falls within the parameters of the ban and yet fails to implicate the interests allegedly supporting the ban": "Here, unlike in *Clark*, demonstrations involving lying down and sleeping on a sidewalk are unlikely to pose the risks that the ban seeks to avoid, in light of the precautions routinely taken by protest organizers and police."[3] The public-sleeping ban is not narrowly tailored to the governmental interests of protecting vulnerable sleeping persons from the dangers of the streets and protecting pedestrians from the obstruction of sleeping persons. And since the ban includes not only innocent conduct but innocent conduct with an expressive function—a protest vigil—it is thus unconstitutionally overbroad.

There is, however, a more obvious difference between *Clark* and *Metropolitan Council* than the question of a governmental interest served or not served by enforcement of the ban: in *Clark* the protesters are homeless, whereas in *Metropolitan Council* the protesters are housed. I do not mean this as a flippant and cynical uncovering of judicial prejudice and inconsistency; rather, I argue that the status of housed citizen is essential to make sleeping in public, in the courts' eyes, a *signifying* event, worthy of protection. The court in *Metropolitan Council* makes this clear, though in an indirect way, when it seeks to narrow the scope of its ruling. In order to allay fears that it is introducing a slippery slope that could result in the unconstitutionality of any and all forms of public-sleeping prohibition, the court reassures the city of "the obvious and dramatic difference between the conduct at which the ban is aimed, . . . 'intoxicated individuals that sleep on the sidewalk or homeless persons that sleep on the sidewalk,' . . . and the organized, constrained protest . . . that is at issue here." Furthermore, "the City has offered no evidence that those who sleep on the sidewalks while intoxicated and/or homeless (the instances cited by the City) will implicate the First Amendment at all."[4]

For this logic to work and to square with the decision in *Clark*, the category of "demonstrator" must be restricted to home-dwelling citizens. Indeed, sleeping in the park by homeless people, even as part of a tent city protest, was not deemed expressive speech to the same extent, according to the district court, because its main role was in "facilitat[ing] a continuous presence in the parks and the attraction of homeless people to the tent city."[5] As Justice Byron White argues, writing for the Supreme Court in *Clark*, "Although we have assumed for present purposes that the sleeping banned in this case would have an expressive element, it is evident that its major value to this demonstration would be facilitative. Without a permit to sleep, it would be difficult to get the poor and homeless to participate or to be present at all." In the rent control protest, by contrast, "sleeping plays a more significant expressive role relative to other aspects of the protest and is not primarily facilitative."[6]

It is worth noting the irony of these two cases read together. They permit housed citizens to engage in symbolic public sleeping to protest their *potential* homelessness but prevent homeless citizens from occupying a tent city to protest their *actual* homelessness. The rent-control activists' overnight vigil—despite its effort to politicize issues of housing security and homelessness—is sharply distinguished from both public sleeping by "homeless persons" (and "intoxicated individuals") and politicized homeless encampments, such as the one whose occupation was prevented in *Clark*. In other words, the renters' group gets the right to protest the looming possibility of homelessness only by virtue of the court's distinction between their protest and the sleeping in public of actual homeless persons. The district court confidently asserts an "obvious and dramatic difference" between a homeless person sleeping on the sidewalk and the proposed overnight vigil, despite the fact that it is precisely such homeless sidewalk-sleeping that is being "symbolized" in the protest.[7]

It appears, then, that Anatole France's searing indictment of legal impartiality—the poor "must labour in the face of the majestic equality of the laws, which forbid rich and poor alike to sleep under the bridges, to beg in the streets, and to steal their bread"—will have to be modified.[8] The law in its majesty does *not* equally prevent the rich and the poor from sleeping in public: housed citizens may sleep in public as a form of protected speech. The housed citizen sleeping on the sidewalk and the empty tent on the Mall are both forms of political expression worthy of constitutional protection—but a homeless citizen sleeping in public does not signify in the same way. According to the logic of these cases, homeless people, because they *must* sleep in public space, do not engage in expressive conduct when they do so. This is why a tent city for homeless persons can be considered "facilitative" but not "expressive." A citizen can "symbolically" sleep in public because he or she can return to his or her home, but a homeless person sleeps in public out of necessity, and for that reason a homeless protest is not as "significantly expressive."

Lurking behind the distinction between a governmental interest served by the sleeping ban in *Clark* and the lack of such an interest in *Metropolitan Council* is a distinction, in the courts' imaginings, between bounded speech and unbridled need, between a "constrained" and symbolic protest by housed citizens who "do not spill out of the protest area" and an unconstrained and "facilitative" protest aimed at "attract[ing] . . . homeless people to the tent city."[9] The homeless, marked by necessity, threaten to overwhelm the public spaces they inhabit. A homeless tent camp is not an act of speech but a potentially out-of-control obstruction of public space; therefore, it can enter the realm of symbolic speech only through the erasure of homeless bodies.

In allowing a housed citizens' overnight vigil while preventing occupation of a homeless tent city, these cases produce an exclusionary vision of "expressive" citizenship in opposition to a subordinate status of bare life. The tenants'-rights group sleeps in public as citizens, whereas homeless persons (and intoxicated individuals) sleep in public as outlawed bare life. As bare life, the homeless are banned—hence the *empty* tent. In a circular logic, it is the law's exclusion of the homeless from the tent that constitutes them as abandoned bare life, but it is the status of the homeless as bare life—as incapable of expressive speech—that justifies their exclusion from the tent. For the tent to signify as a public, political protest and as an expressive act, it must not be occupied by a body that *needs* to sleep there. It is now clear that when law guards the empty tent from occupation by homeless activists, it is also guarding the category of citizenship from occupation by the homeless.[10]

In response to this double standard—to law's rigorous separation of citizenship and expression from bare life and homeless bodies—movements and practices such as politicized homeless encampments (and the street newspaper movement) undermine the distinction between expressive citizenship and bare life.[11] A politicized homeless encampment troubles the boundary between public and private: it provides needed protection from the elements *and* the space for civic involvement, shields the body *and* facilitates action, provides a space of withdrawal *and* expresses a critique of the injustices of homelessness. I argue that one way to nurture "critical responsiveness" toward such pluralizing movements as homeless encampments—deconstructing the rigid oppositions between need and expression, bare life and citizenship—is to think through what it means to "dwell" and to think of public space as a space of common dwelling.

Guidance toward overcoming the distinction between bare life and citizenship through a notion of common dwelling can be found in another court case, *Tobe v. Santa Ana* (1994). Unlike *Metropolitan Council*—which takes a set of facts that brought homeless and housed together (housed citizens protesting possible homelessness) and then proceeds to distinguish rigorously the constitutionally protected expression of housed citizens from the "normal circumstances" of "intoxicated individuals . . . or homeless persons who sleep on the sidewalk"[12]—the California appeals court in *Tobe* undermines the distinction between homeless and housed. The appeals court, sustaining an overbreadth challenge to a public-sleeping ban, recognizes a common human experience of dwelling that draws housed and homeless together. In so doing, it points the way, I argue, to what Agamben calls "a politics in which bare life is no longer separated and excepted, either in the state order or in the figure of human rights."[13]

Santa Ana's long history of harassing the homeless and seeking to drive them out of the city culminated in a roundup of homeless persons in 1990 for various misdemeanor offenses, after which those arrested were chained to benches in a stadium (as described in the introduction), where police chalked numbers on their clothing. In 1992, after agreeing to stop trying to drive the homeless out of Santa Ana, the city passed into law an anticamping ordinance, arguing that the ban represented a departure from its past abusive policies. The ordinance, phrased in neutral language, declared that "it shall be unlawful for any person to camp, occupy camp facilities or use camp paraphernalia" in public spaces of the city. It defined "camping" as "to pitch or occupy camp facilities; to live temporarily in a camp facility or outdoors; to use camp paraphernalia." The ordinance also made it illegal to store personal property in public spaces.[14]

The California appeals court declared the camping ban unconstitutional on several grounds: that it violated the Eighth Amendment prohibition of cruel and unusual punishment by punishing the involuntary status of homelessness,[15] that it violated a fundamental constitutional right to travel, and that it was unconstitutionally vague and overbroad. Here I want to explore the last of these claims.

The appellate court finds the Santa Ana camping ordinance unconstitutionally vague and overbroad because it fails to provide fair warning as to what constitutes punishable conduct, and leaves enforcement "to the virtually unfettered discretion of the police." The vague definitions of "camp paraphernalia" and "camp facilities" "provide no distinction between picnicking and camping or students' backpacks and 'camp paraphernalia.'" Likewise, the definition of camping—"to live temporarily in a camp facility or outdoors"—is unconstitutionally vague: "Most of us do that every day because all our activities are part of living." And finally, the prohibition against "storing" items in public spaces is struck down because the definition of the verb "to store" is overbroad: "The city may have been aiming at shopping carts and bedrolls; but it has hit bicycles, automobiles, delivery vehicles of every description, beach towels at public pools and wet umbrellas in library foyers."[16]

The court's specific argument is that the language of the ordinance is unconstitutionally vague and overbroad. But the legal reasoning has a further rhetorical power in drawing the homeless into the tent of citizenship by, ironically, turning domiciled citizens into potential lawbreakers; it gestures toward universality in a deconstructive direction by drawing the domiciled into the category of the outlaw: "The statute is vague and overbroad as applied to anyone, be they homeless, picnickers, or scouts engaged in a field exercise."[17] For the appellate court, taking the statute at face value means distancing ourselves from the common sense that the law is directly targeting the homeless: we *all* store belongings in public from time to time, and we *all* live temporarily out of doors to the extent that we are all residents of public space. The "majestic equality of the laws" in forbidding the rich *and* the poor to sleep under bridges has turned into the unconstitutional overreaching of the law that prevents rich and poor alike from living temporarily outside.

This legal reasoning resists the call to convert homeless difference into absolute otherness. It attacks the political and material exclusion of the homeless not by referencing a common and abstract humanity that binds us together but rather by thinking through the connections between the dwelling activities of homeless persons and the dwelling activities of housed persons. The appeals court incorporates a recognition of *our common dwelling* into its reading of the law. By thinking of housed citizens as potential outlaws of public space, the court avoids some of the pitfalls of status-crime arguments that protect homeless persons only by carving out a subordinate legal status of helpless bare life.[18] In so doing, it reflects an appreciation of two facts: that the homeless, too, dwell and that domesticated citizens, too, dwell in places outside the normatively enshrined home.

The *Tobe* decision was reversed by the California state supreme court, which distances the homeless and reasserts dwelling as something that only those with homes properly do. This distancing maneuver is unfortunate, since recognition that housed and homeless alike *must dwell* can constitute a central ethical principle for evaluating responses to the economic, cultural, and political injustices of homelessness and promoting democratic pluralization. The California supreme court, reversing the appeals court, articulates a form of common sense to deny the claims of vagueness and overbreadth. The court says that we all know the difference between camping and picnicking, between living temporarily in public space and living permanently in public space; therefore, there is no troubling vagueness, "no possibility that any law enforcement agent would believe that a picnic in public constituted 'camping.'" According to Judge Marvin Baxter,

"The Court of Appeal's strained interpretation of 'living,' reasoning that we all use public facilities for 'living' since all of our activities are part of living, ignores the context of the ordinance which prohibits living not in the sense of existing, but dwelling or residing on public property."[19] Whereas the appeals court tries to expand (and "strain") the meaning of "living" out of doors, the state supreme court says that common sense ought to inflect our reading of the camping ban, and this common sense renders the terms "living," "camping," and "storing" precise and not subject to interpretive uncertainty. There is living as existing, and living as dwelling—and dwelling is a specific activity, something one (properly) does only in the home.

One might ask, though, *for whom* is the distinction between living "in the sense of existing" and living as "dwelling or residing on public property" commonsensical? From the standpoint of someone who is excluded from all private spaces, someone who has no private dwelling space, is the distinction obvious? And for someone who must take care of all his or her bodily needs in public spaces—sleeping, resting, eating, urinating, defecating—is a "picnic" of a categorical order different from sleeping? Thus, despite asserting that the camping law is nondiscriminatory (in preventing homeless and housed alike from sleeping in public), by articulating the common sense underpinnings of the statute, the court unwittingly exposes the thoroughly domesticated nature of that common sense and the discriminatory bias that lurks beneath the universalistic rhetoric of the camping ban. If legitimate dwelling is confined to the space of homes, homeless dwelling becomes an "improper use" of public space.

The California supreme court narrows the meaning of living-as-dwelling and then confines legitimate dwelling to the home. We can better understand this maneuver by drawing upon Heidegger's writings on the meaning of dwelling. Heidegger criticizes the modern tendency to forget dwelling as the basic character of human being in the world and to obscure this meaning with modern notions of dwelling as one activity we perform (at home, in our lodging place) among many: "When we speak of dwelling, we usually think of an activity that man performs alongside many other activities. We work here and dwell there. We do not merely dwell—that would be virtual inactivity—we practice a profession, we do business." To this modern narrowing of dwelling, reflected in the California supreme court's opinion, Heidegger counterposes "the way in which you are and I am, the manner in which we humans *are* on the earth, is *buan*, dwelling." In its broader sense, dwelling involves constructing and cultivating, building and preserving; in its broadest sense, dwelling comprises the rhythms and habits that define the prereflective everyday life of people. As dwelling becomes telescoped in modern experience to residential lodging, "dwelling is not experienced as man's Being; dwelling is never thought of as the basic character of human being."[20]

This wider sense of dwelling can be seen in precapitalist societies, before the private, commodified home was enshrined as the locus of human dwelling. As Iris Young argues, in many times and places, "dwelling in a wider sense occurs outdoors and/or in collective spaces, both sheltered and not." Additionally, she shows that not all citizens of liberal capitalist societies have become enamored of civic privatism and the contemporary home ideal: "Even in modern capitalist societies some people 'live' more in their neighborhood or on their block than in their houses. They sit in squares, on stoops, in bars and coffee houses, going to their houses mostly to sleep." Young refuses a simple endorsement or rejection of modern constructions of home, criticizing the "attachment of personal identity to commodified houses and their contents" and the ways in which the comforts of home have "come at women's expense," while at the same time recognizing that homemaking is also a positive process of sustaining habitats by "endowing things with living meaning."[21] The appellate court in *Tobe*, too, refuses a simple endorsement of civic privatism and a domesticated approach to dwelling by insisting that we *all* "live temporarily outdoors." Even though common sense tells us all that the framers of the ordinance did not mean to include picnicking, strolling along the sidewalks, and moving through public spaces in the course of daily life, the appellate court reads the statute "naively" and rejects the implicit assumption of home as the proper and only place of dwelling, for homeless and non-homeless alike.

In a further critique of civic privatism and the preoccupation with "fortified" and "secure" home spaces that imagine security in terms of separation, seclusion, and the sealing-off of private domestic spaces, Samira Kawash suggests that we look for a way of being in the world that links security not to withdrawal and fortification but rather to interdependence, connection, and relation.[22] Heidegger's wider sense of dwelling might serve as a path to the recognition of this interdependence.

An ethic of dwelling does not involve stripping away superficial differences to find the essential human beneath. Rather, this ethic involves thinking through the commonalities that manifest themselves through differences, recognizing the alternative habits of dwelling that are, nonetheless, common *as* habits of dwelling. Such an "ethos of critical responsiveness" toward difference, as Connolly argues, fosters not a simple tolerance of the other but an active pluralization that can result in changes to dominant identities (such as the identity of the home-dwelling citizen).[23] In this respect, it is helpful for a court to declare that the ban on living out of doors snares home-dwellers' picnics in its net along with homeless persons' public camping. Such arguments might lead us to consider public space as a shared space of dwelling and not simply a space for the free circulation of consumers and commodities which can be blocked by homeless bare life.

As I have argued in the preceding chapters, the development of a normative home ideal, the reduction of housing options that is its consequence, and the evolution of a purified vision of public space as a complement to the home ideal, all work not to *unify* but to *fragment* and *polarize*. As Connolly puts it, "The most powerful contemporary pressures to social fragmentation flow from struggles between contending, dogmatic identities, each hell bent on installing itself as the universal to which everyone and everything must conform."[24] In this context, critical responsiveness to homeless dwelling promotes pluralization and resists the polarized opposition of home-dwelling citizen and homeless bare life. A call to recognize habits of dwelling is not just a call to let the homeless be but a call to resist the pressures to consolidate a fortified home space against a threatening outside and a call to promote the occupation of public space by homeless and housed citizens alike. An ethos of critical responsiveness to homeless dwelling can lead to a loosening of the norms of home-dwelling citizenship as spaces become, in Bickford's words, "fuzzy and multilayered." Treating public space as a site of dwelling, a space of "outside togetherness" for all of us, is a way to resist the pressures of spatial exclusion and identity purification.[25]

A wider conception of dwelling entails, as a first step, the recognition that the homeless, too, though deprived of private homes, dwell. A forgetting of our common dwelling is entailed in the misrecognition of the homeless as bare life. It is all too easy, April Veness argues, to place the homeless in a kind of nonspace nonexistence, an absolute condition of "time and space limbo" to be remedied only by some form of compassionate intervention. The *Seattle Post-Intelligencer* editorial critiquing a homeless encampment (see chapter 3) makes such a gesture—envisioning the help of the Safe Harbors plan to end homelessness at some distant point in the future—giving little thought to what homeless street persons should do now, little thought to what homeless street persons are able to do, given the legally sanctioned attempts to prevent them from dwelling. To recognize that the homeless, too, dwell is to avoid this easy forgetting: "'Homeless' people live *somewhere;* they carry out personal activities in real places even though those activities may be curtailed and constrained."[26]

Veness describes the placemaking strategies of persons called homeless: "Some poor people have recreated homes in habitats that outsiders condemn, such as subway cars, cardboard encampments, abandoned railroad tunnels, foyers outside automatic teller machines, airports, the living room floors of friend and family, and deteriorated dwellings." For other street-dwellers, "home is created around temporal rhythms and self-determined habits."[27] Mitchell Duneier, in his study of New York City sidewalk vendors and panhandlers, points out that "the men who live and work on Sixth Avenue share a common history, and a collective self-consciousness; having come to the avenue, they have remained there because it is a habitat that can sustain a person's minimal existence."[28]

The California appellate court's claims in *Tobe* of vagueness and overbreadth in the Santa Ana ordinance did not win out, ultimately, and a wider conception of dwelling that could break down the political, legal, and discursive opposition between home-dwelling citizens and homeless outlaws was replaced by the state supreme court's "commonsensical" version of domestic dwelling. But the appellate court's argument opens up political space for contesting punitive policies toward the homeless by articulating linkages between the conduct of homeless persons and the conduct of domiciled persons (linkages denied by the court in *Metropolitan Council* when it separates an expressive, symbolic protest by homedwelling citizens from the punishable public sleeping of homeless bare life). This argument indicates that it is possible to critique and contest urban camping ordinances without creating the image of the involuntarily homeless person as helpless, defined by biological necessity and therefore exempt from punishment as the result of a special (and subordinate) status. Rather than make the homeless innocent, excepted from the criminal law by virtue of their complete identification with biological necessity, the vagueness challenge makes home-dwellers "guilty" by virtue of our common engagement in the habits of dwelling. And this recognition of our common engagement in the habits of dwelling—this deconstruction of the home/homeless opposition—is a useful starting point for considering policies and programs aimed at ending homelessness.

Recognizing our common dwelling plight means recognizing that those displaced from "house" and "home" must dwell—will seek out sustaining habitats as best they can, despite their abandonment by law—and that public policy should be oriented toward enabling dwelling, not criminalizing it or reducing it to the stripped-down client relationship of the shelter. Solutions to homelessness should build upon the efforts by homeless persons to create sustaining habitats rather than, as in shelterization, seeking to disrupt these efforts by isolating the individual homeless person (whether as bare life or as client with pathologies) for treatment and shelter. The denial of homeless placemaking activities and the attempt to disrupt these habits of dwelling is common to both punitive policies targeting "disorder" and therapeutic efforts to isolate and reform the homeless client. Wagner and other scholars such as Hoch and Slayton describe the role played by helping agencies in *disconnecting* homeless persons from their sustaining habitats and networks of mutual support and thereby fostering the dependencies the agencies seek to overcome. Wagner argues that the subcultures and networks of homeless persons should be employed rather than attacked by the therapeutic welfare state and that entails "recognition of the homeless as a community." And Hoch and Slayton argue that preserving and constructing single-room-occupancy hotels is a way of providing affordable housing, embedded in working-class communities, without the cultural stigmatization that accompanies the shelter system.[29] Given the cultural, political, and economic injustices of homelessness, recognizing and enabling the dwelling activities of the displaced is a worthy goal, neither self-defeating nor antidemocratic.

Attending to these cultural, political, and economic injustices means refusing the consignment of street-dwellers to an invisible, shadowy, outlaw existence, excluded from the empty tent of citizenship by the ban on bare life. And as home and public space become pluralized, home-dwelling citizens might start to work on an identity that was itself partly constituted in opposition to homeless bare life. All of us, dwellers in a wider sense, are neither abstract citizens capable of symbolic speech only by virtue of our domestic dwelling nor bare biological life banned from the tent and consigned to the shadowy existence of the outlaw. Rather, we are members of a pluralizing polity in which these rigid distinctions begin to break down. Such a political ethic is not utopian, but it is, I think, democratic. It seeks to unsettle the dream of home and a purified public sphere with an attunement toward the dwelling habits of people as they are now, and it points to a politics no longer premised on the isolation and exclusion of bare life.

NOTES

INTRODUCTION

1. Atlanta Union Mission website (2001), http://www.aumcares.org.
2. See, for instance, Priscilla Painton, "Shrugging Off the Homeless," *Time,* April 16, 1990, pp. 14–16; Isabel Wilkerson, "Shift in Feelings on the Homeless: Empathy Turns to Frustration," *New York Times,* September 2, 1991, p. 1.
3. Samira Kawash, "The Homeless Body," *Public Culture* 10 (winter 1998): 326.
4. A comprehensive overview of these punitive policies is presented in a series of reports by the National Law Center on Homelessness and Poverty (NLCHP). Its 1999 report, *Out of Sight—Out of Mind? A Report on Anti-Homeless Laws, Litigation and Alternatives in 50 United States Cities* (Washington, D.C.: NLCHP, 1999), documents that of the fifty largest cities in the United States, seven prohibited sleeping in all public spaces, eleven prohibited sleeping in particular public spaces, ten outlawed camping in all public spaces, and nineteen banned camping in particular public spaces. (Some ordinances define "camping" so broadly as to include sleeping in public, storing any personal belongings in public, and lying down in public.) Ten cities prohibited sitting or lying down on particular sidewalks. Twelve cities prohibited panhandling citywide, twenty-six prohibited begging in particular public spaces such as near automatic teller machines (ATMs), in subway stations, or near bus stops and outdoor cafes. Twenty-five cities have "aggressive panhandling" ordinances.
5. This summary of the events is taken from a California state appellate court's review of Santa Ana's subsequent "urban camping" ordinance: *Tobe v. City of Santa Ana,* 27 Cal. Rptr. 2d 386 (Cal. App. 4 Dist. 1994); reversed, 40 Cal. Rptr. 2d 402 (Cal. 1995). On these arrests, see also Harry Simon, "Towns without Pity: A Constitutional and Historical Analysis of Official Efforts to Drive Homeless Persons from American Cities," *Tulane Law Review* 66 (1992): 631–676.
6. David Rhode, "Federal Judge Upholds Giuliani's Policy on Arresting the Homeless," *New York Times,* December 29, 2000, http://www.nytimes.com/2000/12/29/nyregion/29HOME.html. The statute was upheld as constitutional in *Betancourt v. Giuliani,* 2000 U.S. Dist LEXIS 18516.
7. National Law Center on Homelessness and Poverty, *Illegal to Be Homeless* (Washington, D.C.: NLCHP, 2002), p. 91.

8. The ordinance is cited in *Johnson v. Dallas,* 860 F. Supp 344 (N.D. Tex. 1994); reversed and vacated for lack of standing, 61 F. 3d 442 (5th Cir. 1995). (I discuss this case in chapter 2.) Since the time of the law's passage, the NLCHP (*Illegal to be Homeless,* p. 95) has reported that the public-sleeping ban is enforced by police on a daily basis.

9. NLCHP, *Out of Sight, Out of Mind,* p. i. See also Judith Failer, "Homelessness in the Criminal Law," in *From Social Justice to Criminal Justice,* ed. William C. Hefferman and John Kleinig (New York: Oxford University Press, 2000), p. 251; and Maria Foscarinis, "Downward Spiral: Homelessness and Its Criminalization," *Yale Law and Policy Review* 14 (1996): 26.

10. See, for instance, Rosalyn Deutsche, *Evictions: Art and Spatial Politics* (Cambridge, Mass.: MIT Press, 1996); Don Mitchell, "The End of Public Space? People's Park, Definitions of the Public, and Democracy," *Annals of the Association of American Geographers* 85 (1995): 108–133; and Kawash, "Homeless Body."

11. Andrew Mair, "The Homeless and the Postindustrial City," *Political Geography Quarterly* 5 (1986): 351–368; Don Mitchell, "The Annihilation of Space by Law: The Roots and Implications of Anti-homeless Laws in the United States," *Antipode* 29 (1997): 303–355; Mitchell, "The End of Public Space?" 108–133; and A. R. Veness, "Home and Homelessness in the United States: Changing Ideals and Realities," *Environment and Planning D: Society and Space* 10 (1992): 445–468.

12. Kim Hopper and Jim Baumohl, "Redefining the Cursed Word: A Historical Interpretation of American Homelessness," in *Homelessness in America,* ed. Jim Baumohl (Phoenix, Ariz.: Oryx Press, 1996).

13. Kawash, "Homeless Body."

14. Richard Campbell and Jimmie L. Reeves, "Covering the Homeless: The Joyce Brown Story," *Critical Studies in Mass Communication* 6 (1989): 21–42.

15. Deutsche, *Evictions.*

16. Veness, "Home and Homelessness," p. 464.

17. Ernesto Laclau and Chantal Mouffe, *Hegemony and Socialist Strategy: Towards a Radical Democratic Politics* (London: Verso, 1985).

18. Kawash, "Homeless Body," p. 325.

19. Kim Hopper, "More Than Passing Strange: Homelessness and Mental Illness in New York City," *American Ethnologist* 14 (1987): 163.

20. See, for instance, Kenneth L. Kusmer, *Down and Out, On the Road: The Homeless in American History* (Oxford: Oxford University Press, 2002), p. 11.

21. Indeed, San Francisco's "Matrix" program in the early 1990s brought together, in an "interdepartmental effort," policies and services that at first glance seem incompatible: confiscation of shopping carts, arrests for aggressive panhandling and sleeping in parks and obstructing sidewalks combined with nonpunitive outreach efforts offering shelter, medical care, and information about available services. The Matrix program was upheld as constitutional in *Joyce v. San Francisco,* 846 F. Supp. 843 (N.D. Cal. 1994); No. C-93-4149 (N.D. Cal. August 18, 1995); vacated, 87 F. 3d 1320 (9th Cir. 1996). (See chapter 2.)

22. On welfare as a form of social control, see Frances Fox Piven and Richard A. Cloward, *Regulating the Poor: The Functions of Public Welfare* (New York: Pantheon, 1971), p. 33.

23. Ingrid Sahlin, "Enclosure or Inclusion? Urban Control and Homeless People" (paper presented at the joint meeting of the Law and Society Association and the Research Committee on Sociology of Law [ISA], Budapest, Hungary, July 4–7 2001), p. 15.

24. Wendy Brown makes this point in *States of Injury: Power and Freedom in Late Modernity* (Princeton: Princeton University Press, 1995), p. 15.

25. See, for instance, Eungjun Min, ed., *Reading the Homeless: The Media's Image of Homeless Culture* (Westport, Conn: Praeger, 1999).

26. My consideration of complexity in representation does not take into consideration the great diversity in the homeless population—gender, age, race, family status (single, married, with or without children), class, disability—and in people's experiences of homelessness, which many valuable studies have examined. But the polarities I am exploring have a tendency to recur across and beyond these variations. They are ideological; they do not reflect particular facts and experiences of homelessness but rather provide the frameworks through which to view those facts and experiences. One important project is to show how these ideological polarities are contradicted by the diversity and complexity of homeless experiences and subcultures. (I draw on some of this material, especially in chapter 3.) But as Samira Kawash ("Homeless Body," p. 322) and Rosalyn Deutsche (*Evictions*, p. 277) argue, it is also necessary to scrutinize and critique the internal logic and material effects of the dominant representational patterns themselves.

27. The phrase comes from Mary Douglas, *Purity and Danger: An Analysis of Concepts of Pollution and Taboo* (Middlesex, U.K.: Penguin, 1970), p. 48.

28. See Linda K. Fuller, "From Tramps to Truth-Seekers: Images of the Homeless in the Motion Pictures," in Min, *Reading the Homeless,* esp. 169.

29. Kathleen Arnold, "Homelessness, Citizenship, and Identity" (Ph.D. diss., UCLA, 1998), p. 231.

30. Thomas Dumm, *United States* (Ithaca: Cornell University Press, 1994), pp. 169, 162 (emphasis added).

31. Ibid., pp. 156, 163.

32. Robert Tier, "Restoring Order in Urban Public Spaces," *Texas Review of Law and Politics* 2, no. 2 (1998): 259, 261, 263.

33. Affidavit of Dr. Donald Burnes and Alice Baum in *Joyce v. San Francisco*, quoted in Tier, "Restoring Order," p. 263.

34. Tier, "Restoring Order," p. 264.

35. Howard M. Bahr, *Skid Row: An Introduction to Disaffiliation* (New York: Oxford University Press, 1973); Howard M. Bahr and Theodore Caplow, *Old Men Drunk and Sober* (New York: New York University Press, 1973).

36. Bahr, *Skid Row,* pp. 41 (emphasis added), 42.

37. Charles Hoch and Robert A. Slayton, *New Homeless and Old: Community and the Skid Row Hotel* (Philadelphia: Temple University Press, 1989).

38. Doug Stenberg, "Tom's a-Cold: Transformation and Redemption in *King Lear* and *The Fisher King,*" *Literature Film Quarterly* 22, no. 3 (1994): 167.

39. Fuller, "From Tramps to Truth-Seekers," p. 169.

40. Richard LaGravenese, *The Fisher King: The Book of the Film* (New York: Applause Theater, 1991), pp. 62–63.

41. Ibid., p. 59.

42. Piven and Cloward, *Regulating the Poor,* p. 3.

43. LaGravenese, *Fisher King,* pp. 111–112.

44. Perhaps as recognition of the need to supplement the sit-com scene as decisive, the original film script included a subsequent scene in which Jack returns to one of Parry's hangouts only to find the "hippie bum" being carted away, dead, in an ambulance. Disney rejected the scene as "too dark." (See Richard LaGravenese, "In Search of the Holy Reel," in *Fisher King.*)

45. Christine Di Stefano, "Autonomy in the Light of Difference," in *Revisioning the Political: Feminist Reconstructions of Traditional Concepts in Western Political Theory,* ed. Nancy J. Hirshmann and Christine Di Stefano (Boulder, Colo.: Westview, 1996), p.

107. See also Iris Young, *Justice and the Politics of Difference* (Princeton: Princeton University Press, 1990), chapter 5.

46. Hopper and Baumohl, "Redefining the Cursed Word," pp. 4–5. Arnold ("Homelessness," p. 7) suggests that the homeless are an "uncanny Other, both familiar and yet strange."

47. For the importance of a "political institutional" approach to identity/difference relations in addition to psychoanalyses of culture, see Susan Bickford, "Constructing Inequality: City Spaces and the Architecture of Citizenship," *Political Theory* 28 (June 2000): 366.

48. Giorgio Agamben, *Homo Sacer: Sovereign Power and Bare Life,* trans. Daniel Heller-Roazen (Stanford: Stanford University Press, 1998), pp. 2, 7.

49. Ibid., pp. 83, 109, 7.

50. Ibid., pp. 28, 110.

51. Peter Fitzpatrick, "Bare Sovereignty: *Homo Sacer* and the Insistence of Law," *Theory and Event* 5, no. 2 (2001): para. 6.

52. Agamben, in *Homo Sacer,* seeks to disconnect the doubleness of the ban from any account of the duality of sacredness itself (rejecting this treatment of the sacred, as both holy and impure) as a symptom of the modern psychologizing of religious experience. As Fitzpatrick writes ("Bare Sovereignty," para. 9), "In *Homo Sacer . . .* there is a stark but inexplicit reversal of this standard idea of the sacred. The ambivalence is now denied and the transgressive attributed to a modern neurosis." Agamben's purpose, however, I think is to assert that any ambiguity or ambivalence derives from the doubleness of the ban itself (*Homo Sacer,* p. 110). Bare life is both sacred and profane, but this duality emerges from politics, not religion.

53. Agamben, *Language and Death: The Place of Negativity,* trans. Karen E. Pinkus with Michael Hardt (Minneapolis: University of Minnesota Press. 1991), p. 105.

54. Agamben, *Homo Sacer,* p. 83.

55. Ibid., p. 110. The ban, Agamben writes, originally meant both excluded and free.

56. See Agamben, *Homo Sacer,* p. 9; and Fitzpatrick, "Bare Sovereignty," para. 13.

57. Agamben, *Homo Sacer,* pp. 133–134.

58. Ibid., pp. 9, 106 (original emphasis).

59. As Nassar Hussain and Melissa Ptacek write in "Thresholds: Sovereignty and the Sacred," *Law and Society Review* 34 (2000): 512, "Another version of this question would ask if the citizen is really a fiction, as Agamben asserts, or rather a precarious reality that grants (even if the fiction, perhaps necessarily, describes this as a preservation of) our 'natural' rights."

60. Agamben, *Homo Sacer,* p. 181.

61. Failer ("Homelessness," p. 250) describes subordinate legal statuses within the contemporary liberal state as "relics of the law of persons" and "persisting echoes of the old system." In chapter 1, though, I explore some of the discontinuities between contemporary exclusions of homeless persons from full citizenship and the earlier regime of vagrancy law.

62. Thus, Agamben's account of the political isolation of bare life as a founding act of sovereign power complements Judith Failer's analysis of homelessness as a legal status.

63. On the problems with such an approach, see Andrew Norris, "Giorgio Agamben and the Politics of the Living Dead," *Diacritics* 30, no. 4 (2000): 51.

64. Hannah Arendt, *The Origins of Totalitarianism* (San Diego, Calif.: Harcourt, Brace, 1973), p. 296. See also Norris, "Giorgio Agamben," p. 51.

65. William Connolly, *The Ethos of Pluralization* (Minneapolis: University of Minnesota Press, 1995), pp. 88, 184 (emphasis in original).

66. Breakaway nationalist movements each seeking its own national home lead to an endlessly repeated process of partition.

67. Nicholas Xenos, "Refugees: The Modern Political Condition," *Alternatives* 18 (1993): 427. Interestingly, one of Agamben's few concrete proposals for responding to the situation of refugees manifests the pluralizing impulse, the proposal to make Jerusalem the capital of two states simultaneously: "Instead of two national states separated by uncertain and threatening boundaries, it might be possible to imagine two political communities insisting on the same region and in a condition of exodus from each other." Giorgio Agamben, *Means without End*, trans. Vincenzo Binetti and Cesare Casarino (Minneapolis: University of Minnesota Press, 2000), p. 24.

68. Connolly, *Ethos of Pluralization*, pp. 88, xii. Samira Kawash, "Safe House? Body, Building, and the Question of Security," *Cultural Critique* 45 (spring 2000): 185–221, discusses the increasing preoccupation with security as fortification in contemporary constructions (both material and ideal) of home.

69. Connolly, *Ethos of Pluralization*, p. 198.

70. Ibid., p. 180.

71. Richard Sennett, *Flesh and Stone: The Body and the City in Western Civilization* (New York: Norton, 1994), pp. 309–310.

72. Hannah Arendt, *The Human Condition* (Chicago: University of Chicago Press, 1958).

1. FROM VAGRANCY LAW TO CONTEMPORARY ANTI-HOMELESS POLICY

1. Simon, "Towns without Pity," pp. 633–634.

.2. Robert Humphreys, *No Fixed Abode: A History of Responses to the Roofless and Rootless in Britain* (New York: St. Martin's, 1999), p. 1.

3. Mitchell, "Annihilation of Space by Law," p. 306.

4. Robert Tier, "Maintaining Safety and Civility in Public Spaces: A Constitutional Approach to Aggressive Begging," *Louisiana Law Review* 54 (1993): 300, 303, 294.

5. To be sure, my own account, following Agamben, of the relationship between sovereign power and bare life may suffer in a similar way from the assertion of an ahistorical dynamic of political exclusion. Agamben's approach, however, is sensitive to historical shifts in the regulation of bare life—from *homo sacer* in Roman law to the modern refugee's relation to a modern regime of natural, human rights, for instance.

6. Michel Foucault, *Madness and Civilization: A History of Insanity in the Age of Reason*, trans. Richard Howard (New York: Vintage, 1988), pp. 46, 56, 57.

7. A. L. Beier, *The Problem of the Poor in Tudor and Early Stuart England* (London: Methuen, 1983), pp. 6, 18.

8. Robert Hitchcock, *A Politic Plat for the Honour of the Prince, the Great Profit of the Public State, Relief of the Poor, Preservation of the Rich, Reformation of Rogues and Idle Persons, and the Wealth of Thousands That Know Not How to Live* (1580), quoted in A. L. Beier, *Masterless Men: The Vagrancy Problem in England, 1560–1640* (London: Methuen, 1985), p. 150.

9. Beier, *Masterless Men*, p. 164.

10. William J. Chambliss, "The Law of Vagrancy," in *Crime and the Legal Process*, ed. William J. Chambliss (New York: McGraw-Hill, 1969), pp. 51–62.

11. Tier, "Maintaining Safety," p. 298.

12. Kusmer, *Down and Out*, pp. 137, 38, 47.

13. Caleb Foote, "Vagrancy-Type Law and Its Administration," in Chambliss, *Crime and the Legal Process*, p. 310.

14. William Blackstone, *Commentaries on the Laws of England,* vol. 4, *Of Public Wrongs (1769),* facsimile of the first edition (1765–1769; Chicago: University of Chicago Press, 1979), p. 162.

15. Foote, "Vagrancy-type Law," p. 299.

16. Blackstone, *Commentaries,* pp. 169, 170.

17. Blackstone, *Commentaries,* pp. 170–171.

18. Blackstone, *Commentaries,* pp. 174–175.

19. Alan Hunt, *Governance of the Consuming Passions: A History of Sumptuary Law* (New York: St. Martin's, 1996), pp. 285, 290, 274.

20. Vagrancy ordinances were also struck down by lower courts on the grounds that they criminalized status, which, in an extension of the doctrine on status crimes in *Robinson v. California,* 370 U.S. 660 (1962), constituted cruel and unusual punishment in violation of the Eighth Amendment (see Simon, "Towns without Pity," p. 642).

21. Jacksonville Ordinance Code § 26–57, quoted in *Papachristou v. City of Jacksonville,* 405 U.S. 156 (1972), 156–157 n. 1.

22. *Papachristou v. Jacksonville,* 161.

23. *Ledwith v. Roberts* (1937), quoted in *Papachristou v. Jacksonville,* 162.

24. *Papachristou v. Jacksonville,* 162, 164. The California appeals court performs a similar subversion in *Tobe v. Santa Ana,* describing Santa Ana's camping ban as unconstitutionally vague and overbroad (see chapter 5).

25. *Papachristou v. Jacksonville,* 169.

26. Daniel Bell, *The Cultural Contradictions of Capitalism* (New York: Basic Books, 1976).

27. Warren I. Susman, *Culture as History: The Transformation of American Society in the Twentieth Century* (New York: Pantheon, 1984), p. xx, cited in Lendol Calder, *Financing the American Dream: A Cultural History of Consumer Credit* (Princeton: Princeton University Press, 1999), pp. 8–9.

28. Jean Baudrillard, "Consumer Society," in *Consumer Society in American History: A Reader,* ed. Lawrence B. Glickman (Ithaca: Cornell University Press, 1999), pp. 49, 51.

29. Nikolas Rose, *Powers of Freedom: Reframing Political Thought* (Cambridge, U.K.: Cambridge University Press, 1999), p. 166.

30. Baudrillard, "Consumer Society," p. 51.

31. Rose, *Powers of Freedom,* pp. 87, 164.

32. See Deutsche, *Evictions,* p. 57; Gerald Frug, "Public Cities/Private Cities" (paper presented at the Law and Society Association annual meeting, Miami, Florida, 2000); and Bickford, "Constructing Inequality."

33. Oskar Negt and Alexander Kluge, *Public Sphere and Experience,* trans. Peter Labanyi, Jamie Owen Daniel, and Assenka Oksiloff (Minneapolis: University of Minnesota Press, 1993), quoted in Deutsche, *Evictions,* p. 59. See also Frug, "Public Cities/Private Cities," p. 9.

34. Bickford, "Constructing Inequality," p. 356.

35. Mike Davis, *City of Quartz* (New York: Vintage, 1992), p. 226; Clarissa Ryle Hayward, "Between 'The Street' and 'The Mall': Social Space and Democratic Possibility" (paper presented at the Midwest Political Science Association meeting, Chicago, 2001), pp. 3, 6. Hayward prefers "nonpublic" to "postpublic" precisely to avoid the dangers of nostalgia for an "authentic" public space that we have supposedly lost. The idea of "nonpublic" space, however, gets at only one side of the dynamic (exclusion, purification, etc.); like "postpublic" space, it misses the constitution of a "public" through exclusionary processes.

36. Hayward, ("Between 'The Street' and 'The Mall,'" p. 3) identifies these as features of "nonpublic urban space."

37. Deutsche, *Evictions*, p. 283.

38. Ibid., p. 290. This is also Kawash's approach ("The Homeless Body") in examining how a "disembodied" public is constituted through the war against the homeless.

39. Hayward, "Between 'The Street' and 'The Mall,'" p. 14. Hayward ultimately expresses reservations about this ideal of publicness, urging a reorientation of democratic theory and practice aspiring "not to realize the ideal of 'the street,' so much as to challenge the inter-municipal political inequalities produced by local autonomy in the context of spatial differentiation" (p. 19).

40. Bickford, "Constructing Inequality," p. 358.

41. Deutsche, *Evictions*, pp. 289, 322.

42. Connolly, *Ethos of Pluralization*, p. xiv.

43. Bickford, "Constructing Inequality," p. 361.

44. Deutsche, *Evictions*, p. 278.

45. Mair, "The Homeless and the Postindustrial City," pp. 352, 362, 363. See also David Wagner, *Checkerboard Square: Culture and Resistance in a Homeless Community* (Boulder, Colo.: Westview, 1993); and Talmadge Wright, *Out of Place: Homeless Mobilizations, Subcities, and Contested Landscapes* (Albany: State University of New York Press, 1997), for ethnographies of homeless populations as resistant subcultures.

46. Santa Monica's aggressive solicitation ordinance, quoted in *Doucette v. Santa Monica*, 955 F. Supp. 1192 (C.D. Cal. September 30, 1996). The federal district court upheld the ordinance as constitutional.

47. Prior to the passage of an aggressive panhandling ordinance, the Baltimore City Council commissioned a study titled "Persons Causing Anxiety." The study is cited in *Patton v. Baltimore City*, Civil No. S93–2389 (D. Md. August 19, 1994) (Memorandum Opinion).

48. These new legal barriers around the consumptive pathways of middle-class urban life extend even to the consumption of refuse: several cities have made it illegal to search through public trash bins.

49. David A. Snow and Leon Anderson, *Down on Their Luck: A Study of Homeless Street People* (Berkeley: University of California Press, 1993), p. 104.

50. The targeting of consumption by the homeless reflects what Anne Norton, *Republic of Signs* (Chicago: University of Chicago Press, 1993), p. 58, sees as a general anxiety in American popular culture surrounding the consumptive practices of marginalized groups.

51. Kawash, "Homeless Body," pp. 329–330.

52. See William M. Berg, "*Roulette v. City of Seattle* : A City Lives with Its Homeless," *Seattle University Law Review* 18 (1994): 170–171, for full text of the ordinance.

53. *Roulette v. City of Seattle*, 850 F. Supp 1442 (W.D. Wash. 1994), 1445; affirmed, 97 F. 3d 300 (9th Cir. 1996).

54. Mark Sidran, quoted in Constantine Angelos, "Opponents of Sidewalk Ordinance File Challenge," *Seattle Times*, November 11, 1993, B-1.

55. Defendants' Memorandum cited in Berg, "*Roulette,*" p. 172.

56. Sennett, *Flesh and Stone*, pp. 309–310.

57. For more on the ideology of motion in punitive anti-homeless policy, see Jeremy Waldron, "Homelessness and the Issue of Freedom," *UCLA Law Review* 39 (December 1991): 301.

58. Mark Sidran, "Establishing Standards of Civil Behavior," *Seattle Times*, August 10, 1994, B-5. Sidran's insistence upon using the word "lounging" in his brief to the

Ninth Circuit Court of Appeals seems to call forth notions of "idleness" that hark back to vagrancy law. Sidran says he uses this term to encompass both sitting and lying down on sidewalks, but the word connotes a kind of irresponsible leisure and passivity that rhetorically bolsters his argument.

59. *Roulette v. City of Seattle* (1996), 302.

60. Mitchell, "Annihilation of Space," p. 321.

61. See the chapter "Spatiality and Policy Discourse: Reading the Global City," in Michael Shapiro, *Reading the Postmodern Polity* (Minneapolis: University of Minnesota Press, 1992).

62. Kawash, "Homeless Body," pp. 320, 325.

63. Seattle, Wash., Code 15.48.040–050, cited in Berg, "*Roulette,*" pp. 170–171 n. 173.

64. Baltimore city had a vagrancy law on the books (repealed approximately three months after passage of the aggressive-panhandling law) which, echoing the statute struck down by the Supreme Court in *Papachristou,* defines "pauper" as one who "has no visible means of maintenance from property or personal labor or is not permanently supported by his or her friends or relatives and lives idle without employment"; a "habitual beggar" as someone who panhandles on the streets; and a "vagrant" as a wanderer in public space with no fixed abode (cited in *Patton v. Baltimore City,* 7).

65. "Aggressive Panhandling Ordinance," Ordinance 275, Baltimore Md., Code art. 19, § 249 (1994), cited in *Patton v. Baltimore City,* 6.

66. Ordinance 1768, cited in *Doucette v. Santa Monica,* 1201.

67. The combination of the punitive ban on bare life and normalizing strategies of assimilation is a combination of (Agamben's) sovereignty and (Foucault's) biopower—what Fitzpatrick ("Bare Sovereignty," para. 14) terms "'the commandment' . . . to death *and* to life, to a negating exclusion and to an encompassing inclusion." See also Arnold, "Homelessness," for a discussion of these two strategies in Foucauldian terms.

68. Kawash, "Homeless Body," p. 321.

69. North Beach Citizens, "Community Coupons" (2001), http://www.north-beachcitizens.org/html/cc.html (emphasis added). Thanks to Patchen Markell for informing me about this program.

70. North Beach Citizens, "About Us" (2001), http://www.northbeachcitizens.org/html/au.html#step.

71. See Davis, *City of Quartz,* p. 224. The combination of welfare-state rollback and punitive-state intensification is also explored in Andrew Gamble, *The Free Economy and the Strong State* (London: Macmillan, 1994).

72. Robert Desjarlais, *Shelter Blues: Sanity and Selfhood among the Homeless* (Philadelphia: University of Pennsylvania Press, 1997), p. 104.

73. Sanford F. Schram, *After Welfare: The Culture of Postindustrial Social Policy* (New York: New York University Press, 2000).

74. While the Supreme Court in *Papachristou v. Jacksonville* overturned a vagrancy law for vagueness—failing to give notice to a citizen of what conduct is prohibited, and criminalizing conduct considered innocent by modern standards—lower federal courts and state courts around the same time also struck down vagrancy laws on the grounds that they punished status, not conduct, in violation of the Eighth Amendment.

75. George L. Kelling and Catherine M. Coles, *Fixing Broken Windows* (New York: Free Press, 1996), pp. 40, 51, 57.

76. Arendt, *Origins,* p. 286.

77. This criminalization of the homeless is linked to other punitive politics of "individual responsibility," such as welfare reform. In the context of welfare reform and

the discourse of "personal responsibility," Schram (*After Welfare*, p. 53) argues "The text of behavior is in need of a subtext of identity, added after the fact to lend coherence to what is described." Enter the "welfare queen"—the accountable, choosing subject behind the irresponsible deeds: "Welfare discourse calls for its own welfare queens in order to make its criticisms convincing and the behavior it condemns as the product of people's choices." In addition, the development of the status/conduct distinction connects anti-homeless policy with the "Don't Ask, Don't Tell, Don't Pursue" policy of the armed forces concerning gays and lesbians. Whereas the old military policy made *being* gay or lesbian itself grounds for discharge, and vagrancy law made the status of being a vagrant or "habitual loafer" a crime, the newer policies articulate a focus on conduct. Nevertheless, both sets of policies perform a double gesture: claiming to provide protection to "being" by "merely" prohibiting certain harmful and disruptive "doings," yet deconstructing *being* into its various doings so as to target the being itself. The military's "Don't Ask, Don't Tell" policy, like the public-space ordinances concerning panhandling and public sleeping, demonstrates how the status/conduct distinction gets manipulated in ways that superficially accord legal protection to disfavored minorities while underneath they expand the net of illegalities to which such persons are subject. Janet Halley shows how the move from status- to conduct-based regulation is really a "bad faith" claim that enables the regulation of status to proceed "with new subtlety." See Francisco Valdes, "Sexual Minorities in the Military: Charting the Constitutional Frontiers of Status and Conduct," *Creighton Law Review* 27 (1994): 473–474; and Janet E. Halley, *Don't: A Reader's Guide to the Military's Anti-Gay Policy* (Durham, N.C.: Duke University Press, 1999), p. 63.

78. Sidran, "Establishing Standards of Civil Behavior," B-5.

79. This discourse manifests the combination of a "myth of community" emphasizing harmony and an ethic of rugged individualism emphasizing personal responsibility. See the concluding chapter in Carol J. Greenhouse, Barbara Yngvesson, and David Engel, *Law and Community in Three American Towns* (Ithaca: Cornell University Press, 1994).

80. Kelling and Coles, *Fixing Broken Windows*, p. 20.

81. James Q. Wilson and George L. Kelling, "Broken Windows: The Police and Neighborhood Safety," *Atlantic Monthly*, March 1982, p. 34.

82. Schram, *After Welfare*, p. 53.

83. Kelling and Coles, *Fixing Broken Windows*, p. 26.

84. Security Task Force Report, p. 11, cited in *Patton v. Baltimore City*, 5.

85. Richard Sennett, *The Uses of Disorder* (New York: Norton, 1970), pp. 138–139 (emphasis added), 82, 145.

86. Bickford, "Constructing Inequality," pp. 363, 365, 366.

87. Ibid., p. 362.

88. Mitchell Duneier, *Sidewalk* (New York: Farrar, Straus & Giroux, 1999), pp. 43, 71.

89. Ibid., p. 289.

2. THE LEGAL CONSTRUCTION OF THE HOMELESS AS BARE LIFE

1. For a full account of the range of ordinances in effect and the various rulings of federal district and appellate courts, and state courts see NLCHP, *Out of Sight—Out of Mind?* and *Illegal to be Homeless*.

2. In *Robinson v. California*, the Supreme Court found that punishing a person for being a drug addict constituted cruel and unusual punishment for status.

3. The idea of homelessness as a process of disaffiliation from society was first developed in the sociology of Bahr, *Skid Row;* and Bahr and Caplow, *Old Men Drunk and Sober.*

4. The major exception is Wes Daniels, "'Derelicts, Recurring Misfortune, Economic Hard Times, and Lifestyle Choices: Judicial Images of Homeless Litigants and Implications for Legal Advocates," *Buffalo Law Review* 45 (fall 1997): 687–737.

5. Failer, "Homelessness," p. 257.

6. *Pottinger v. City of Miami,* 810 F. Supp. 1551 (S.D. Fla. 1992); remanded, 40 F. 3d 1155 (11th Cir. 1994).

7. *Joyce v. San Francisco,* 857.

8. *Robinson v. California,* cited in *Joyce v. San Francisco.*

9. *Joyce v. San Francisco,* 857.

10. Ibid. (emphasis added).

11. Halley, *Don't,* pp. 31, 30.

12. *Joyce v San Francisco,* 857, 858 (emphasis added).

13. William Connolly, *Political Theory and Modernity* (Oxford: Basil Blackwell, 1988), p. 156.

14. *Love v. City of Chicago* No. 96-C-0396, 1996 U.S. Dist. LEXIS 16041 (N.D. Ill. October 23, 1996), 7, 14–15; WL 60804, 1998 U.S. Dist. LEXIS 1386 (N.D. Ill. February 5, 1998).

15. One could argue that consumption by homeless persons threatens the coherence of the consumptive public sphere.

16. *Love v. Chicago* (1998), 15, 13, 31.

17. Ibid., 36 (emphasis added).

18. Kawash, "Homeless Body," p. 331.

19. See Norton, *Republic of Signs.* And as I argued in chapter 1, it is consumption by middle-class city dwellers that is being protected by these ordinances and police practices.

20. Ted Kilian, "Public and Private, Power and Space," in *The Production of Public Space,* ed. Andrew Light and Jonathan Smith (New York: Rowman, Littlefield, 1998), pp. 115–134.

21. Daniela Gobetti, "Humankind as a System: Private and Public Agency at the Origins of Modern Liberalism," in *Public and Private in Thought and Practice,* ed. Jeff Weintraub and Krishan Kumar (Chicago: University of Chicago Press, 1997), p. 104.

22. The jurisdictional distinction between the state and the individual is a distinction formed within civil society and founded upon the private realm of family and household, argues Carole Pateman, "Feminist Critiques of the Public/Private Dichotomy," in *The Disorder of Women* (Cambridge: Polity, 1990), pp. 121–122. See also Jeff Weintraub, "The Theory and Politics of the Public/Private Distinction" in Weintraub and Kumar, *Public and Private.*

23. The court imagines the homeless to be unduly burdening the city with their demand that the city "insure" their property against theft (by vandals?), when plaintiffs are in fact simply asking city officials to stop confiscating the property themselves.

24. I am grateful to Samira Kawash, personal communication, for this formulation.

25. These cases are: *Pottinger v. Miami* (1992); *Johnson v. Dallas* (1994); *Tobe v. City of Santa Ana* (1994).

26. *Tobe v. City of Santa Ana* (1995); and *Johnson v. Dallas* (1995). Neither of these procedural reversals delved substantially into the substance of the Eighth Amendment challenge. The *Johnson* court simply ruled that since the plaintiffs had not been convicted of a crime under the sleeping ordinance, they did not have standing. Similarly, the *Tobe* court claimed that the plaintiffs had not perfected an "as-applied" challenge to the

ordinance, and the camping ban, on its face, did not unconstitutionally punish the status of homelessness since the words of the statute made no distinction between the homeless and the housed. I discuss *Tobe* in greater depth in the conclusion.

27. Edward J. Walters, "No Way Out: Eighth Amendment Protection for Do-Or-Die Acts of the Homeless," *University of Chicago Law Review* 62 (1995): 1643, 1645.

28. Ibid., 1620. See also Juliette Smith "Arresting the Homeless for Sleeping in Public: A Paradigm for Expanding the Robinson Doctrine," *Columbia Journal of Law and Social Problems* 29 (1996): 293–335; and Foscarinis, "Downward Spiral" pp. 1–63.

29. Tier, "Maintaining Safety," p. 322; Tier, "Restoring Order," p. 268.

30. Daniels, "Derelicts," p. 706.

31. *Pottinger v. Miami* (1992), 1563, 1564.

32. Ibid., 1564.

33. Ibid.

34. *Pottinger v. Miami*, No. 88–2406-CIV-ATKINS (S.D. Fla. April 7, 1995), slip op, 8 n. 7, quoted in Daniels, "Derelicts," p. 731.

35. *Johnson v. City of Dallas* (1994), 350.

36. Ibid.

37. As Daniels ("Derelicts," p. 731) argues, "Even when criminalization lawsuits are successful, the rights established are negative rights, in that at most they restrict the ways in which government can punish homeless people for engaging in certain types of behavior. . . . And the state can remove the constitutional barrier to official punitive measures, a barrier cognizable only in the context of 'involuntary' homelessness, by offering homeless people even the most minimal of alternatives, such as 'beds' in emergency shelters, or even a 'shelter's floor.'"

38. Kawash, "Homeless Body," p. 331.

39. An illuminating contrast is presented by the charitable efforts to assist victims of Hurricane Andrew: Joseph B. Treaser, "After the Storm: New Home Humble, but Is Welcomed," *New York Times,* September 3, 1992, p. A-18, reported that National Guard troops spruced up the encampments with various amenities and then went out and talked up the amenities to disaster victims in an attempt to persuade them to come to the camps.

40. Daniels, "Derelicts," p. 731.

41. NLCHP, *Illegal to be Homeless,* p. 67.

42. Ibid. The shelter is a hybrid space, neither simply a space of confinement nor simply a space of refuge and safety. Chapter 3 explores the stigmatizing effects of homeless shelters. Here, my concern is with the legal constitution of the shelter as a particular kind of space.

43. *Joel v. Orlando,* 232 F. 3d 1353 (11th Cir. 2000), 1362; cert denied 149 L. Ed. 2d 480 (2001).

44. Waldron, "Homelessness," p. 303; Dumm, *United States.*

45. The subsequent history of the case is complicated: An appeals court reversed Judge Lippmann, but while the case was on appeal to the state supreme court, Brown was ordered released from Bellevue rather than forcibly medicated. See *In the Matter of Billie Boggs, Petitioner,* 136 Misc. 2d 1082 (NY Supreme Ct., NY County, 1987); reversed 132 A.D. 2d 340 (1987); appeal dismissed as moot, 70 N.Y. 2d 972 (1988). For details of the case history, see Judith Failer, *Who Qualifies For Rights: Homelessness, Mental Illness, and Civil Commitment* (Ithaca: Cornell University Press, 2002).

46. *In the Matter of Billie Boggs, Petitioner* (1987), 411.

47. Ibid., 412.

48. Ibid.

3. REDISTRIBUTION, RECOGNITION, AND THE SOVEREIGN BAN

1. See *Tobe v. Santa Ana* (1994), 387–388, 392 n. 4, discussing municipal memoranda that articulate the goal of forcing homeless people out of Santa Ana entirely. The appeals court decision was overturned by the California Supreme Court in *Tobe v. Santa Ana* (1995). See chapter 5.

2. See Foscarinis, "Downward Spiral."

3. Quoted in Michelle Roberts, "Homeless Camping Ban Voided," *Oregonian,* September 28, 2000, p. E-1. Katz was responding to the ruling in *State v. Wicks,* Nos. 2711742 and 2711743 (Ore. Cir. Ct. Multnomah County, 2000).

4. Evelyn Nieves, "Santa Cruz Journal: Furious Debate Rages on Sleeping in Public," *New York Times,* May 28, 2000, A-14.

5. Kelling and Coles, *Broken Windows,* pp. 228, 220.

6. See, for instance, Michael W. McCann, *Rights at Work: Pay Equity Reform and the Politics of Legal Mobilization* (Chicago: University of Chicago Press, 1994), pp. 139–140.

7. Fraser's works are cited in notes 9–13.

8. I borrow this term from Bonnie Honig, *Political Theory and the Displacement of Politics* (Ithaca: Cornell University Press, 1993).

9. Nancy Fraser, *Justice Interruptus: Critical Reflections on the 'Postsocialist' Condition* (New York: Routledge, 1997), p. 2. The first version of Fraser's argument was published in "From Redistribution to Recognition? Dilemmas of Justice in a 'Post-Socialist' Age," *New Left Review* 212 (July/August 1995): 68–93, a revised version of which appears as the first chapter in *Justice Interruptions.*

10. Nancy Fraser, "A Rejoinder to Iris Young," *New Left Review* 223 (May/June 1997): 126.

11. Fraser, "From Redistribution to Recognition?" pp. 69, 88.

12. Fraser, *Justice Interruptus,* p. 25.

13. In four subsequent articles, Fraser has clarified, and complicated, her argument: "Heterosexism, Misrecognition, and Capitalism: A Response to Judith Butler," *New Left Review* 1/228 (March/April 1998): 140–149; "A Rejoinder to Iris Young"; "Social Justice in the Age of Identity Politics: Redistribution, Recognition, and Participation," in *Tanner Lectures on Human Values* (Salt Lake City: University of Utah Press, 1997), pp. 1–67; and "Rethinking Recognition," *New Left Review* 3 (May/June 2000): 107–120. In "Social Justice," Fraser argues that different recognition strategies are needed at different times and in different contexts, and judgments about the appropriateness of a deconstructive approach or a multiculturalist approach cannot be made theoretically and a priori. Fraser argues further that "real-world" social classes are probably bivalent, not purely economic, and that an exploited class might need a cultural politics of recognition in order to combat internalized stereotypes and push for redistributive justice. Finally, in "Rethinking Recognition," she urges a shift from an "identity" model of recognition politics to a "status" model. Yet even this status model does not entail specific attention to the production of specifically political-status injustices such as the state's relegation of some to a subordinate legal status. Fraser's model is more centered on the social than on the political.

14. I am not suggesting that the political theorists discussed below support punitive policies such as public-sleeping bans. My point rather is to show certain resonances between the respective arguments.

15. David Harvey, "Class Relations, Social Justice, and the Politics of Difference," in *Place and the Politics of Identity,* ed. Michael Keith and Steve Pile (London: Routledge, 1993), p. 64.

16. Edward Said, "The Politics of Knowledge," *Raritan* 11 (1991): 31.

17. Fraser ("From Redistribution to Recognition," p. 76.) uses this phrase to describe the group dedifferentiating goal of a socialist revolution in relation to the proletariat.

18. Ibid.

19. Wright, *Out of Place*, p. 12.

20. Peter Marcuse, "Neutralizing Homelessness," *Socialist Review* 18 (1988): 73–74.

21. At least exploitation is not one of the defining markers of the condition of homelessness. Many homeless men work as day laborers; for example, a company called, "Labor Ready" exists to facilitate (and profit from) day labor. But any exploitation is a function of homeless person's status as a subpopulation of the working class, not a function of homelessness per se.

22. See Waldron, "Homelessness," p. 299.

23. Fraser, *Justice Interruptus*, p. 17.

24. Further, I do not believe that much rides on the question of whether homelessness is an economic phenomenon with derivative cultural injustices or a bivalent category with autonomous economic and cultural injustice. What is important is acknowledging and exploring the cultural and economic injustices.

25. Fraser, "Social Justice," p. 19.

26. This categorization of public forms of misrecognition and stigmatization of the homeless draws upon David Wagner's threefold distinction (*Checkerboard Square*, p. 176) between a conservative-individualist frame, a charity/compassion frame and a therapeutic frame.

27. These four forms of misrecognition are not clearly distinct from one another in actual discourses and practices; furthermore, the bare-life predicament significantly inflects all four.

28. Patchen Markell, "The Recognition of Politics: A Comment on Emcke and Tully," *Constellations* 7, no. 4 (2000): 502.

29. Susan Bickford ("Constructing Inequality") insightfully analyzes practices of spatial segregation in U.S. cities and suburbs, which, by "zoning out" undesirable populations, make media representations all the more important as citizens' main source of information about those others whom they cease to contact in everyday life.

30. Richard Campbell and Jimmie L. Reeves, "Covering the Homeless: The Joyce Brown Story," *Critical Studies in Mass Communication* 6 (1989): 27–28. See also Jimmie L. Reeves, "Re-Covering the Homeless: Hindsights on the Joyce Brown Story," in Min, *Reading the Homeless*.

31. Campbell and Reeves, "Covering the Homeless," pp. 28, 29.

32. Desjarlais, *Shelter Blues*, pp. 124, 125.

33. Steven VanderStaay, *Street Lives: An Oral History of Homeless Americans* (Philadelphia: New Society, 1992), p. 24.

34. Sidran, "Establishing Standards of Civil Behavior."

35. See Kawash, "Homeless Body"; and Deutsche, *Evictions*.

36. VanderStaay, *Street Lives*, p. 24.

37. A compelling theory of injustice "must make visible and criticizable, both the cultural subtexts of apparently economic processes and the economic subtexts of apparently cultural practices" (Fraser, "Social Justice," p. 42).

38. Doug A. Timmer, D. Stanley Eitzen, and Kathryn D. Talley, *Paths to Homelessness* (Boulder, Colo.: Westview, 1994), p. 184.

39. See in particular Hoch and Slayton, *New Homeless and Old*, chap. 11.

40. Timmer, Eitzen, and Talley, *Paths to Homelessness*, p. 107.

41. See Bobby Burns, *Shelter: One Man's Journey from Homelessness to Hope* (Tucson: University of Arizona Press, 1998), pp. 32, 108–109, for a good description of the stigmatizing effects of an emergency shelter.

42. Hoch and Slayton, *New Homeless and Old,* pp. 227–228.

43. Arnold, "Homelessness," p. 224.

44. See Hoch and Slayton, *New Homeless and Old;* Timmer, Eitzen, and Talley, *Paths to Homelessness.*

45. Hoch and Slayton, *New Homeless and Old,* p. 219.

46. Sahlin, "Enclosure or Inclusion?" p. 21.

47. Michel Foucault, "The Subject and Power," in Herbert Dreyfus and Paul Rabinow, *Michel Foucault: Beyond Structuralism and Hermeneutics* (Chicago: University of Chicago Press, 1982), p. 208.

48. Timmer, Eitzen and Talley, *Paths to Homelessness,* pp. 104, 105.

49. Neil Swan, "In Birmingham Alabama: Access to Housing and Job Training Helps Recovering Homeless People Stay Drug Free" (1997), http://www.nida.nih.gov/NIDA_Notes/NNVol12N4/Access.html.

50. Timmer, Eitzen and Talley, *Paths to Homelessness,* p. 187.

51. NLCHP, *Illegal to be Homeless,* p. 73. As Kathleen Arnold writes ("Homelessness," p. 220), "Like a penal institution, a shelter can be the ultimate representation of the means to which the marginalized can be controlled, documented, observed and molded."

52. See Wagner, *Checkerboard Square;* and Hoch and Slayton, *New Homeless and Old.*

53. Michel Foucault, *Discipline and Punish,* trans. Alan Sheridan (New York: Vintage, 1979), p. 143.

54. Desjarlais, *Shelter Blues,* p. 104. This threat is well described in Elliot Liebow's study of shelters for homeless women, *Tell Them Who I Am: The Lives of Homeless Women* (New York: Penguin, 1995), pp. 121–122.

55. For Foucault's neglect of state power (notwithstanding the late essays on governmentality), see Brown, *States of Injury,* pp. 16–17. Agamben (*Homo Sacer,* p. 9) explicitly contends that his theory of sovereign power over bare life completes Foucault's account of modern biopower.

56. Fraser, "Social Justice," p. 55.

57. Treating the state as secondary, subsidiary to fundamental economic and cultural processes, may also help further the notion that the state as an agent of cultural injustice acts primarily in terms of the misrecognition (stigmatization) or nonrecognition (invisibility) of an already existing group. But treating the state as primary would point to its deeper "performative" role in constituting the very terms of identities and collectivities in the first place. Nation, race, and ethnicity appear from a state-centric viewpoint not as preexisting social entities which the political order correctly recognizes, misrecognizes, or fails to recognize at all but rather as productive classifications that are fundamentally tied to the political order, such as the status of bare life.

58. Brown, *States of Injury,* pp. 195, 18.

59. Fraser ("Rethinking Recognition," pp. 116–117) continues: "I do not develop this possibility here, however, but confine myself to maldistribution and misrecognition, while leaving the analysis of political obstacles to participatory parity for another occasion."

60. Myra Marx Ferree and William A. Gamson make a related point in their study of abortion politics in Germany and the U.S., "The Gendering of Governance and the Governance of Gender" (paper presented at the conference "Fifty Years of the Federal Republic of Germany through a Gendered Lens," University of North Carolina, 1999) pp.

1–2: "Nancy Fraser's useful distinction between redistribution and recognition as paradigms for justice rests in part on Weber's classic distinction between class, status and power. Unlike Weber, however, Fraser only utilizes the first two of these dimensions . . . The dimension of power is not wholly incorporated in either of these. Because the political relationship between individual and community is theoretically separable from the axes of cultural recognition of the actors and redistribution of their goods, there are distinctive issues of justice to be considered." See http://www.unc.edu/depts/europe/conferences/Germany_celeb9900/abstracts/marx%20ferree_myra.html.

61. "Tent City Not the Answer, but Real Solution Coming" (editorial), *Seattle Post-Intelligencer*, Wednesday May 10, 2000, http://seattlepi.nwsource.com/opinion/lessed/shtml.

62. Agamben, *Homo Sacer*, p. 28.

63. Mark Sidran letter, quoted in Bob Redmond, "Sidran: 'No Answer' for Homeless," *Real Change* 6 (July 1999): 4.

64. Arendt, *Origins of Totalitarianism*, pp. 295–296.

65. The National Coalition for the Homeless sponsors a Voting Rights Project that presses for the adoption of a model homeless registration voting act. An on-line listing of all fifty states' policies on registration for people living in shelters and on the streets is available at http://www.nationalhomeless.org/civilrights/voting.html#1.

66. Failer, "Homelessness," p. 250.

67. Wagner, *Checkerboard Square*, pp. 99, 104.

68. "Dignity Village is Not a Solution" (editorial), *Oregonian*, December 19, 2002, B6.

69. Wright, *Out of Place*, p. 255.

70. Ibid, pp. 282, 266.

71. Ibid, p. 227.

72. In making these distinctions I am inspired by, and draw upon, Fraser's earlier work on the politics of welfare and need interpretation—in particular the distinction between "official-political" and "discursive-political." See Nancy Fraser, *Unruly Practices* (Minneapolis: University of Minnesota Press, 1989), p. 166.

73. Fraser, *Justice Interruptus*, pp. 173–174.

74. James Tully, "Struggles over Recognition and Distribution," *Constellations* 7, no. 4 (2000): 469.

75. Tully ("Struggles," p. 472) does allow that theorists will still make observations about the goals of justice of particular movements, but he argues that their doing so will be an exercise of "practical reason," not "above the fray" theoretical truth. I agree with this claim, but I disagree with the need to prioritize "the struggles themselves as the primary thing." The problematic implication of this argument is that whereas comments on the goals of justice will be an exercise of mere practical reason, a theory of the democratic process in which those goals are put forth is an exercise of a different kind of reason altogether.

76. Connolly, *Ethos of Pluralization*, p. 184.

4. HOUSING DIVERSITY AND DEMOCRATIC PLURALISM

1. See Calvin Trillin, "U.S. Journal, San Francisco: 'Some Thoughts on the International Hotel Controversy,'" *New Yorker*, December 19, 1977, pp. 116–120; and Paul Groth, *Living Downtown: The History of Residential Hotels in the United States* (Berkeley: University of California Press, 1994). At long last, plans are underway to build on the site a 104-unit apartment complex for low-income elderly, an elementary school,

and a museum. The development is scheduled for completion in 2005. See Bernice Yeung, "The 'I' Is for Irony," *SFWeekly,* June 6, 2001, http://www.sfweekly.com/issues/2001–06–06/bayview.html, and Angela Watercutter, "Site in Manilatown Will Once Again House Elderly Tenants," *San Francisco Examiner,* August 5, 2002, http://www.examiner.com/headlines/default.jsp?story=n.manilatown.0805w.

2. Agamben, *Homo Sacer.* See the introduction and chapter 2, for fuller discussion of Agamben's concept of bare life.

3. Veness, "Home and Homelessness," discusses the strengthening of the home ideal and reduction of alternative forms of dwelling in the 1980s. Groth, *Living Downtown,* and Hoch and Slayton, *New Homeless and Old,* discuss in particular the disappearance of the SRO hotel.

4. This argument is a simplification of the literature. Veness ("Home and Homelessness"), for one, argues that the home ideal was most open in the 1970s, but she too sees a trend of consolidation through the 1970s around the modern nuclear family and its fully detached house and points to the end of the nineteenth century as a time when the types of housing were most numerous.

5. Kawash, "Safe House?" pp. 185–186; Nancy Rosenblum, *Membership and Morals* (Princeton: Princeton University Press, 1998), p. 122; Veness, "Home and Homelessness," pp. 460–462.

6. Bonnie Honig, "Difference, Dilemmas, and the Politics of Home," *Social Research* 61, no. 3 (1994): 567. See also Honig, *Political Theory and the Displacement of Politics;* Connolly, *Political Theory and Modernity* and *The Ethos of Pluralization;* and Chantal Mouffe, *The Return of the Political* (London: Verso, 1993).

7. See, for instance, Susan Okin, *Justice, Gender, and the Family* (New York: Basic Books, 1989); Pateman, "Feminist Critiques of the Public/Private Dichotomy"; and Christopher Philip Long, "A Fissure in the Distinction: Hannah Arendt, the Family, and the Public/Private Dichotomy," *Philosophy and Social Criticism* 24, no. 5 (1998): 85–104.

8. Groth, *Living Downtown,* p. 7.

9. Hoch and Slayton, *New Homeless and Old,* p. 23.

10. Pete Yamamoto quoted in Yeung, "The 'I' Is For Irony."

11. Hoch and Slayton, *New Homeless and Old,* p. 173.

12. Roy Lubove, *The Progressives and the Slums: Tenement House Reform in New York City, 1890–1917* (Pittsburgh: University of Pittsburgh Press, 1963), pp. 174, 98.

13. Hoch and Slayton, *New Homeless and Old,* p. 182; Hopper, "More Than Passing Strange."

14. Groth, *Living Downtown,* p. 295; Hoch and Slayton, *New Homeless and Old,* p. 188.

15. Hoch and Slayton, *New Homeless and Old,* pp. 173, 7. See also Hopper, "More Than Passing Strange."

16. Hoch and Slayton, *New Homeless and Old,* p. 219.

17. This is not to say that Progressive Era housing reformers read political theory or that there is some causal relationship between political theory texts and policy developments. Rather, it is to say that certain clusters of ideas, given more extended theoretical articulation by political theorists, are also present in the discourses of housing reform and are implicated in the reduction of housing options.

18. If, in Arendt's terms, the household as a sphere of withdrawal is essential to maintaining the plurality of the public sphere, I contend that such concern for the maintenance of plurality must be extended back to the realm of the household itself. A rigid

home ideal beyond contestation exacerbates the problems of displacement, of rightlessness, that Arendt identifies in her discussion of refugees. (I develop this argument below.)

19. I take the distinction between integrationist and participationist visions from Seyla Benhabib's contrast in *Situating the Self* (Cambridge, U.K.: Polity Press, 1997) between two forms of communitarianism: one that emphasizes participation in a community and in collective decision-making, and one that emphasizes integration of the individual into a tradition-based social order.

20. Arendt, *Origins of Totalitarianism*, p. 475; Hannah Arendt, *The Human Condition* (Chicago: University of Chicago Press, 1958), p. 57.

21. Arendt, *Human Condition*, pp. 30–31, 37, 64, 29–30.

22. Arendt, *Origins of Totalitarianism*, pp. 293, 296.

23. Sen. Charles Percy, campaign address, "A New Dawn for Our Cities" (Chicago, September 15, 1966), quoted in Peter Marcuse, "Residential Alienation, Homeownership, and the Limits of Shelter Policy," *Journal of Sociology and Social Welfare* 3 (November 1975): 193.

24. Lawrence Veiller, "The Housing Problem in American Cities," *Annals of the American Academy of Political and Social Science* 25 (1905): 253, 254.

25. Veiller, "Housing Problem," pp. 255–256.

26. Veiller, "Housing Problem," p. 256.

27. For an Arendtian account of the historical development of ideas of intimacy and their dangerous extension into political life, see Richard Sennett, *The Fall of Public Man* (New York: Norton, 1976), pp. 308–312.

28. Michael Walzer, *Spheres of Justice: A Defense of Pluralism and Equality* (New York: Basic Books, 1983), p. 9.

29. Michael Walzer, "Liberalism and the Art of Separation," *Political Theory* 12 (August 1984): 321, 315; Walzer, *Spheres of Justice*, p. 17.

30. Walzer, *Spheres of Justice*, pp. 229, 232.

31. Mary Douglas, "The Idea of Home: A Kind of Space," *Social Research* 58 (spring 1991): 297, 302 (citing Marcel Mauss, *The Gift*, trans. W. D. Halls [London: Routledge, 1990]), 305, 306.

32. Walzer, *Spheres of Justice*, p. 6.

33. Ibid., p. 19.

34. Walzer, *Interpretation and Social Criticism* (Cambridge, Mass: Harvard University Press, 1987), p. 14.

35. Ibid., pp. 14–15.

36. Franz Kafka, quoted in Walzer, *Interpretation*, p. 15.

37. Walzer, *Interpretation*, pp. 15–16.

38. Bonnie Honig ("Difference, Dilemmas, and the Politics of Home," p. 585) describes this ever expanding dream of home: "The phantasmatic imaginary of home (as safe haven in a heartless world) leaks into the politics of its bearers, animating a longing for a more homelike, (would-be) womb-like universe unriven by difference, conflicts, or dilemmas, a well-ordered and welcoming place."

39. Walzer, "Liberalism," p. 323.

40. Sennett, *Fall of Public Man*, p. 297.

41. See Lubove, *Progressives and the Slums*, pp. 229–230.

42. Groth, *Living Downtown*, p. 304.

43. Lawrence Veiller, *Housing Reform: A Hand-Book for Practical Use in American Cities* (New York: Charities Publication Committee, 1910), p. 109.

44. Ibid., pp. 113, 110.

45. Lubove, *Progressives and the Slums,* pp. 66, 82, 174.

46. Veiller, *Housing Reform,* p. 120.

47. Groth, *Living Downtown,* p. 214.

48. Shapiro, *Reading the Postmodern Polity,* p. 94.

49. Groth, *Living Downtown,* p. 230.

50. See Mark E. Kann, "Individualism, Civic Virtue, and Gender in America," in *Studies in American Political Development* (New Haven: Yale University Press, 1990), 4:46–81, on the ideal of civic virtue nurtured by women in the domestic sphere as tempering the unruly passions of individualistic male heads of household in American political thought.

51. The home ideal is noncommodified in the sense that relations between home-dwellers are not governed by the norms of buying and selling, as Mary Douglas ("Idea of Home") explains in the contrast between home and hotel. The home itself, however, is a kind of commodity—bought and sold in the market, and furnished with other commodities that, as we all know from catalogues, home-decorating magazines, and television advertising, are presented as precisely what turns a "house" into a "home."

52. See Kawash, "Safe House?" p. 194.

53. Kawash, "Safe House?" pp. 213, 192.

54. Connolly, *Ethos of Pluralization,* pp. 183, 194.

55. Ibid., p. xii: "The American pluralist imagination, in particular, remains too stingy, cramped, and defensive for the world we now inhabit."

56. See April Veness, "Neither Homed nor Homeless: Contested Definitions and the Personal Worlds of the Poor," *Political Geography* 12 (July 1993): 319–340, on the importance of resisting this relativist posture toward "home."

57. Robert Frost, "Mending Wall," in *Poems of Today: A Collection of the Contemporary Verse of American and Great Britian,* ed. Alice Cecilia Cooper (Modesto, Calif.: Ginn, 1924), p. 120.

CONCLUSION

1. *Clark v. Community for Creative Nonviolence* [CCNV], 468 U.S. 288 (1984), 292.

2. Ibid., 298.

3. *Metropolitan Council, Inc v. Safir,* 99 F. Supp. 2d 438 (SDNY 2000), 446, 447.

4. Ibid.

5. Ibid., 446 n. 11.

6. *Clark v. CCNV,* 296; *Metropolitan Council,* 446 n. 11.

7. *Metropolitan Council* 446.

8. Anatole France, *The Red Lily (Le Lys rouge),* trans. Winifred Stephens (London: John Lane, The Bodley Head, 1922), p. 95.

9. *Metropolitan Council,* 445, 446.

10. The ruling in *Clark* illustrates in a surprising way Claude Lefort's account in *Democracy and Political Theory,* trans. David Macey (Cambridge U.K.: Polity Press, 1988), of power in democracy as constituted by an empty space.

11. The North American Street Newspaper Association represents forty-seven member newspapers in U.S. cities. See http://www.speakeasy.org/nasna/.

12. Defendants' council (transcript), cited in *Metropolitan Council,* 446.

13. Agamben, *Homo Sacer,* p. 134.

14. Santa Ana Mun. Code, ch. 10, art. VIII, § 10–402, cited in *Tobe v. Santa Ana* (1994), 389 n. 3.

15. Although the appeals court upholds plaintiffs' Eighth Amendment claim, its logic is much less well developed than that of the federal district court opinions in *Pottinger* and *Johnson*, which similarly held that camping and public-sleeping bans violate the Eighth Amendment. See chapter 2 on the involuntariness argument and the accompanying vision of the homeless as bare life.

16. *Tobe v. Santa Ana* (1994), 394, 395.

17. Ibid., 395 n. 14.

18. The appeals court in *Tobe* also made the Eighth Amendment a basis for striking down the camping ban, cursorily citing the *Pottinger* case, but its discussion of homelessness as an involuntary status is less well developed than its the overbreadth and vagueness discussion.

19. *Tobe v. Santa Ana* (1995), 425.

20. Martin Heidegger, "Building Dwelling Thinking," in his *Basic Writings*, ed. David Farrell Krell (New York: HarperCollins, 1993), pp. 349, 350.

21. Iris Young, *Intersecting Voices: Dilemmas of Gender, Political Philosophy, and Policy* (Princeton: Princeton University Press, 1997), pp. 142, 135, 134, 152.

22. Kawash, "Safe House?"

23. Connolly writes: "To alter your recognition of difference . . . is to revise your own terms of self-recognition as well. Critical responsiveness thus moves on two registers: to redefine its relation to others a constituency must also modify the shape of its own identity" (*Ethos of Pluralization*, p. xvi).

24. Ibid., 26.

25. Bickford, "Constructing Inequality," pp. 369, 370.

26. Veness, "Neither Homed Nor Homeless," pp. 324–325.

27. Ibid.

28. Duneier, *Sidewalk*, p. 153.

29. Wagner, *Checkerboard Square*, p. 181; Hoch and Slayton, *New Homeless and Old*.

BIBLIOGRAPHY

Agamben, Giorgio. *Homo Sacer: Sovereign Power and Bare Life.* Trans. Daniel Heller Roazen. Stanford, Calif.: Stanford University Press, 1998.
——. *Language and Death: The Place of Negativity.* Trans. Karen E. Pinkus with Michael Hardt. Minneapolis: University of Minnesota Press, 1991.
——. *Means without End: Notes on Politics.* Trans. Vincenzo Binetti and Cesare Casarino. Minneapolis: University of Minnesota Press, 2000.
——. "We Refugees." Trans. Michael Rocke. *Symposium* 49 (summer 1995): 114–119.
Angelos, Constantine. "Opponents of Sidewalk Ordinance File Challenge." *Seattle Times,* November 11, 1993, p. B-1
Arendt, Hannah. *The Human Condition.* Chicago: University of Chicago Press, 1958.
——. *The Origins of Totalitarianism.* San Diego: Harcourt, Brace, 1973.
Arnold, Kathleen. "Homelessness, Citizenship, and Identity." Ph.D. diss., University of California, Los Angeles, 1998.
Atlanta Union Mission Website. 2001. http://www.aumcares.org.
Bahr, Howard M. *Skid Row: An Introduction to Disaffiliation.* New York: Oxford University Press, 1973.
Bahr, Howard M., and Theodore Caplow. *Old Men Drunk and Sober.* New York: New York University Press, 1973.
Baudrillard, Jean. "Consumer Society." In *Consumer Society in American History: A Reader,* ed. Lawrence B. Glickman. Ithaca: Cornell University Press, 1999.
Beier, A. L. *Masterless Men: The Vagrancy Problem in England 1560–1640.* London: Methuen, 1985.
——. *The Problem of the Poor in Tudor and Early Stuart England.* London: Methuen, 1983.
Bell, Daniel. *The Cultural Contradictions of Capitalism.* New York: Basic Books, 1976.
Benhabib, Seyla. "Citizens, Residents, and Aliens in a Changing World: Political Membership in the Global Era." *Social Research* 66 (fall 1999): 709–744.
——. *Situating the Self.* Cambridge, U.K.: Polity Press, 1997.
Berg, William M. "*Roulette v. City of Seattle* : A City Lives with Its Homeless." *Seattle University Law Review* 18 (1994): 147–195.

Bickford, Susan. "Constructing Inequality: City Spaces and the Architecture of Citizenship." *Political Theory* 28 (June 2000): 355–376.

Blackstone, William. *Commentaries on the Laws of England,* vol. 4, *Of Public Wrongs (1769).* Facsimile of first edition (1765–1769). Chicago: University of Chicago Press, 1979.

Bourdieu, Pierre. *Distinction: A Social Critique of the Judgment of Taste.* Trans. Richard Nice. Cambridge, Mass.: Harvard University Press, 1984.

Brown, Wendy. *States of Injury: Power and Freedom in Late Modernity.* Princeton: Princeton University Press, 1995.

Burns, Bobby. *Shelter: One Man's Journey from Homelessness to Hope.* Tucson: University of Arizona Press, 1998.

Butler, Judith. *Bodies That Matter: On the Discursive Limits of "Sex."* New York: Routledge, 1993.

——. *Excitable Speech.* New York: Routledge, 1997.

——. "Merely Cultural." *New Left Review* 227 (January/February 1998): 33–44.

Calder, Lendol. *Financing the American Dream: A Cultural History of Consumer Credit.* Princeton: Princeton University Press, 1999.

Campbell, Richard, and Jimmie L. Reeves. "Covering the Homeless: The Joyce Brown Story." *Critical Studies in Mass Communication* 6 (1989): 21–42.

Chambliss, William J. "The Law of Vagrancy." In *Crime and the Legal Process,* ed. William J. Chambliss. New York: McGraw-Hill, 1969.

Ciampi, Maria. "A Buberian Approach to Constitutional Analysis: So That We May Be Able to Face Our Poorer Brethren Eye to Eye." *St. John's Law Review* 65 (1991): 325–364.

Cohen, Richard, dir. *Taylor's Campaign.* Videorecording. Santa Monica, Calif.: Raindog Films, 1997.

Connolly, William. "Discipline, Politics, and Ambiguity." *Political Theory* 11 (August 1983): 325–341.

——. *The Ethos of Pluralization.* Minneapolis: University of Minnesota Press, 1995.

——. *Political Theory and Modernity.* Oxford: Basil Blackwell, 1988.

Daniels, Wes. "'Derelicts, Recurring Misfortune, Economic Hard Times, and Lifestyle Choices: Judicial Images of Homeless Litigants and Implications for Legal Advocates." *Buffalo Law Review* 45 (fall 1997): 687—737.

Davis, Mike. *City of Quartz.* New York: Vintage, 1992.

Desjarlais, Robert. *Shelter Blues: Sanity and Selfhood among the Homeless.* Philadelphia: University of Pennsylvania Press, 1997.

Deutsche, Rosalyn. *Evictions: Art and Spatial Politics.* Cambridge, Mass: MIT Press, 1996.

"Dignity Village Is Not a Solution" *Oregonian,* December 19, 2002, p. B-6.

Di Stefano, Christine. "Autonomy in the Light of Difference." In *Revisioning the Political: Feminist Reconstructions of Traditional Concepts in Western Political Theory,* ed. Nancy J. Hirschmann and Christine Di Stefano. Boulder, Colo.: Westview, 1996.

Douglas, Mary. "The Idea of Home: A Kind of Space," *Social Research* 58 (spring 1991): 287–307.

——. *Purity and Danger: An Analysis of Concepts of Pollution and Taboo.* New York: Praeger, 1966.

Dreyfus, Herbert, and Paul Rabinow. *Michel Foucault: Beyond Structuralism and Hermeneutics.* Chicago: University of Chicago Press, 1982.

Dumm, Thomas. *United States.* Ithaca: Cornell University Press, 1994.

Duneier, Mitchell. *Sidewalk.* New York: Farrar, Straus & Giroux, 1999.

Failer, Judith. "Homelessness in the Criminal Law." In *From Social Justice to Criminal Justice,* ed. William C. Hefferman and John Kleinig, pp. 248–263. New York: Oxford University Press, 2000.

———. *Who Qualifies for Rights: Homelessness, Mental Illness, and Civil Commitment.* Ithaca: Cornell University Press, 2002.

Ferree, Myra Marx, and William A. Gamson. "The Gendering of Governance and the Governance of Gender." Paper presented at the conference "Fifty Years of the Federal Republic of Germany through a Gendered Lens," University of North Carolina, 1999. http://www.unc.edu/depts/europe/conferences/Germany_celeb9900/abstracts/marx%20ferree_myra.html.

Fitzpatrick, Peter. "Bare Sovereignty: *Homo Sacer* and the Insistence of Law." *Theory and Event* 5, no. 2 (2001).

Foote, Caleb. "Vagrancy-Type Law and Its Administration." In *Crime and the Legal Process,* ed. William J. Chambliss. New York: McGraw-Hill, 1969.

Foscarinis, Maria. "Downward Spiral: Homelessness and Its Criminalization." *Yale Law and Policy Review* 14 (1996): 1–63.

Foucault, Michel. *Discipline and Punish.* Trans. Alan Sheridan. New York: Vintage, 1979.

———. *Madness and Civilization: A History of Insanity in the Age of Reason.* Trans. Richard Howard. New York: Vintage, 1988.

France, Anatole. *The Red Lily (Le Lys rouge).* Trans. Winifred Stephens. London: John Lane, The Bodley Head, 1922.

Fraser, Nancy. "From Redistribution to Recognition? Dilemmas of Justice in a 'Post-Socialist' Age." *New Left Review* 212 (July/August 1995): 68–93.

———. "Heterosexism, Misrecognition and Capitalism: A Response to Judith Butler." *New Left Review* 228 (March/April 1998): 140–149.

———. *Justice Interruptus: Critical Reflections on the 'Postsocialist' Condition.* New York: Routledge, 1997.

———. "A Rejoinder to Iris Young." *New Left Review* 223 (May/June 1997): 126–129.

———. "Rethinking Recognition." *New Left Review* 3 (May/June 2000): 107–120.

———. "Social Justice in the Age of Identity Politics: Redistribution, Recognition, and Participation." In *Tanner Lectures on Human Values,* 18:1–67. Salt Lake City: University of Utah Press, 1997.

———. *Unruly Practices.* Minneapolis: University of Minnesota Press, 1989.

Frost, Robert. "Mending Wall." In *Poems of Today: A Collection of the Contemporary Verse of America and Great Britian,* ed. Alice Cecilia Cooper. Modesto, Calif.: Ginn, 1924.

Frug, Gerald. "Public Cities/Private Cities." Paper presented at the Law and Society Association annual meeting, Miami, Florida, 2000.

Fuller, Linda K. "From Tramps to Truth-Seekers: Images of the Homeless in the Motion Pictures." In *Reading the Homeless: The Media's Image of Homeless Culture,* ed. Eungjun Min. Westport, Conn.: Praeger, 1999.

Gamble, Andrew. *The Free Economy and the Strong State.* London: Macmillan, 1994.

Gobetti, Daniela. "Humankind as a System: Private and Public Agency at the Origins of Modern Liberalism." In *Public and Private in Thought and Practice,* ed. Jeff Weintraub and Krishan Kumar. Chicago: University of Chicago Press, 1997.

Greenhouse, Carol J., Barbara Yngvesson, and David Engel. *Law and Community in Three American Towns.* Ithaca: Cornell University Press, 1994.

Groth, Paul. *Living Downtown: The History of Residential Hotels in the United States.* Berkeley: University of California Press, 1994.

Halley, Janet E. *Don't: A Reader's Guide to the Military's Anti-Gay Policy.* Durham, N.C.: Duke University Press, 1999.

Hanssen, Beatrice. *Critique of Violence.* New York: Routledge, 2000.

Harvey, David. "Class Relations, Social Justice, and the Politics of Difference." In *Place and the Politics of Identity,* ed. Michael Keith and Steve Pile. London: Routledge, 1993.

Hayward, Clarissa Ryle. "Between 'The Street' and 'The Mall': Social Space and Democratic Possibility." Paper presented at the Midwest Political Science Association meeting, Chicago, Illinois, 2001.

Heidegger, Martin. "Building Dwelling Thinking." In *Basic Writings,* ed. David Farrell Krell. New York: HarperCollins, 1993.

——. "Letter on Humanism." In *Basic Writings,* ed. David Farell Krell. New York: HarperCollins, 1993.

Hoch, Charles, and Robert A. Slayton. *New Homeless and Old: Community and the Skid Row Hotel.* Philadelphia: Temple University Press, 1989.

Honig, Bonnie. "Difference, Dilemmas, and the Politics of Home." *Social Research* 61 (fall 1994): 563–597.

——. *Political Theory and the Displacement of Politics.* Ithaca: Cornell University Press, 1993.

Hopper, Kim. "More Than Passing Strange: Homelessness and Mental Illness in New York City." *American Ethnologist* (1987): 155–167.

Hopper, Kim, and Jim Baumohl. "Redefining the Cursed Word: A Historical Interpretation of American Homelessness." In *Homelessness in America.* ed. Jim Baumohl. Phoenix, Ariz.: Oryx Press, 1996.

Humphreys, Robert. *No Fixed Abode: A History of Responses to the Roofless and Rootless in Britain.* New York: St. Martin's, 1999.

Hunt, Alan. *Governance of the Consuming Passions: A History of Sumptuary Law.* New York: St. Martin's, 1996.

Hussain, Nasser, and Melissa Ptacek. "Thresholds: Sovereignty and the Sacred." *Law and Society Review* 34 (2000): 495–515.

Hyde, Alan. *Bodies of Law.* Princeton: Princeton University Press, 1997.

Isaac, Jeffrey C. *Democracy in Dark Times.* Ithaca: Cornell University Press, 1998.

Kann, Mark E. "Individualism, Civic Virtue, and Gender in America." In *Studies in American Political Development,* 4:46–81. New Haven: Yale University Press, 1990.

Kawash, Samira. "The Homeless Body." *Public Culture* 10 (winter 1998): 319–339.

——. "Safe House? Body, Building, and the Question of Security." *Cultural Critique* 45 (spring 2000): 185–221.

Kelling, George L., and Catherine M. Coles. *Fixing Broken Windows.* New York: Free Press, 1996.

Kilian, Ted. "Public and Private, Power and Space." In *The Production of Public Space,* ed. Andrew Light and Jonathan Smith, 115–134. New York: Rowman, Littlefield, 1998.

Kusmer, Kenneth L. *Down and Out, On the Road: The Homeless in American History.* Oxford: Oxford University Press, 2002.

Laclau, Ernesto, and Chantal Mouffe. *Hegemony and Socialist Strategy: Towards a Radical Democratic Politics.* London: Verso, 1985.

LaGravenese, Richard. *The Fisher King: The Book of the Film.* New York: Applause Theater, 1991.

Lefort, Claude. *Democracy and Political Theory.* Trans. David Macey. Cambridge, U.K.: Polity Press, 1988.

Liebow, Elliot. *Tell Them Who I Am: The Lives of Homeless Women.* New York: Penguin, 1995.

Link, Bruce G., et al. "Public Knowledge, Attitudes, and Beliefs about Homeless People: Evidence for Compassion Fatigue?" *American Journal of Community Psychology* 23 (1995): 533–555.

Long, Christopher Philip. "A Fissure in the Distinction: Hannah Arendt, the Family, and the Public/Private Dichotomy." *Philosophy and Social Criticism* 24 (1998): 85–104.

Lubove, Roy. *The Progressives and the Slums: Tenement House Reform in New York City, 1890–1917.* Pittsburgh: University of Pittsburgh Press, 1962.

McCann, Michael W. *Rights at Work: Pay Equity Reform and the Politics of Legal Mobilization.* Chicago: University of Chicago Press, 1994.

Mair, Andrew. "The Homeless and the Postindustrial City." *Political Geography Quarterly* 5 (October 1986): 351–368.

Marcuse, Peter. "Neutralizing Homelessness." *Socialist Review* 18 (1988): 69–96.

——. "Residential Alienation, Homeownership, and the Limits of Shelter Policy." *Journal of Sociology and Social Welfare,* November 1975, pp. 181–203.

Markell, Patchen. "The Recognition of Politics: A Comment on Emcke and Tully." *Constellations* 7 (2000): 496–506.

Min, Eungjun, ed. *Reading the Homeless: The Media's Image of Homeless Culture.* Westport, Conn.: Praeger, 1999.

Mitchell, Don. "The Annihilation of Space By Law: The Roots and Implications of Anti-homeless Laws in The United States." *Antipode* 29 (1997): 303–355.

——. "Anti-homeless Laws and Public Space: II. Further Constitutional Issues," *Urban Geography* 19 (1998).

——. "The End of Public Space? People's Park, Definitions of the Public, and Democracy." *Annals of the Association of American Geographers* 85 (1995): 108–133.

Mouffe, Chantal. *The Return of the Political.* London: Verso, 1993.

National Law Center on Homelessness and Poverty. *Illegal to be Homeless.* Washington, D.C.: NLCHP, 2002.

——. *Out of Sight—Out of Mind? A Report on Anti-Homeless Laws, Litigation, and Alternatives in 50 United States Cities.* Washington, D.C.: NLCHP, 1999.

——. *No Homeless People Allowed : A Report on Anti-Homeless Laws, Litigation, and Alternatives in 49 United States Cities.* Washington, D.C.: NLCHP, 1994.

Negt, Oskar, and Alexander Kluge. *Public Sphere and Experience.* Trans. Peter Labanyi, Jamie Owen Daniel, and Assenka Oksiloff. Minneapolis: University of Minnesota Press, 1993.

Nietzsche, Friedrich. *On the Genealogy of Morals and Ecce Homo.* Trans. Walter Kaufmann and R.J. Hollingdale. New York: Vintage, 1989.

Nieves, Evelyn. "Santa Cruz Journal: Furious Debate Rages on Sleeping in Public." *New York Times,* May 28, 2000, p. A-14.

Norris, Andrew. "Giorgio Agamben and the Politics of the Living Dead." *Diacritics* 30, no. 4 (2000): 38–58.

North Beach Citizens. "Community Coupons" (2001). http://www.northbeachcitizens.org/html/cc.html.

Norton, Anne. *Republic of Signs.* Chicago: University of Chicago Press, 1993.

Okin, Susan. *Justice, Gender, and the Family.* New York: Basic Books, 1989.

Painton, Priscilla. "Shrugging Off the Homeless: The Nation's Toughest Urbanites Lose Patience with the Homeless." *Time,* April 16, 1990, pp. 14–16.

Pateman, Carole. "Feminist Critiques of the Public/Private Dichotomy." In *The Disorder of Women*. Cambridge: Polity, 1990.

Piven, Frances Fox, and Richard A. Cloward. *Regulating the Poor: The Functions of Public Welfare*. New York: Pantheon, 1971.

Redmond, Bob. "Sidran: 'No Answer' for Homeless." *Real Change* 6 (July 1999): 4.

Reeves, Jimmie L. "Re-Covering the Homeless: Hindsights on the Joyce Brown Story." In *Reading the Homeless*, ed. Eungjun Min. Westport, Conn.: Praeger, 1999.

Rhode, David. "Federal Judge Upholds Giuliani's Policy on Arresting the Homeless." *New York Times*, December 29, 2000. http://www/nytimes.com/2000/12/29/nyregion/29HOME.html.

Roberts, Michelle. "Homeless Camping Ban Voided," *Oregonian*, September 28, 2000, p. E-1.

Rose, Nikolas. *Powers of Freedom: Reframing Political Thought*. Cambridge, U.K.: Cambridge University Press, 1999.

Rosenblum, Nancy. *Membership and Morals*. Princeton: Princeton University Press, 1998.

Rousseau, Jean-Jacques. *Discourse on the Origin of Inequality*. Trans. Donald A. Cress. Indianapolis: Hackett, 1992.

Rushdie, Salman. *The Ground beneath Her Feet*. New York: Henry Holt, 1999.

Sahlin, Ingrid. "Enclosure or Inclusion? Urban Control and Homeless People." Paper presented at the joint meeting of the Law and Society Association and the Research Committee on Sociology of Law (ISA), Budapest, Hungary, 2001.

Sahlins, Marshall. "Food as a Symbolic Code." In *Culture and Society: Contemporary Debates*, ed. Jeffrey C. Alexander and Steven Seidman. Cambridge, U.K.: Cambridge University Press, 1990.

Said, Edward. "The Politics of Knowledge." *Raritan* 11 (1991): 17–31.

Schram, Sanford F. *After Welfare: The Culture of Postindustrial Social Policy*. New York: New York University Press, 2000.

Sennett, Richard. *The Fall of Public Man*. New York: Norton, 1976.

——. *Flesh and Stone: The Body and the City in Western Civilization*. New York: Norton, 1994.

——. *The Uses of Disorder*. New York: Norton, 1970.

Shapiro, Michael. *Reading the Postmodern Polity*. Minneapolis: University of Minnesota Press, 1992.

Sidran, Mark. "Establishing Standards of Civil Behavior." *Seattle Times*, August 10, 1994, p. B-5.

Simon, Harry. "Towns without Pity: A Constitutional and Historical Analysis of Official Efforts to Drive Homeless Persons from American Cities." *Tulane Law Review* 66 (1992): 631–676.

Smith, Juliette. "Arresting the Homeless for Sleeping in Public: A Paradigm for Expanding the Robinson Doctrine." *Columbia Journal of Law and Social Problems* 29 (1996): 293–335.

Snow, David A., and Leon Anderson. *Down on Their Luck: A Study of Homeless Street People*. Berkeley: University of California Press, 1993.

Stenberg, Doug. "Tom's a-Cold: Transformation and Redemption in *King Lear* and *The Fisher King*." *Literature Film Quarterly* 22, no. 3 (1994): 160–169.

Swan, Neil. "In Birmingham Alabama: Access to Housing and Job Training Helps Recovering Homeless People Stay Drug Free." NIDA Website. 1997. http://www.nida.nih.gov/NIDA_Notes/NNVol12N4/Access.html.

"Tent City Not the Answer, but Real Solution Coming." *Seattle Post-Intelligencer*, May 10, 2000.

Tier, Robert. "Maintaining Safety and Civility in Public Spaces: A Constitutional Approach to Aggressive Begging." *Louisiana Law Review* 54 (1993): 285–338.

———. "Restoring Order in Urban Public Spaces." *Texas Review of Law and Politics* 2 (1998): 256–290.

Timmer, Doug A., D. Stanley Eitzen, and Kathryn D. Talley. *Paths to Homelessness.* Boulder Colo.: Westview, 1994.

Treaser, Joseph, B. "After the Storm: New Home Humble, but Is Welcomed." *New York Times,* September 3, 1992, p. A-18.

Trillin, Calvin. "U.S. Journal: San Francisco: 'Some Thoughts on the International Hotel Controversy.'" *New Yorker,* December 19, 1977, pp. 116–120.

Tully, James. "Struggles over Recognition and Distribution." *Constellations* 7 (2000): 469–482.

Valdes, Francisco. "Sexual Minorities in the Military: Charting the Constitutional Frontiers of Status and Conduct." *Creighton Law Review* 27 (1994): 384–475.

VanderStaay, Steven. *Street Lives: An Oral History of Homeless Americans.* Philadelphia: New Society, 1992.

Veiller, Lawrence. "The Housing Problem in American Cities." *Annals of the American Academy of Political and Social Science* 25 (1905): 248–272.

———. *Housing Reform: A Hand-book for Practical Use in American Cities.* New York: Charities Publication Committee, 1910.

Veness, April R. "Home and Homelessness in the United States: Changing Ideals and Realities." *Environment and Planning D: Society and Space* 10 (1992): 445–468.

———. "Neither Homed nor Homeless: Contested Definitions and the Personal Worlds of the Poor." *Political Geography* 12 (July 1993): 319–340.

Wagner, David. *Checkerboard Square: Culture and Resistance in a Homeless Community.* Boulder, Colo.: Westview, 1993.

Waldron, Jeremy. "Homelessness and the Issue of Freedom." *UCLA Law Review* 39 (December 1991): 295–324.

Walters, Edward J. "No Way Out: Eighth Amendment Protection for Do-or-Die Acts of the Homeless." *University of Chicago Law Review* 62 (1995): 1619–1649.

Walzer, Michael. *Interpretation and Social Criticism.* Cambridge, Mass.: Harvard University Press, 1987.

———. "Liberalism and the Art of Separation." *Political Theory* 12 (August 1984).

———. *Spheres of Justice: A Defense of Pluralism and Equality.* New York: Basic Books, 1983.

Watercutter, Angela. "Site in Manilatown Will Once Again Hose Elderly Tenants." *San Francisco Examiner,* August 5, 2002. http://www.examiner.com/headlines/default. jsp?story=n.manilatown.0805w.

Weintraub, Jeff. "The Theory and Politics of the Public/Private Distinction." In *Public and Private in Thought and Practice,* ed. Jeff Weintraub and Krishan Kumar. Chicago: University of Chicago Press, 1997.

Wilkerson, Isabel. "Shift in Feelings on the Homeless: Empathy Turns to Frustration." *New York Times,* September 2, 1991, p. 1.

Williams, Raymond. *Marxism and Literature.* Oxford: Oxford University Press, 1977.

Wilson, James Q., and George L. Kelling, "Broken Windows: The Police and Neighborhood Safety." *Atlantic Monthly,* March 1982, pp. 29–38.

Wright, Talmadge. *Out of Place: Homeless Mobilizations, Subcities, and Contested Landscapes.* Albany: State University of New York Press, 1997.

Xenos, Nicholas. "Refugees: The Modern Political Condition." *Alternatives* 18 (1993): 419–430.

Yeung, Bernice. "The 'I' Is for Irony." *SFWeekly*, June 6, 2001. http://www.sfweekly.com/issues/2001-06-06/bayview.html.

Young, Alison. *Imagining Crime: Textual Outlaws and Criminal Conversations.* London: Sage, 1996.

Young, Iris Marion. *Intersecting Voices: Dilemmas of Gender, Political Philosophy, and Policy.* Princeton: Princeton University Press, 1997.

———. *Justice and the Politics of Difference.* Princeton: Princeton University Press, 1990.

———. "Unruly Categories: A Critique of Nancy Fraser's Dual Systems Theory." *New Left Review* 222 (1997): 147–160.

CASES CITED

Betancourt v. Guiliani, 2000 U.S. Dist. LEXIS 18516.

Chad v. Ft. Lauderdale, 861 F. Supp. 1057 (S.D. Fla. 1994).

Clark v. Community for Creative Nonviolence, 468 U.S. 288 (1984).

Doucette v. Santa Monica, 955 F. Supp. 1192 (C.D. Cal. September 30, 1996).

In the Matter of Billie Boggs, Petitioner, 136 Misc. 2d 1082 (NY Supreme Ct., NY County, 1987); reversed, 132 A.D. 2d 340 (1987); appeal dismissed as moot, 70 N.Y. 2d 972 (1988).

Joel v. Orlando, 232 F. 3d 1353 (11th Cir. 2000); cert denied 149 L. Ed. 2d 480 (2001).

Johnson v. Dallas, 860 F. Supp 344 (N.D. Tex. 1994); reversed and vacated for lack of standing, 61 F. 3d 442 (5th Cir. 1995).

Joyce v. San Francisco, 846 F. Supp. 843 (N.D. Cal. 1994); No. C-93–4149 (N.D. Cal. August 18, 1995); vacated, 87 F. 3d 1320 (9th Cir. 1996).

Love v. City of Chicago, No. 96-C-0396, 1996 U.S. Dist. LEXIS 16041 (N.D. Ill. October 23, 1996); WL 60804, 1998 U.S. Dist LEXIS 1386 (N.D. Ill. February 5, 1998).

Metropolitan Council, Inc. v. Safir, 99 F. Supp. 2d 438 (SDNY 2000).

Papachristou v. City of Jacksonville, 405 U.S. 156 (1972).

Patton v. Baltimore City, Civil No. S93-2389 (D. Md. August 19, 1994) (Memorandum Opinion).

Pottinger v. City of Miami, 810 F. Supp. 1551 (S.D. Fla. 1992); remanded, 40 F. 3d 1155 (11th Cir. 1994).

Robinson v. California, 370 U.S. 660 (1962).

Roulette v. City of Seattle, 850 F. Supp. 1442 (W.D. Wash. 1994); affirmed, 97 F. 3d 300 (9th Cir. 1996).

State v. Wicks, Nos. 2711742 and 2711743 (Ore. Cit. Ct. Multnomah County, 2000).

Tobe v. City of Santa Ana, 27 Cal. Rptr. 2d 386 (Cal. App. 4 Dist. 1994); reversed, 40 Cal. Rptr. 2d 402 (Cal. 1995).

Young v. New York City Transit Authority, 903 F. 2d 146 (2d Cir. 1990).

INDEX